CUTTING THE WIRE

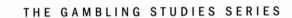

THE GAMBLING STUDIES SERIES

CUTTING THE WIRE

GAMBLING PROHIBITION AND THE INTERNET

DAVID G. SCHWARTZ

University of Nevada Press / Reno & Las Vegas

The Gambling Studies Series

Series Editor: William R. Eadington

University of Nevada Press, Reno, Nevada 89557 USA

Manufactured in the United States of America

Design by Carrie House

Library of Congress Cataloging-in-Publication Data

Schwartz, David G., 1973–

Cutting the wire : gambling prohibition and the Internet /

David G. Schwartz.— 1st ed.

p. cm. — (The gambling studies series)

Includes bibliographical references and index.

ISBN 0-87417-619-0 (hardcover : alk. paper)

ISBN 0-87417-620-4 (pbk. : alk. paper)

1. Internet gambling—Law and legislation—United States—Criminal

provisions. 2. Gambling—Law and legislation—United States—Criminal

provisions. 3. Gambling—United States—History. I. Title. II. Series.

KF9440.S39 2005

345.73′0272′02854678—dc22   2005010632

The paper used in this book meets the requirements of American

National Standard for Information Sciences—Permanence of

Paper for Printed Library Materials, ANSI Z.48-1984. Binding

materials were selected for strength and durability.

FIRST PRINTING

14 13 12 11 10 09 08 07 06 05

5 4 3 2 1

This book is dedicated to the memory of Shannon L. Bybee Jr., gaming regulator, industry leader, and educator.

Shannon helped to write the laws that govern legal Nevada gaming, and I wish that he could be with us to see gaming law fully adapt to the digital era. His wise counsel and good advice, I'm sure, would help us immeasurably. He was a mentor and friend who encouraged me, like so many other people, by his example and with his support.

CONTENTS

PREFACE

My first book, *Suburban Xanadu: The Casino Resort on the Las Vegas Strip and Beyond*, grew out of my doctoral dissertation in U.S. history at UCLA. Since I grew up with the casino industry in Atlantic City, New Jersey, the history of casinos was a rather obvious topic for my dissertation. To tell a story about that world and help people better understand the place of casinos in American society just came naturally.

Where to go from there? The explosion of Internet gaming, I thought, was just as shrouded in mystery as the origins of casinos. The current American irresolution over Internet gaming provided the impetus for this book. With a better understanding of the past, both sides of the current debate might be more thoughtfully conducted. I think that history has great lessons for both those who are in the business of gaming and those who oppose gaming expansion — and certainly for those charged with creating and enforcing the laws that deal with gaming.

This book begins with an introduction, followed by seven chapters and an epilogue. The introduction, "Kennedy's War Continues," discusses how the Wire Act symbolizes the uneasy American pursuit of gaming and gives a brief introduction to the act. The first chapter, "Legal Vices and Illicit Diversions," sums up the history of legal and illegal American gaming, describes the long connections between gaming and technology, and explains the development of the race wire service. Chapter 2, "The Anxious Decade," describes the harried investigations into organized crime of the 1950s. The revelations brought to light by these investigations convinced Americans that they faced a profoundly powerful "enemy within" — organized crime — and that a favored pastime, gaming, directly funded this enemy.

With the first two chapters setting the stage, the third chapter, "Camelot Strikes Back," provides an in-depth look at the circumstances attending the birth of the Wire Act. The act was part of Attorney General Robert F. Kennedy's larger initiative to "get organized crime," and it is necessary to see it in that light. I also gauge public reaction to the act and describe its immediate impact. Chapter 4, "Booking the Bookies," traces the legacy of the Wire Act over the next three decades.

In chapter 5, "A Money Jungle From Sea to Sea," I explore the growth of gaming in the last quarter of the twentieth century, culminating in the introduction of Internet gaming. This provides the context for better understanding the development of online gaming in the 1990s, a subject covered in chapter 6, "Point, Click, and Bet." Chapter 7, "March Madness," focuses on two court cases involving the Wire Act: the successful prosecution of Jay Cohen and Antigua's resulting challenge of U.S. enforcement actions before the World Trade Organization. Finally, in the epilogue, "Prohibition in a Borderless America," I offer my own thoughts on the track record of Americans in chasing gaming and the place of the Internet in American life.

Dozens of people helped me with the writing of this book. I'm sure I'll neglect to mention many of them, but here are those whose contributions are particularly fresh in my mind.

Joanne O'Hare at the University of Nevada Press saved the day when I had almost given up on seeing this book published at all. A note for any struggling author—when in doubt, stick to your convictions, and someone will see the value of your work.

The University of Nevada, Las Vegas, boasts the world's leading gaming collection, so even if I didn't work there, I would have spent a great deal of time there. Everyone at UNLV Special Collections—Peter Michel, Su Kim Chung, Jonnie Kennedy, Joyce Marshall, Kathy War, Claytee White, and the helpful student staff—doubled as coworkers and people who helped me with the research. Also within UNLV Libraries, Dean Kenneth Marks, Lee Scroggins, Vicki Nozero, Chris Wiatroski, Susie Skarl, Tim Skeers, and Nancy Master all helped in various ways. Hal Rothman, chair of the Department of History, gave me much-appreciated opportunities to teach and some significant inspiration. Petula Iu read parts of the draft manuscript and gave me excellent ideas for revision.

At the Library of Congress, everyone at the Main Reading Room in the Jefferson Building, the Law Library, and the Special Collections Room deserves thanks, as do the helpful staff of the U.S. National Archives and Records Administration: Archives II, College Park, Research Room of Motion Picture, Sound, and Video Recording, part of the Special Media Division. Laura Craig-Mason at the National Criminal Justice Reference Service gave me invaluable help there.

At the Federal Bureau of Investigation, Bruce Yarborough, Daron Borst, Fred Bradford, and Kathleen Magnafici all helped me get a better handle on past and current federal anti–illegal gaming efforts.

On the other side of the law (at the time), Jay Cohen kindly assented to an interview and gave me both material and inspiration.

Attorney Bob Blumenfeld helped me grasp the current legal ramifications of my research and generously offered comments on the manuscript.

I've been lucky to follow in the footsteps of several gaming experts. I'd like to acknowledge the assistance of gaming attorneys Anthony Cabot and I. Nelson Rose and of Judy Cornelius and Bill Eadington of the University of Nevada, Reno, which was particularly timely.

Of course, none of this would have been possible without the support of my family, friends, and the hundreds of random people I've gotten to know, even if only ephemerally, through my work on the Web at *http://gaming.unlv .edu* and my personal site, *http://www.dieiscast.com*.

Finally, thanks to you, the reader. As I tell my students, research and writing are a worthless diversion without an audience, and I appreciate your giving me the chance to share a compelling story. If you want to learn more about my work, check out the Web sites mentioned above.

CUTTING THE WIRE

Introduction: Kennedy's War Continues

Jay Cohen's defiant hope, Bobby Kennedy's first crusade, and the relevance of a 1961 anti-mob statute to Internet gaming today.

February 24, 2002. Southern District Court, New York City. Honorable Thomas P. Griesa presiding.

Until the judge started giving the jury its instructions, Jay Cohen felt pretty confident that he'd be back at his desk at the World Sports Exchange in a week or two. Sure, the prosecutors had shown the jury lots of evidence proving that his company had accepted bets from undercover agents over the phone and on the Web. But they had never proved that he intended to break the law, defraud anyone, or do anything but run a legal, licensed business.

Throughout the trial, Cohen's attorney, Benjamin Brafman, had conceded that his client had been the president of the World Sports Exchange. He couldn't have denied it if he had wanted to—Cohen had appeared in *Sports Illustrated* and the *Wall Street Journal*, and had even testified before Congress. That he was a founder of one of the most reputable, innovative sports betting Web sites wasn't at issue, Cohen thought. The trial was about whether he had broken the law. And Cohen was sure he had not. After all, taking bets online was legal in Antigua, and it didn't seem to be illegal in New York. He'd consciously patterned the WSE on Capital OTB, an off-track betting concern that paid millions in taxes each year. As he watched Brafman deliver his closing argument to the jury, Cohen felt good about his chances.

Judge Griesa had started out innocuously enough, telling the jurors the importance of weighing the evidence, and of the consideration of witness credibility. Cohen knew he couldn't have been more credible; he took the stand in his own defense and laid out his case for the jurors, plain and simple. He'd studied this new business, sought the best legal and financial advice, and acted accordingly. Moving to Antigua while still paying for a condo in the Bay Area hadn't been a day at the beach. He missed the little things that everyone living in the United States takes for granted—cheeseburgers, for God's sake. His family, too, for that matter. He'd followed all the rules. The jury would have to see that and acquit him.

But as the judge continued, Cohen felt his heart start to beat faster; even Brafman began to look a little nervous. When Griesa said, "I want to start by discussing with you the law that is applicable, and that is a statute which we refer to as Title 18 United States Code Section 1084," Cohen's day in court turned into a nightmare. He listened, speechless, as the judge told the jury that it didn't matter whether Cohen's business was licensed in Antigua, or that off-track betting was legal in New York. The judge then instructed the jury that to find Cohen guilty, they only had to conclude that Cohen was in the business of accepting bets and that his service had provided betting information to undercover officers—something that Brafman had conceded at the start of his case. Suddenly, coming back to New York to fight charges of violating the Wire Act didn't seem like such a good idea.

So Jay Cohen wasn't that optimistic when, four days later, after fruitless objections by his attorneys, the jury filed back into the courtroom and he stood awaiting their verdict.

As the deputy court clerk asked them how they found in the case of *United States v. Cohen*, 98Cr. 434, count 1, the foreman answered "guilty." On each of eight counts, for every possible clause, the response was the same: guilty.

As Joseph DeMarco, the lead assistant U.S. attorney presenting the government's case, started to smile, Cohen remembered a fragment of his opening statement: "A federal law known as Title 18 United States Code Section 1084 makes it a crime for bookies like Cohen to take bets using the phone lines."

How am I a bookie? Cohen wondered. And where did this Section 1084 come from, anyway? How, if Congress was still debating an Internet gambling prohibition, was a law passed in 1961 being used to put him in prison?

Cohen's questions have answers. Section 1084 (the Wire Act) became law as the result of a convergence of public anxiety, political opportunity, and personal opprobrium, and it remains law because of America's habitual ambivalence over gambling, an ambivalence that has only become more striking in a generation during which states have parlayed gaming legalization into increasingly large fiscal stakes. Though Section 1084 can trace its lineage to the turn of the twentieth century, it became law only because of the energetic advocacy of one of the most charismatic figures of the turbulent 1960s—Robert F. Kennedy.

Profiles in Prosecution

Bobby Kennedy hated gamblers. Not your two-dollars-a-race bettors or guys who played poker once a week to unwind—they were just real men looking to let off some steam. For Kennedy, a "gambler" meant boss gamblers, the shadowy men who controlled the action, running illegal numbers games or taking off-the-books bets on legal horse racing. These men didn't really gamble. They set the odds, always unfairly, and rode the foolish hopes of anyone naive enough to play—rode them all the way to the bank. The big gamblers were infesting America, hiding behind protective layers of underlings who always took the fall and laughing at the efforts of reformers to drive them out. They were parasites who leeched working people and gave nothing back to society. With their goons and guns, they acted like tough guys, but they weren't really tough. These gamblers might threaten and intimidate, and they could scare most people, but they weren't tough in the quiet, confident way of the NYPD detectives who fought to break up the rackets.

After his brother convinced him to become attorney general, Kennedy decided that the rackets would be his top target. He'd made some inroads in the fight against them with the McClellan Committee. Serving as chief counsel, he'd made even fake-tough Jimmy Hoffa squirm—but he hadn't put him in jail. Even if he had, another would have stepped into Hoffa's place at the union, all too eager to take the crooked money of the racketeers. To beat the rackets once and for all, Kennedy thought, he'd have to hit them where it really hurt—in the wallet. If he could take their gambling profits away, he just might smash them permanently.

Kennedy was assisted by a pliant Congress, which passed five pieces of anti-crime legislation in 1961 to help the new attorney general fight organized crime and racketeering. The laws were a mixed lot. Two of them had no real connection to the actual business of organized crime but fit under the vague rubric of "anti-crime legislation." These statutes enlarged the Fugitive Felon Act and amended the Federal Firearms Act to prohibit felons from trafficking in firearms.[1]

The remaining three bills took more direct action against those who profited from crime. In sum, they made it a crime to use interstate travel or facilities to conduct an illegal gambling, liquor, narcotics, or prostitution business, to transport betting paraphernalia across state lines, and to use interstate wire communications facilities to transmit bets or information that assisted in the placing of bets. The Senate passed this final law, S. 1656, known as the "Wire Act" or "Wire Wager Act," on July 28. The House followed suit on August 21, and on September 13, 1961, President Kennedy signed it and its companion antigambling/anti-racketeering statutes into law.[2] In his brief remarks upon signing the bills, the president noted that the three new laws were "the culmination . . . of years of effort by the Federal

Government and the Congress to place more effective tools in the hands of local, State, and national police."[3]

The Wire Act made several changes in federal law. First, it amended § 1081 of Title 18 of the United States Code to better describe the term "wire communication facility" as:

> Any and all instrumentalities, personnel, and services (among other things, the receipt, forwarding, or delivery of communications) used or useful in the transmission of writings, signs, pictures, and sounds of all kinds by aid of wire, cable, or other like connection between the points of origin and reception of such transmission.[4]

After this prelude, the statute added a new section, 1084. Section 1084 had four paragraphs. The first paragraph levied no more than a $10,000 fine or two years imprisonment on anyone who knowingly used a wire communication facility to transmit bets or wagers on sporting events, or information assisting in the placing of such wagers. In addition, a final provision made it clear that gambling for either money or credit was illegal.[5]

The rest of Section 1084 further clarified the new prohibition. The second paragraph specifically exempted news reporting of sports events and bets sent between two states where such wagers were legal, thus making the world safe for ESPN and horse race simulcasting, respectively. The third ensured that Section 1084 could not be used to prevent prosecution under any state law. The final paragraph of the new section obligated "common carriers" (i.e., telecommunications companies) to "discontinue or refuse" service to a subject after notification in writing by a law enforcement agency "acting within its jurisdiction." In addition to compelling the halt of service, this paragraph indemnified the carrier from civil or criminal penalty for doing so and allowed for the right of the carrier to "secure an appropriate determination" as to whether service should be discontinued or restored.[6]

How did law enforcement use Section 1084? Federal investigators and police used the Wire Act to effectively disrupt interstate illegal gaming networks, and they managed to ensnare a handful of those involved in legal Nevada sportsbooks in Wire Act prosecutions. But by and large, the original premise of the Wire Act, that it be used to smash organized crime, did not long outlive Robert Kennedy's tenure as attorney general. The Racketeer Influenced and Corrupt Organizations Act (RICO), passed in 1970, provided a far more flexible tool for targeting organized crime. Successful prosecutions of illegal and offshore bookmakers certainly satisfied the letter of the law but at the same time strayed far from its original spirit.

Though in retrospect the Wire Act seems to have been a specific outgrowth of the Kennedy administration, it represented a longtime desire to involve the federal government in the suppression of gambling. To understand why the Wire Act passed, one must consider more than a century's worth of anti-gambling panic and Kennedy's urgent personal need to fight the mob. And to appreciate the role of this law in the Internet age, one has to better understand just how it has been used to fight illegal bookmaking and organized crime, two practices that are often—but not always—linked.

An Uneasy Obsession With Gambling

In fighting gambling, Robert Kennedy was swimming upstream. From Virginia cavaliers "bowling in the streets" to Mississippi River roustabouts rolling dice to stock traders buying futures contracts on the O. J. Simpson verdict, gambling has been an integral part of many Americans' identities. Historians, philosophers, and self-appointed authors of virtue have agreed that Americans seemingly cannot escape their desire to gamble, but few said it as perfectly as Frank Costello when he remarked that "ninety-nine percent of a human being is gamble-minded" and that, even if the law prohibited a person from gambling, "he'll find some trick to do it."[7]

Therein lay the rub. For although gambling was enjoyable, by its very nature it had a lucky winner and a downcast loser. When gamblers remained personal acquaintances linked by social ties, this was no great problem, as there was a fair chance today's loser would become tomorrow's winner. But the rise of professional gamblers meant that most players would inevitably lose. This realization triggered the rage against American lotteries that resulted in their demise during the Jacksonian era.

The professional gambler (distinguished from the recreational player) had an implacable foe: the antigambler. Sometimes the antigambler opposed the very act of gambling for moral reasons and would denounce schoolgirls pitching pennies for ribbons just as vehemently as gambling kingpins who monopolized bookmaking citywide. Other times, they opposed only the gamblers that Robert Kennedy did, those more accurately described as professional gaming operators. The evolution of the antigambler mirrors the progressive growth of professional (or mercantile) gambling over the past three centuries.

The original Puritan strictures against gambling condemned it more as idleness than as economic folly, and in any event few colonists were likely to forfeit much of their wealth to playing backgammon at the local tavern. But gamblers soon began playing for dangerously high stakes. The rise of the cash economy in the early nineteenth century—a development historians have termed the Market Revolution—removed much of the safety net of the "moral economy" of early America. Merchants now charged what the traffic could bear rather than what was socially acceptable; banks stood ready to foreclose on homes and farms; and itinerant gamblers sauntered about the nation's rivers and railroads, ready to cheat their marks before slipping off into the anonymous night.

In this world, the professional gambler emerged as the scourge of an honest society whose victims were the hopeful souls seduced into placing foolhardy bets. Opponents of gambling into the Progressive Era lamented the fates of those who were tempted to try their luck and ended up penniless. As the nation became more economically polarized during the late nineteenth century and the political corruption that nourished ostensibly illegal gaming operations became increasingly noisome to reformers and their constituents, a new backlash against gaming commenced. The first congressional action against gaming ended the interstate transportation of lottery materials in a successful attempt to strike down the Louisiana lottery. Throughout the nation, legislators rejected existing schemes of state-sponsored betting. Legalized gaming shrank nearly to extinction.

Still, Americans continued to gamble, and many of them began to believe that legalizing and taxing gaming might help states navigate their way out of straitened economic circumstances without imposing additional taxes. So the American embrace of gaming entered a new phase, with states turning to pari-mutuel betting as a kind of wagering in the public interest. At the same time, charitable gaming—certainly a cruel oxymoron to anti-gaming moralists like Anthony Comstock—also gained credibility, as Americans began frequenting Monte Carlo nights and church bingo games. Gambling could, just maybe, be socially beneficial.

Though society now sanctioned this public-interest gambling, there were those who sought to skim profit from it. Much like pirates lurking near trade routes and plundering cargo at their pleasure, "organized gamblers" sent runners to racetracks (and, when denied racetracks, to trees and other vantage points around them) to obtain race information and results. These results fed a national telegraph network known as the race wire, which terminated in thousands of illegal, untaxed betting dens and bookie stands.

The race wire outraged defenders of the public order because it subverted the entire scheme of public-interest gaming. Its operators took information and profited from it, denying the state a cut of the proceeds. Bettors frequenting horse rooms were not at racetracks, and dollars bet in the illicit outlets fed by the race wire were denied to the racetracks and, in turn, to the state, which garnered a share of each bet. An information monopoly maintained on violence and intimidation, the race wire was all the more sinister because it siphoned profits from state-sponsored gaming, mocking the premise that gaming could be channeled to the social good.

Local and state police might arrest bookmakers, and district attorneys might even hope to indict the leaders of citywide gambling rings, but so long as the race wire existed no one would lose money if he bet that, before long, someone would be taking bets again. Powerless against the national reach of the race wire, local law enforcement begged federal authorities for help.

Help did not come until 1961, after the use of the race wire had already begun to decline, the victim of the shift from race betting to sports betting. Robert Kennedy believed that in dismantling the race wire he might fight a decisive battle in his war on organized crime, and he successfully pressed Congress for such a law. The Wire Act was, on its surface, an attempt to make criminal the transmission of race information, but it spoke to a deeper desire to deny criminals access to the American information and communications infrastructure. Facing an enemy within, Kennedy vowed that he would not let it gain power from the same wires that linked Americans in pursuit of economic gain. Telegraphs and telephones might have brought Americans closer, but they would no longer help professional gamblers take bets.

Kennedy's statute did not criminalize placing bets, ostensibly because of potential nightmares over enforcement but also because of an enduring American belief that gaming, in and of itself, is no crime. But the Wire Act did purport to give prosecutors a weapon against those who profited from gaming. The framers of the 1961 law realized that information is essentially power, and they hoped that without access to information organized gambling would die, taking with it organized crime.

But organized gambling did not die; instead, states and eventually the federal government (through its sanction of tribal government gaming) wrested control of most gaming from organized and disorganized criminal elements.

Licensing and taxing casinos, establishing lottery monopolies, taking a cut of pari-mutuel wagering, and permitting charitable gaming, American governments became increasingly dependent on gaming for revenue in the final third of the twentieth century. Derailing Internet gaming, the cynical say, is not about protecting Americans from the scourge of fraud or compulsive gambling; it's about governments eliminating an untaxed competitor.

Kennedy's Law in Bush's America

Legislation changes far more slowly than society does. Any enterprising middle-schooler could run a quick Internet search of state and federal statutes to find laws on the books that are hopelessly archaic. The U.S. Congress, for example, still has the legal wherewithal to authorize piracy, as the eleventh clause of section 8 of the Constitution gives that body the power to grant letters of marque and reprisal. The Wire Act, originally meant to fight mobsters who enriched themselves by running bookmaking organizations that used telegraphs and telephones to send horse race information across state lines, remains the law of the land. Changes in technology have pushed that law into places that Robert Kennedy could never have foreseen.

Technology advances continuously, and gaming operators have usually been quick to seize on technical innovations in order to facilitate their wagering businesses. The operators of horse rooms in the 1920s, for example, used telephone and telegraph transmissions of the latest odds and racing results to stimulate play. By the 1940s, law enforcement observers considered control of the race wire tantamount to control of organized crime: The master of racing information could use his position to take control of illicit gaming and, ultimately, other racketeering sectors (usually, however, it was the other way around — the most powerful underworld presence would seize the most lucrative racket). With the growing popularity of the Internet in the early 1990s, smart offshore sportsbooks saw a new way to take bets. In May 1995, Interactive Gaming and Communications Corporation, previously an offshore telephone sportsbook operating out of Grenada, began taking online wagers. Online bets quickly grew to become 40 percent of Interactive Gaming's total business, an estimated $35.4 million in 1996.[8]

By 1997 about two hundred gambling sites existed, though many of these featured free-play games that merely simulated casino action using imaginary chips. A few live betting sites that accepted real-money wagers opened in Antigua, chiefly because the government there had taken the initiative and begun issuing online gambling licenses. The Caribbean island also had a technical edge over competing jurisdictions, with an undersea fiber-optic link to the United States that guaranteed American Net gamblers continuous telecommunications access, even in the event of a hurricane.[9]

Media coverage of this new phenomenon—the online bookie—usually afforded cautious praise to those who sought to pioneer in the new medium. Jay Cohen and Steve Schillinger, founders of the World Sports Exchange, emerged as articulate, engaging advocates for their chosen trade in an April 1997 *Wall Street Journal* article about online sportsbooks. The two met while working as stock traders in San Francisco, and Cohen recommended that Schillinger transfer a burgeoning "office pool" of betting on the floor of the Pacific Stock Exchange to the Web. Armed with $600,000 in start-up capital, the two opened the World Sports Exchange in January 1997.[10]

By May of that year cyberbooks like the World Sports Exchange had attracted the attention of major sports leagues, which demanded that the sites stop accepting bets from the United States and that they refrain from using league and team trademarks. Cohen and Schillinger refused to shut down but changed their practices by naming only cities and not teams. Removing the league and team insignia, they thought, would insulate them from any trademark suits. As they were running a legal, licensed business, they imagined that the sports leagues would have nothing further to say.[11]

At this point, Cohen's supporters allege, the National Football League (through its law firm Debevoise and Plimpton) investigated Cohen and others and asked the Justice Department to bring charges against operators of Caribbean books.[12] These requests culminated in the "March Madness" prosecutions. In March 1998 federal prosecutors charged twenty-two defendants with conspiracy to violate the Wire Act and with several substantive violations of the law. Of those charged, ten pled guilty to conspiracy charges, three pled guilty to misdemeanor counts, and seven, including Cohen's partners in the World Sports Exchange, remained technically fugitives from the law and continued their businesses in the Caribbean.[13] Cohen himself, who wanted to clear his name and felt that he had solid legal standing, returned to the United States to face trial. After a two-week trial, Cohen was convicted in Manhattan federal court on February 28, 2000. He ultimately served seventeen months at Federal Prison Camp Nellis, within sight of the Las Vegas Strip, before his release in March 2004. To date, Cohen is the only American to have been found guilty of running an illegal betting business online under Section 1084 while operating a licensed Internet sportsbook in another country.

The Cohen verdict did little to stop online wagering. By 2004 annual revenue from online casinos and sportsbooks was estimated at $5 to $7 billion, with about 50 percent coming from Americans.[14] Cohen appealed his case and failed to get the verdict overturned. In 2003 the government of Antigua successfully brought suit against the United States in the World Trade Organization, charging that federal prosecutions of Antigua-based sites had violated trade statutes guaranteeing cross-market access.[15] The United States has appealed, and it seems that continuing cross-border legal squabbles over Internet gaming are inevitable. Thus the Cohen case distills the collision of gaming, technology, and international commerce brought about by two simple facts—that Americans love to bet on sports and that in most of the United States they are barred from doing so legally. A people unsure of their convictions vis-à-vis gaming have produced a world in which a gaming entrepreneur can be transformed from being the toast of the *Wall Street Journal* to being a federal inmate simply by offering the public what it wants.

A Long Way From Camelot

The Wire Act is more than an artifact of the Kennedy years—it is a living piece of legislation that is, to date, the preeminent tool the federal government uses to curtail Internet gambling. A thorough reexamination of this law is necessary, both to better understand the world that created it and to comprehend the world that we have created around ourselves.

Americans in the Kennedy years, it seems, were just waking up to the realization that organized crime was a mammoth part of American life. Within a few years anxieties about organized crime would be displaced by far more pressing issues, as fissures of race, gender, age, and politics threatened to tear the nation asunder during the Johnson and Nixon years. Today, in a nation grappling with drug abuse, street violence, war, and economic anxiety, to say nothing of the specter of terrorism, legislation cracking down on the interstate transportation of wagering paraphernalia seems quaint. Yet Americans in 1961 had good reason to believe that a strike against gaming was the first necessary stab at organized crime, a national menace.

Considering the conditions attendant upon the passage of the Wire Act, it is important to remember where America once stood and now stands on the question of legalized gaming. In 1950, when similar legislation was proposed to Congress, the attorney general of the United States could tell civic leaders without hesitation that, despite several states' permitting legal parimutuel betting and one allowing virtually unrestricted gaming, "throughout the United States there is, and has existed for many years, a public policy that condemns organized gambling and makes its activities criminal."[16] In 1961 the legislative situation remained much the same. But by 1998, when the Wire Act was turned against Antigua's Internet sportsbooks, gaming had become an inextricable part of the social and fiscal policies of every state in the nation except two, Utah and Hawaii. When state governments actively encourage citizens to buy lottery tickets, it is difficult to argue that a national public policy justifying the use of federal resources to fight illegal gaming truly exists.

The Wire Act can teach us a few things about our own approach to gaming and crime. Public officials should translate the lessons learned by reflecting on the Wire Act into a more rational approach to both gambling and the challenges of new technology. Today, perhaps, is not that much different from the days when Attorney General Kennedy vowed to throttle organized crime. Now, as then, we face domestic problems set against an ominous backdrop of simmering, uncertain foreign aggression. Now, as then, Americans are about a decade removed from defeating a menacing adversary and in the midst of a confrontation with a seemingly more insidious one. And, of course, now, as then, Americans love to gamble and hate to think about what that means.

1   Legal Vices and Illicit Diversions

For more than two centuries, Americans have vacillated between their desires to permit and to control gaming, creating an erratic record of legalized gaming initiatives and a distasteful legacy of illegal gaming and corruption.

No matter where races are held in the land, the transmission by telegraph and telephone of race-track news makes betting possible here. As a result, gambling in poolrooms and by means of handbooks is practically as active in winter as during the summer, when our own tracks are open. Betting on horses, as it is conducted here, is one of the worst forms of gambling. It is impossible to beat the game. The jails, the poorhouses are crowded with men who have tried it.

When Russia stopped the traffic in vodka there were those who predicted that the Empire would fall. Instead the Nation has been infinitely enriched, mentally, morally, and physically. Race-track gambling, that hopeless chase of the golden will-o'-the-wisp, is sapping American manhood, destroying countless homes, wrecking countless lives. It is not improving the breed of horses, and it is playing havoc with the breed of men.

— *New York Globe* editorial, February 24, 1916

AMERICANS HAVE NEVER QUITE AGREED on what to do about gaming. They inherited a legislative indecision about gaming along with the rest of the corpus of English law. "The common law and the early English statutes on gambling were not consistent," wrote a New York judge as he surveyed gaming law in 1950. "Toleration and prohibitions of gambling went hand in hand."[1] Gaming conducted in a private house might not be criminal, but the same game played in a public place might be prosecuted as a breach of the peace or as corrupting to public morals. Often, authorities considered cheating at gambling, rather than gaming itself, to be a criminal act. Though the liberal attitude expressed in early common law gave way to statutory restrictions on gaming, an essential tension remained: Gaming, if not completely legal, was never completely illegal either.

A gaming casino is legal in Nevada, legal in Illinois if it has one of the ten permitted licenses and is waterborne, and illegal under any circumstances in Tennessee. Betting on horses is legal in New York on track and at OTB shops, legal in Nevada sportsbooks unaffiliated with any track, and illegal in Mississippi. What makes a gaming operator an honest living in one state will get him imprisoned in another one. Furthermore, gaming statutes are notoriously unstable; legislators constantly experiment with new forms of legalized gaming, often rejecting them in the face of mounting public dissatisfaction. What was illegal in 1934 may have become legal in 1935, but there was no guarantee that it would remain legal in 1936.

Legal uncertainty about gaming often translated into government support of various schemes of legalized (and taxed) gaming. Never shy about experimenting with licensing and taxing a supposed vice to enrich the public coffers, Americans have not been exactly resolute in their determination to harness gaming for the public benefit either. But because that same public rarely paused in its zeal for betting, gaming continued. Now officially illegal, it contributed no revenue to the state and operated under a presumed cloak of secrecy. Over the decades illegal gambling grew by leaps and bounds, while legal gambling sputtered forward.

Gambling Prohibition: Is There a Rhyme or Reason?

Americans have gambled for a very long time. Many times, they had no problem with keeping gaming ostensibly illegal, but at other times they resolved to legalize, regulate, and tax gaming. Surprisingly, these efforts most often proved transitory, ending in scandal, failure, and recriminalization. The Wire Act is best seen in the context of these cycles of legalization and criminalization. This law did not come hurtling down to Earth from the inky reaches of space; it was the end result of ten years of serious congressional discussion and drew upon more than a century's worth of anti-gaming legislation on the state level and seventy years' worth of hesitant federal anti-gaming efforts. Without understanding the legal backdrop of gaming in the United States, it is impossible to fix exactly the motives of the Wire Act's authors and the law's intended consequences.

The standard framework for viewing American flirtations with legalized gaming has been the "three waves" model, which, according to gaming law expert I. Nelson Rose, suggests that the United States has seen three major waves of gaming legalization.[2] The first wave, beginning "during the colonial period," ended before the Civil War. The second wave started with the Civil War (or more accurately, with Reconstruction), as the devastated South turned to lotteries for quick revenues. This wave ended with the disgrace of the Louisiana lottery in the 1890s and resulted in "imposition of stiff federal laws and state constitutional restrictions" against legal gaming. A third wave, which started in 1964 with the first state lottery of the twentieth century, the New Hampshire Sweepstakes, continues today.[3]

But this framework has limitations. The legal status of the lottery divorced from other laws against gaming and, indeed, the social, cultural, and economic context of the law itself do not really explain why Americans have turned toward, then away from, legal gaming. Rather than a neat series of three longitudinal waves, the American experience with gaming has been characterized by pragmatic experimentation as citizens sought to balance a desire for social control and a lingering distrust of gamblers with the need to channel gaming to benefit society. As befits a federal system, this experimentation took place primarily on the state and even county levels, rendering attempts to construct national interpretations of gaming legislation nearly inconsequential.

A model in which large waves regularly sweep the landscape, leaving uniform change in their wake, hardly describes the pell-mell history of legal gaming in the United States. Instead, we might be better off thinking of legal gaming as a weather system. Rain in Washington tonight does not mean that Philadelphians are grabbing their umbrellas, to say nothing of citizens of Phoenix. Local forces, such as topography, interact with larger global ones, such as the Gulf Stream, to produce understandable, though not always predictable, patterns. Similarly, legal gaming schemes owed much to big-picture national developments, such as the fluctuations of economic fortune, but they manifested themselves in ways unique to their local environments. This model is not as tidy as wave theory, which is itself vaguely rooted in the cyclical nature of the economy (not the law), but it helps us to better understand what actually happened.

Or perhaps it is best to say that there is no simple framework for understanding why gambling is legal at some times in some places and illegal in others. Historians still cannot (or perhaps should not) give pat explanations for the fall of the Roman Empire, the disappearance of the civilization that built Mohenjo-daro, or countless other phenomena. Perhaps it's only natural that Americans, as people living in an imperfect world and working with imperfect information, have experimented with legal gaming with no eye for the big picture and no real master plan.

Betting in a New World

Gambling in America is older than the nation itself. The first inhabitants of North America wagered avidly, and the "American culture of chance" that developed with the American nation ultimately, according to historian Jackson Lears, fused African, Native American, and European Catholic traditions with a dominant British-American-Protestant culture of control that ostensibly disapproved of frivolities like games of chance but never quite eradicated them.[4] The records of the earliest European trappers, colonists, and missionaries in what would become the United States are so rife with descriptions of Indian rituals that intertwined gambling and divination that gaming could be labeled a nearly universal element in Native American cultures. Even before European settlement, North America witnessed much gambling, all of it public and legal.

The Anglo-American forebears of the Republic did not embrace gaming as unapologetically, but as gaming was an essential part of life in the mother country, it was certainly widespread from the earliest days of British North America. The first expeditions to the New World, financed by stock companies, were themselves a form of wagering. Perhaps a subscriber's ship might land safely and its crew discover gold, or land amenable to exploitation, yielding a pretty dividend; perhaps it would capsize in a storm before even sighting land, meaning a total loss. The stock subscriber stood to gain profit or suffer loss depending on the outcome of an event ultimately beyond his control—the very definition of gambling.

Those who crossed the Atlantic in search of a new life or simply to extract as much as possible from the New World before returning to the Old were gamblers too, whether they were dauntless adventurers or God-fearing men and women in search of religious and civic utopia. The element of risk inherent in any such enterprise that asks its participants to abandon the lives they know for an unknown future means that all those who chose to seek a fortune in the new land were wagering on a better tomorrow.

So when historian John Findlay labels Americans a "people of chance," he is quite accurate. The earliest British gambles on "plantations" in America in the 1570s and 1580s ended in failure, so risk shadowed the settlers of the early seventeenth century, who gambled that they could somehow succeed where all others had failed. Notably, the joint stock company charged with the settlement of Virginia helped to defray its debts by running a lottery in

England. After running the lottery (and settlements in the Chesapeake Bay) from 1612 to 1621, the Virginia Company remained in the red. Its subscribers must have known the frustration of the gambler who, as she walks away from her slot machine, sees the next gambler at the same machine hit the big jackpot; after the company was dissolved and Virginia declared a crown colony, the discovery that tobacco could be raised and sold profitably made the enterprise a lucrative one.[5]

Of the two earliest permanent British settlements, the Virginia plantations and the Massachusetts Bay Colony, the tidewater cavaliers of Jamestown and its environs have secured a reputation as the more notorious gamblers. But there was nothing peculiar to the Chesapeake that transformed industrious Englishmen into dissolute plungers. Instead, it must be remembered, the colonization of America took place during the "seventeenth-century explosion" of English gaming. Hand in glove with the growth of international trade, the rise of a cash and credit economy, and the development of a probabilistic, rationalist mind-set came an upswing in the popularity of gaming. As sociologist Gerda Reith argues in *The Age of Chance*, this eruption of gaming took three primary forms: speculation in chancy economic ventures, betting between individuals, and gambling at games of chance.[6] All of these were found, to one degree or another, in every American colony.

Though the Calvinist Puritans of Massachusetts Bay, fervid believers in predestination and sober industriousness, sanctimoniously abhorred gambling, playing games nonetheless took root, particularly as the colony continued its declension from the theocratic republic of the "city on a hill" to the bustling commercial nexus of New England, home to fishermen, mechanics, and merchants. Yet the desire to stamp out gaming remained, as can be judged from the fact that, for Harvard graduate students in the late seventeenth century, wagering was, fiscally, the ultimate sin; if caught playing cards they could be fined 5 shillings, the highest penalty (drunkenness, at 3 shillings, and profaning the Lord's name, at 1.6 shillings, were comparatively mild offenses).[7]

Colonial antigambling laws were more often aimed at guarding against idleness or the "nuisances" associated with gaming than the activity itself. The first antigambling law passed in the colonies, a 1646 Massachusetts edict, was directed not against those who profited from gambling but rather against "houses of entertainment," which were defined as places allowing shuffleboard and bowling, for within these places "much precious time is spent unprofitably, and much waste of beer and wine occasioned."[8] Where laws did exist against gaming, they usually prohibited not the activity itself but rather the excesses involved in public tavern gaming, a milieu described as wasteful and dissolute.[9] In the South, early statutes addressed cheating, fighting, and economic dislocation caused by large-scale gaming losses, and laws against gaming were irregular, "patch-quilt affairs, with specific evils being subject to prohibition as they arose."[10]

So gambling thrived in the British North American colonies. Since most of the betting took place among private citizens, it usually escaped the attentions of the law and the scythe of historical harvest, and its true reach can only be speculated. Thus we do not know much about how frequently colonists gambled on horses or cards—merely that they did so often enough to occasion laws that addressed the nuisances caused by gaming but rarely gaming itself. Another, very public, form of gambling was well documented, however—lotteries. Lotteries endorsed by the monarch had been legal in England since the medieval era. In the final years of the seventeenth century, lotteries fell under parliamentary control and were used, beginning in 1694, as tools to raise revenue.[11] The American colonies retained such lotteries.

By the time of the Revolution, gaming was well entrenched. If not always legal, gaming as a generic activity was rarely criminal. So it is really not surprising to read that the Continental Congress authorized a lottery to pay the expenses of the resistance effort, or that George Washington himself gambled, despite his proclamation that his officers and soldiers should forswear gambling, the "cause of evil" and "many a brave and gallant officer's ruin," for working and training. Even Thomas Jefferson patiently endured the swings of fortune as he played backgammon, cards, and lotto while writing the Declaration of Independence.[12] When he was close to death, and his estate appeared unable to settle his debts, he received a charter from the Virginia legislature to sell his real estate via a lottery to satisfy his creditors; the lottery was canceled after Jefferson died, but it shows the propriety of the lottery as a legitimate fiscal tool.[13] The founding fathers looked out on a new nation that undeniably liked to test its luck.

Wolf Traps and Serpents

Gaming, predictably, soon became an inextricable part of the "new order of the ages" of the American nation. The new regime inherited the ambiguous legislation of the colonial period, with lotteries given state sanction, some elements of public gaming disallowed, and private gaming usually left alone.

But as the nation grew economically, and gaming both increased and changed its nature, citizens began to demand stronger antigambling laws. The Market Revolution of the early nineteenth century saw the growth of a domestic market in the United States based on manufacturing, not just exports; in many previously inaccessible parts of the continent, farmers were drawn into the commercial economy—instead of raising food for subsistence, they grew it for the markets. With this new market came banks and capitalism, as well as increased speculation in land and businesses. This chancy wagering on business, so akin to outright gambling, made some rich but ruined others. Andrew Jackson's legendary rage against the Bank of the United States, for example, can be traced to his own failed land investments, an early, brutal introduction to the new world of commercial speculation.[14]

As Americans traveled more and had more currency in their pockets, they naturally had occasion to gamble more often. This situation facilitated the development of professional gamblers, men who made their livings solely from the profits of their gaming. Games of cards and dice were no longer social diversions and now took a decidedly economic cast, with definite winners and losers. By the 1820s, even previously sacrosanct lotteries began to attract negative attention, as professional lottery corporations emerged to manage increasingly lucrative contests, displacing the disinterested, public-minded citizens who had previously run lotteries as a public service. Unlike the part-time managers they replaced, these lottery professionals had no special ties to the community and were usually more interested in maximizing their personal enrichment than in increasing the monies left for the charity or project in question. Such promoters transformed the lottery from a civic exercise in voluntary contribution to a strictly moneymaking proposition.[15] Lotteries, no longer contributing meaningfully to the public good, became viewed as yet another monopoly that preyed upon industrious citizens.

Such a shift in public perceptions augured a slow doom for lotteries. States (starting with Massachusetts in 1833) began abolishing them.[16] While certain particularly noisome incidents of fraud, embezzlement, and suicide sparked the turn against lotteries in the 1830s, it is no coincidence that during these same years, Andrew Jackson waged his war against the Bank of the United States and, in general, privilege and monopoly came under attack.[17] The turn against legal lotteries was not the isolated response of citizens to the excesses of lottery promoters but part of a general mistrust of speculation and special charters. In addition, these years saw the religious revival of the Second Great Awakening, which inspired some citizens to disdain recreations such as gambling and embrace temperance and slow, steady self-improvement. The end of legal lotteries signified not a larger shift in American attitudes toward gaming but rather a specific response to the specific issue of privately run monopolistic lotteries that, more often than not, served no public interest.[18]

Indeed, though laws against public gaming houses remained on the books, Americans did not slow their wagering. If anything, the volume of gaming increased. As the population diffused throughout the opening West, gaming continued to play an important part in everyday life, as Americans on the frontier wagered on horse racing, cockfighting, cards, and dice. States that outlawed gaming permitted wagers between individuals and prohibited only bank games in which a player bet against the house.[19] Such gambling, primarily social in nature, soon acceded to the growing market ethos of the times, and a class of professional gamesters, much like the professional lottery managers, emerged.

With the increase in river commerce and a cash economy in general in the 1820s, blacklegs (as the professionals were called in the popular parlance) saw the opportunity to settle down and allow the gambling trade—primarily those who worked or traveled the river to sell merchandise—to come to them. Transportation hubs like Knoxville, Louisville, Memphis, and particularly Natchez soon sported "outlaws, desperadoes, hardened prostitutes, and unprincipled gamblers."[20] In rough-and-tumble establishments known as gambling hells or low dens, professional gamblers bilked river workers and travelers, usually with few legal consequences. As the volume of river trade increased in the 1830s, this became a growing problem. Still, as long the gamblers kept to their low dens and did not intrude upon "polite society," they were neglected. It was not until 1835 and the discovery of a massive conspiracy linked to gamblers that the river towns took decisive action against professional gamblers.

In June of that year, Mississippians learned that John Murrell, a desperado and gambler, had organized a band of outlaws, gamblers, and opportunists—known as the Clan of the Mystic Confederation—that sought to incite a slave revolt, a terrifying concept for most white Mississippians, slaveholders and non-slaveholders alike. But Murrell was no abolitionist firebrand seeking to liberate the slaves. The conspiracy's ultimate goal was not to topple the cruel regime of slavery but to take advantage of the confusion of the uprising by looting the towns while the white residents quashed the revolt. When the conspiracy was discovered, it unleashed the worst fears of white

Southerners and decisively turned many towns throughout the region violently against gamblers. There was no new official legislation passed to mark this occasion; rather, vigilante committees typically rousted the low dens and forced their denizens to move on under pain of death. In one town, Vicksburg, tensions between "citizens" and the demimonde exploded, as a vigilante group summarily lynched five gamblers after a small riot.[21] Yet for all the sound and fury, Southerners soon found they couldn't bear to hate gamblers. Though the blacklegs never returned to their old river hangouts, they morphed into figures still resonant in American mythology: riverboat gamblers, who cheated to win and moved on. Riverboats would remain notorious haunts of professional gamblers through the Civil War; gambling on the rivers stopped only in the 1860s, when railroads surpassed riverboats as the nation's premier transportation.

In the major cities, professional gaming increased in scope because there were progressively more people with more money. As in the river towns, and as was common throughout Europe, most urban American gambling took place in commercial establishments that were specifically places to gamble. With the increased sophistication of the economy and the development of cities as major commercial centers, a new phenomenon emerged—the gambling house. Originally, taverns or coffeehouses provided tables and even implements of play for their customers, who wagered among themselves. Some such houses eventually became primarily places for gaming, and the proprietors eventually introduced bank games that pitted customers against the house.

This happened in stages. A kind of gaming house known as a wolf-trap, snap house, deadfall, or 10 percent house originated in Cincinnati in the 1830s and quickly spread throughout the nation. In a wolf-trap, anyone could open a game; a faro dealer could walk in with $50, buy chips from the wolf-trap manager, set up at a table, and deal. The house provided the gaming implements and surveillance to guard against player or dealer cheating. If the dealer walked away a winner, the house took 10 percent of the profits; if he lost, the house took nothing. Because players, dealers, and management summarily dealt rough justice to cheaters, games were more or less on the square.[22] Since games like faro gave the house no real advantage over the player, this meant rather small revenues. To truly make money running a gaming house, operators needed a different system.

Such a system soon emerged. By 1835, the same year that legal gaming in New Orleans crashed (temporarily) and the South turned against gaming, a "small and select" number of "very splendid hells" had appeared in New York City, the nation's commercial capital. Upscale houses, "elegantly fitted up," offered their patrons fine dining, good cigars, heady liquors, and the opportunity to play against the house, sometimes fairly. Lower-rent skinning houses offered few pretenses of luxury and generally fleeced out-of-towners; most employed ropers who set upon new arrivals and steered them to the slaughter.[23]

The first of these houses, dating from the 1820s, featured only tables where patrons could play among themselves, but soon gaming houses began offering bank games, at which customers bet against the house—a sign of the rise of the professional gambler. New York City and Washington, D.C., were famous for their illegal (but easy to find) gambling dens, but New Orleans led all cities in the number and quality of its "very splendid hells." Indeed, Herbert Asbury, in his informal history of American gambling, *Sucker's Progress*, considered the Crescent City to be the "fountain-head" of gambling in the United States.[24] Owing to the cultural syncretism of French, Spanish, Native American, African, and Anglo-American traditions, New Orleans had the distinction of fostering a diverse set of games (including, perhaps, craps and poker) and gamblers.

New Orleans's experiment with legalized casino gaming and the circumstances that attended its demise warrant the attention of those interested in how Americans have intertwined gaming and law. Louisiana, which the United States purchased from Napoleon in 1803, inherited French, rather than English, law. Authorities initially permitted gambling, which flourished in New Orleans, an entrepot with many transient people who had large sums of money to spend. But with the advent of Louisiana's statehood in 1811, the legislature outlawed gambling in all areas except New Orleans with the caveat that it be closely supervised there by municipal authorities. These authorities, overworked with maintaining general public order, made little effort to regulate gaming, and in this laissez-faire environment crooked games predominated. In 1820 the state legislature revoked all legal gambling privileges, but this served only to remove gamblers from even token oversight. Gambling continued unabated, and the City of New Orleans was officially no richer for it, though graft from gaming operators unofficially lined the pockets of politicians and police alike.

So in 1823 the state legalized gambling again, permitting six gambling houses to operate for a $5,000 annual license fee each, earmarked for the support of the College of New Orleans and the Charity Hospital. The paying licensees pressured the police to stamp out illegal gambling, and within three years illegal games were rare. The games were reported to be honest, and a portion of gaming revenue was being siphoned off for the public good. Everyone, it seemed, was a winner. These opulent houses attracted imitators, and a score of "clubhouses" opened as the legislature upped the annual license fee to $7,500 and permitted an unlimited number of houses to operate.

But in 1835 the Louisiana legislature turned violently against gamblers, making the act of running a gambling house a felony punishable by a sizable fine and prison time. There are a variety of reasons for this sudden about-face, including the growing political power of certain operators and the rising tide of Southern resentment against professional gamblers, which boiled over that year with the revelations of the Murrell conspiracy.[25] Quite simply, the nouveau riche gamblers lacked the kind of institutional buy-in that might have insulated them from public outrage. Like the professional lottery corporations, these licensed casinos became viewed as another corrupt (and corrupting) monopoly. Still, the state ban was not absolute, as the city began in the 1840s to license and tax casinos once again, a practice that endured into the 1860s.[26] The early colonial statutes that outlawed public gaming hardly dampened the ardor of the betting public. It would not be until the 1950s and a decided turn against illegal urban gaming that Americans would quite get the hang of putting their money behind their convictions. All other things being equal, the gaming in any given time in American history, legal or otherwise, roughly parallels the latest trends in mainstream business organization. So in the earliest years of the Republic, when the rudiments of a capitalist economy were taking shape, most American gaming was still predominantly a community affair. Friends and relations got together at the local tavern and wagered on cards, dice, bowling, or more arcane sports like bear baiting. With the rise of a cash economy, professional gamblers appeared—but usually working on their own and only occasionally banding together.

Before the Civil War, most gaming houses were run by limited partnerships. One or two professional gamblers sought investors and opened a house. As long as revenue outpaced expenses (which included graft as well as salaries, dividends, and payouts to customers), the house remained in business. Occasionally, a single operator owned shares in more than one house. Reuben Parsons, the "Great American Faro Banker," invested in a number of gaming houses and made enough money from his business to invest in real estate and retire from the gaming business. Although he maintained a network of spies and confidants throughout his gambling empire, it had no truly corporate structure; each employee owed personal allegiance to Parsons and was scarcely conscious of working for a larger combine. When Parsons left the "industry," he left behind no organization to speak of.[27]

After the Civil War, however, full-scale gaming syndicates became far more common. Such syndicates ran both opulent, first-class hells and the roughest gaming dens. Combining their finances enabled syndicate members to take larger bets and expand into nearby cities. Syndicates also contracted with police and politicians, systematizing protection for their houses and arranging to shut down rival operators. Again, this mirrored developments in the mainstream of American business, as pools and trusts did virtually the same thing in industries ranging from beef to cigarettes. The most notorious of these syndicates evolved into the "gambling commission" of New York City, which used city police as its active enforcement arm. The "commission" authorized new gaming operations and taxed them by charging a set fee. Any operation that failed to get commission approval or fell behind in its tribute was immediately raided and closed. In 1900 the commission took in more than $3 million from nearly 1,200 different operations.[28] Gaming houses, illegal or not, were a functional part of the American economic and political system.

Likewise, it is important to note that the turn against lotteries and even friendly betting on card games, which intensified in the 1840s and 1850s, represented only a specific reaction to these specific forms of gambling and not evidence of any larger pattern of American intolerance for gaming. Where there was sentiment against the lottery, it was often commingled with anti-bank or anti-commercial feelings. Though some states, such as Mississippi (1857) and Arkansas (1855), made all forms of betting illegal, this does not represent the thundering end of a wave of gaming legalization. In the Far West, card and dice gaming was either legal, as it was in Nevada from 1869 until the end of the century and San Francisco from 1856 to 1860, or simply allowed to flourish unmolested as the result of salutary police neglect. Horse racing remained legal in many states, and in others penalties were so gentle that even professional gamblers continued to operate openly.[29] In New York City, despite the best efforts of antigambling reformers such as the Association for the Suppression of Gambling, there were an estimated six thousand places to gamble, and 25,000 men (one-twentieth of the whole population) who made their living from gambling, if the sources are to be believed.[30]

Some states rolled the dice on legal gaming, with generally poor results.

Florida experimented unsuccessfully with casino gaming in the 1880s before completely abandoning the scheme in 1895. These forays into legal gaming do not show any kind of decisive swing toward legal gaming as a national public policy in the late nineteenth century. One could, in fact, argue the opposite. Congress took its first steps to restrict the national distribution of lottery materials in 1868, when it included a provision in the postal statutes that barred the mailing of such items.[31] Many Southern governments remained in the antigambling camp; Georgia, for example, specifically forbade the legislature from authorizing lotteries at its Reconstruction Constitutional Convention of 1868 and went so far as to outlaw contracts in agricultural futures in 1883, something that several other states, bowing to Granger and Populist pressures, did as well.[32]

As with its early experiment with casinos, Louisiana was the exception rather than the rule. The Reconstruction government of the state, looking for ways to raise funds and mindful of the abundant sale of Havana lottery tickets in New Orleans, was empowered by its new constitution to authorize a lottery company. A concomitant act to legalize all gaming houses upon the payment of a $5,000 annual fee ended in failure, but the Louisiana Lottery Company, known colloquially as the Serpent, prospered. Originally selling tickets only in New Orleans, by 1877 it sold chances in every state of the Union. With daily (except Sunday), monthly, and semiannual drawings, the lottery brought in tremendous sums. This wealth enabled the company's owners to buy influence in the legislature and insulate their monopoly from competition. This corruption eventually so angered the citizens of Louisiana that in 1890 they voted against extending the company's charter, set to expire in 1895, despite fervent lobbying efforts by the lottery.[33]

In 1876, in direct reaction to the Louisiana Lottery Company, Congress strengthened the existing anti-lottery statutes by striking the word "illegal," in effect barring the mailing of even state-sanctioned lottery materials. Finally, Congress passed an even stronger anti-lottery bill in 1890 that decisively barred the use of the mail for lottery advertising or operations. After the Louisiana Lottery Company transferred its operations to the Honduras, Congress responded with an 1895 provision that further barred the importation of foreign lottery materials. This step finally stopped the Serpent, and the Louisiana lottery ceased operations.[34] The anti-lottery federal statutes of the 1890s did not represent a seismic shift in federal attitudes toward gaming; rather they were a specific reaction to the crisis posed by the Louisiana lottery. Only the federal government could legislate control of the postal system, so non-lottery states demanded that Congress follow their lead and act against the interstate sale of lottery tickets. The Louisiana lottery took advantage of the federal system to sell lottery tickets by mail where it could not open legal franchises, and it was this perceived abuse that federal action sought to curtail. Other forms of gaming and betting, more amenable to local control, remained under the prerogative of state control.

As the lottery game played out in Louisiana, gambling continued in the cities and resorts of the North, and in the burgeoning lands of the West, usually illegally. In the major cities, the risky proposition of running a gaming house was rarely an individual effort, as syndicate ownership—which spread the chance of ruin and enlarged the house's bankroll—became the norm. These syndicates, in addition to providing a measure of financial security against the necessary risk of a gaming enterprise, also allowed gaming operators to better coordinate cooperation with the local politico-police regime. While policy had been syndicated since the end of the Civil War, during the 1880s and 1890s bookmaking became syndicated as well. Bookmakers formed local turf associations to regularize relations with racetracks and police and to monopolize the trade for members.[35] Exactly the same development transformed "legitimate" business into a system dominated by pools or trusts, which likewise collectively ameliorated relations with the government and stifled competition.

The wide-open/reform/wide-open pattern of gambling enforcement in the cities, predating the development of formal police in the middle of the nineteenth century, became more regular with the development of big money gaming syndicates in the latter part of the century. The paltry enforcement of anti-gaming statutes was only one in a series of issues that Progressive reformers like Theodore Roosevelt seized upon. Though a personal bugbear for some, it remained a minor part of national reform efforts. Thus, while the Progressive Era saw an ephemeral victory for the anti-gaming forces in previously wide-open Nevada, where all but social wagering was banned in 1910 (though the ban was never effective), the Progressive impetus against gaming never solidified into anything approaching the anti-alcohol effort, which climaxed with the passage of the Eighteenth Amendment in 1919 and the Volstead Act in 1920, which made illegal the manufacture, sale, or transportation of alcoholic beverages (with a few exceptions). Once the trans-state problem of the Louisiana lottery had been dispatched, citizens comfortably returned the task of gaming enforcement to the states. Gaming was simply not a galvanizing national issue; every attempt at federal action against gambling, save the stifling of the Louisiana lottery, failed.

Before too long, gaming proponents began beating the drums for the legalization—or simply decriminalization—of betting. The Nevada experiment with gaming prohibition was almost immediately rolled back, as in 1915 the legislature decriminalized games played for cigars, drinks, or sums less than two dollars. In 1931, looking for a way out of the malaise of the Depression, the legislature would famously inaugurate wide-open casino gaming (along with horse racing and "quickie" six-week divorces) in an attempt to foster economic development, an experiment that has been more than successful. In other states, while lotteries remained beyond the pale of civic consideration, legal betting on horse racing began to spread, as did experiments with slot machines and bingo and charitable gaming.

The Progressive years witnessed the apex of the prohibition of legal gaming. By the early 1920s, legal race betting had been eradicated from nearly every state. Slot machines, gaming houses, betting parlors, and lotteries continued to operate, but they were officially outlawed. With the realization that citizens continued to gamble, many states turned to legalized, regulated pari-mutuel wagering on horse racing for revenue. Some early outcroppings of this trend appeared in 1925, when Florida legalized pari-mutuel wagering, and in 1927, when Illinois did so.[36] In 1933, as Franklin Roosevelt launched the New Deal to lift the nation out of the Depression, a total of ten states moved to legalize race wagering: California, Michigan, New Hampshire, New Mexico, North Carolina, Ohio, Oregon, Texas (which soon returned to prohibition), Washington, and West Virginia.[37] By the 1940s, all northeastern states had sanctioned pari-mutuel wagering, usually under the authority of a regulatory commission.[38] While several states in the South did not legalize pari-mutuel betting, for religious or moral reasons, by World War II many of the most populous and developed states had a direct stake in legal race wagering. In addition, the loosening of antigambling statutes to permit charitable gaming such as bingo gave the 1930s and 1940s an often forgotten boom in state-sanctioned gaming. It is telling that, while the economic doldrums of the 1930s lowered purse sizes, the horse racing industry on the whole thrived, chiefly because state need for pari-mutuel revenues gave governments a vested interest in regulating, if not promoting, the sport.[39]

Some states also toyed with the legalization of slot machines. In 1935, the Florida legislature declared them legal, with counties given the option to forbid them. The regulatory regime, however, could not guarantee any degree of reputability or oversight, and a violent public reaction against slots forced the legislature to recriminalize the machines a scant two years later.[40] A 1937 Montana law permitting religious, fraternal, and charitable groups to operate slots and punchboards (a similarly random game) did little to improve the state's finances, and the governor in fact singled out his signing of those laws as "the two outstanding mistakes" of his administration. In 1945, Idaho legalized slots statewide, but two years later the state turned slots over to local control and ultimately abandoned legal slots entirely.[41] Maryland had a longer fling with one-armed bandits; in 1943 (the same year that an act enabling pari-mutuel wagering passed), the state legislature authorized Anne Arundel County to legalize and tax slots. By 1951 five Maryland counties had legal slot machines. But less-than-anticipated revenues combined with rumors of corruption to persuade the legislature, in 1963, to begin a five-year phaseout of legal gaming.[42]

So as the United States demobilized from World War II and began the anxious prosperity of the "long decade" of the 1950s, there was hardly a national consensus on gaming. Most citizens still made no connection between the slot machines in their corner tavern and the political corruption that marred many city governments. There seemed little reason to press the federal government into action. But within a few years citizens would be clamoring desperately for the federal government to strike back against the "boss gamblers," chiefly because of the increased scope of gaming, particularly slot machines and bookmaking. Against the seemingly favorable backdrop of increased government sanction of gaming, gamblers had upped the ante, a bold bluff that would ultimately backfire.

Any Number Can Win

Horse racing was a popular diversion from the colonial days, and betting was almost always associated with the races. Though often illegal, it boomed along with the general increase in horse racing of the late nineteenth century; the formation of the National Trotting Association in 1870 is evidence of the desire to exercise a degree of central control over the horse racing "industry," which was susceptible to charges of crooked races.[43] Toward the end of the century, "running races" began to supplant "trotting races" as favored amusements.

Variously condoned and condemned throughout the nineteenth century, betting on horses, like other forms of gaming, reached its nadir in the Progressive Era; in 1917 it was legal in only Kentucky and Maryland. The sport of racing, as distinct from legal betting on it, had increased greatly in popularity since the 1870s, but pari-mutuel wagering on horses failed to catch on, largely because existing turf associations worked to keep out this new competition. Some states experimented with permitting legal gaming at the tracks; the Ives Pool Bill, passed by the New York legislature in 1887, sanctioned betting, pool-selling, and bookmaking at prescribed periods for the purposes of "improving the breed," but it was overturned by an 1894 constitutional amendment that prohibited all forms of gaming, including betting on horses.[44] Though many states outlawed wagering on horses, betting at the tracks continued, frequently with little pretense of stealth. The conventional wisdom held that "there is no racing if there be no betting," and, judging from the continued proliferation of racing and betting news in newspapers of the period, there was still an abundance of wagering conducted.[45]

Opponents directly linked the burgeoning racing industry to wagering. An 1895 anti-gaming manifesto, appropriately titled *The Highway to Hell: Shall We Improve the Breed of Horses or Men?*, began by stating that the most vicious evils in the United States associated with chance emanated from "the turf."[46] In addition to wagering at tracks, telegraph technology allowed for the creation of "poolrooms" or horse rooms, in which bettors could lay stakes on races run throughout the country. This created a "mania" for horse wagering, both at the tracks and in the poolrooms. The author of *Highway to Hell* decried the fact that "year by year the fever of gambling on the races increases in intensity and the range of its operations." Even worse, the news media not only tolerated this growing mania but actually fed it by publishing "pointers," advice to bettors that was no more informed than blind guessing but that served the journalistic enterprise by selling papers.[47] From the cities to the tracks, betting on horses could be found nearly anywhere.

Bookmaking increased in complexity as one accepted larger bets. At the first level, a bookmaker, handling small wagers of $2 to $10, entered the business with about $1,000 in capital. His clients made their selection by checking newspapers and scratch sheets, and he determined the winners by checking the newspapers on the following day. Such an operator had a small group of clients, with whom he settled accounts after each day of betting, and he did not need the wire service, since there was no urgency to his clients' bets, or the security of a lay-off service, since he did not accept large bets.[48] The second-tier operator, accepting bets of up to $100 per horse, maintained an office with two to fifteen phones and hired agents to collect bets from industrial and office workplaces. Because he accepted phone and proxy bets in real time, he needed to subscribe to the wire service to keep tabs on changing odds. The larger size of his bets also created the need for a lay-off service, or a larger bookmaker to relieve the risk associated with large amounts wagered on a single horse.[49] Large-scale operators with direct subscriptions to the wire service occupied the third tier.[50] Located in storefronts where the public could watch the changing odds and place bets, these operations both retailed betting to high-end customers and wholesaled it by accepting lay-off bets from smaller bookmakers. Bookmaking was quite a business, and the fact that different sizes of bookmaking operations serviced different parts of the betting market reveals the incredible public appetite for betting on equines.

If Americans had a fondness for wagering on horses, they also evinced a partiality to betting on contests between humans. Prizefighting attracted its share of wagers, but team sports became even more attractive for bettors, particularly with the establishment of professional and collegiate leagues in the late nineteenth century. Even newspapers joined in the mania for betting on sports, with one daily offering an early baseball pool to its readers; the "correct guesser" of the first- and second-place finishers in the (then) three professional leagues received a prize of $500.[51] Another newspaper reported in 1909 an early example of spread betting in a Pennsylvania/Yale Ivy League gridiron matchup:

> The Yale men were offering odds . . . that the blue would triumph over the red and blue by at least twenty points. . . . The Pennsylvanians placed considerable money at these odds, and consequently won. So far as is known not a single Pennsylvania man lost a dollar on this game, in consequence of which the Philadelphians are jubilant and the Yalesians correspondingly downcast. Thus was the game a victory for the Pennsylvania backers, and the presumption is that they got all they lost on the Princeton game and more besides.[52]

Obviously, betting on sports was common enough; that the Penn men had earlier bet on "the Princeton game" is considered a given, providing evidence that betting was customary. This article, incidentally, records a crude version of social spread betting years before most histories report the first professional bookies taking spread bets, suggesting that the practice was not the innovation of one or two isolated operators but rather a widespread phenomenon. In any event, it is clear that betting on games was prevalent, even at the low point of legalized gaming in the United States, the years immediately after World War I.

Gambling on games was so ubiquitous, in fact, that one writer has argued that baseball's National League owes its founding to the need for a "strong" league that would root out gamblers' rampant interference with America's pastime. Gamblers, in this analysis, "operated openly in the stand," and players who accepted bribes to throw games in the most obvious of fashions were never penalized.[53] The Black Sox scandal, in which eight members of the heavily favored Chicago White Sox allegedly accepted bribes ranging from $5,000 to $30,000 to throw the 1919 World Series, was hardly an isolated incident. A major 1877 betting scandal resulted in four players from the Louisville Grays being permanently banished from the sport, and the friendliness of some players, particularly first baseman Hal Chase, with well-known gamblers smacked of collusion.[54] Sports betting exercised an influence so great that it threatened the integrity of the games themselves. Still, while such betting was never exactly legal, because it took place mostly between individuals, few police officers concerned themselves with it.

Illegal betting on sports would develop into a thriving business in the twentieth century. Baseball pool cards, present in New York City from the turn of the century, permitted players to make small bets on several statistical categories, such as which team would lead the league in runs scored. Football pool cards, which required the bettor to select five winning teams from a pool of nine weekly games, became a thriving industry in the 1930s.[55] The popularization of point-spread betting in the 1940s led to increased wagering and the ascendancy of college basketball as a betting vehicle. Despite several major point-shaving scandals, college basketball would remain popular with bettors into the next century.[56] By the middle of the twentieth century, betting on sports had undeniably emerged as a large and apparently profitable illegal business.

If sports betting took time to evolve into a professional business, illegal lotteries were, from the start, strictly business propositions, with no pretense of casual wagering among friends. The switch from policy to numbers in the early part of the twentieth century apparently did not slake the urban public's thirst for chance, as the volume of bets increased.

Numbers operations tended to be uncomplicated, with few barriers to entry. On the street (literally and metaphorically), bettors "purchased" bets from writers or runners, who made a commission of 10 percent. A pickup man picked up cash receipts and books of slips from the writer and delivered them to the bank, where the banker or his employees tabulated the receipts and coordinated payments to winners. Often, numbers banks themselves "laid off" numbers that were particularly strongly played to larger banks.[57] A prospective numbers banker needed only access to runners to employ, a larger bank with which to lay off as insurance against a big hit, and knowledge of the right politico-police palms to grease. Because so little was required to start up a numbers route, it became a popular business for urban entrepreneurs who were denied entry or were unwilling to enter legal business. With the hard economic times of the 1930s, the numbers grew even stronger. In 1936, for example, one anti-gaming author estimated the nation's total bill for "commercialized gambling," including foreign lotteries, the numbers, race betting, and sports pools, to exceed $6.6 billion a year.[58] By the end of World War II the numbers, along with bookmaking, were apparently ubiquitous in the streets and factories of urban America.

If the anti-gaming jeremiads are to be believed, illegal gaming had reached epidemic proportions by the late 1940s. A 1948 *BusinessWeek* study estimated that in the average industrial workplace, one out of every 250 employees supplemented his or her income by working as an agent for a gaming operation; from this work, the agents made up to fifty times their weekly legal wages. In large plants (more than 1,000 employees), about 10 percent of all employees consistently gambled, and about 50 percent gambled occasionally. In smaller plants, either nearly all employees gambled or none of them did. Plant management, the study found, almost certainly tolerated in-plant gaming, and in several cases foremen acted as gambling agents themselves. Preferred forms of betting included numbers, horse races, and sports betting. The article summarizing the results of the study also implied that labor unions were susceptible to corruption from gaming, though it concluded, "Unionism and in-plant gambling don't mix well."[59] It was all too apparent, though, that illegal gaming mixed very well with both the work and the play of blue-collar Americans. In the following year, a *Collier's* article stated that 15 million Americans regularly played the numbers.[60] With illegal bookmaking and a burgeoning sports-betting trade, citizens could be forgiven for assuming that gaming was reaching epidemic proportions.

Examining the history of illegal gaming in the United States brings the reader to the conclusion that Americans seemingly are willing to go to any lengths to gamble. They bet at card games, on horse races, professional baseball, college football, and even presidential elections. For most otherwise law-abiding citizens, making gaming illegal did not make it undesirable. Indeed, in a perverse way, the restrictions may have encouraged gaming by giving it an air of intrigue. Certainly, illegal gaming operations had few oversights to guarantee their customers fair play or equitable resolution of disputes. One can only conclude that most efforts to control gaming by outlawing it either were begun in righteous though naive zeal or were exercises in deception that were never supposed to eliminate gaming.

The Art of Making Money Automatically

Some media outlets treated the advent of Internet wagering in the late 1990s as a slightly humorous novelty. Cartoon images of pockmarked bookies hunting and pecking at keyboards obscured by cigarette smoke implied that there was something fundamentally contrary about the idea of gaming businesses as technological innovators. Looking at the actual history of gaming, though, it is clear that gaming operators have always seized upon the latest technologies to better practice their business. Technology has pushed gaming (and sometimes been pushed by gaming) in two ways. In several instances, smart gaming entrepreneurs latched on to the latest, most state-of-the-art transportation or communication network to provide a better delivery system for existing gaming or to facilitate existing gaming operations. In others, gaming entrepreneurs used emerging technologies to create new ways to gamble.

Gaming, like other forms of entertainment or business, is constantly evolving. There is nothing fixed about the activity of wagering save the nearly universal impulse to court risk, which may be related to the pervasive desire for play.[61] Beyond technical innovations, styles of gaming are constantly changing. No self-respecting Victorian-era British man of means would have neglected the game of whist, yet today the game is nearly dead. In the United States, once-popular card games like brag, boston, and faro have faded from the scene, yielding to blackjack, poker, and baccarat. That gaming will adapt to the latest innovations seems to be as near a historical certainty as can be imagined.

The proliferation of riverboat gaming in the 1830s and 1840s provides an example of the malleability of gaming. The riverboat gambler is an American cultural icon, probably more because of cinematic portrayals of the milieu than because of anything in the actual annals of recorded history. The riverboats that traversed the Mississippi were hardly the stately paddle wheelers of legend, gently gliding past magnolia trees, cloaked in the tranquil night. Rather, they were the most sophisticated—and most dangerous—transit of the time. With little regard for safety measures, steamboat races (a popular bet of the day) often ended in tragedy; in 1838, for example, nearly five hundred people perished in boiler explosions. In an attempt to manage this apparently uncontrollable new technology, Congress in 1852 passed the nation's first major regulatory act, which sought to set standards for boiler construction and the licensing of steamboats.[62]

When professional gamblers descended upon riverboats in search of eager customers, they were simply seeking the most up-to-date delivery system for their product: gaming. Needing to find a fairly transient customer base with discretionary income, they were naturally drawn to the riverboats. That riverboat passengers were more or less anonymous also helped—one never knew if the man sitting across from him (most gaming on the river took place exclusively among men) was an aristocratic planter or an unctuous sneak thief. This was the perfect setting for the professional gambler who was not above using dishonest skill to win a pot.

Yet however perfectly matched professional gamblers and riverboats were, many gamblers made an easy transition to the next mode in the transportation revolution, the train. Like the riverboat, the locomotive-driven train was, in its first years, a risky proposition, but after the Civil War it became an essential part of the transportation network and, many historians have argued, a principal factor in the creation of a national economy and culture. The railroads were the biggest business of the day and, as with Internet startups during the dot-com boom, they made many millionaires but also many paupers. The speculation centering on the railroads was one way in which Americans gambled on railroads, but they also did so in more literal ways. Gamblers readily adapted to this new delivery system; they were just as comfortable fleecing their marks in smoking cars as they had once been doing so on the deck.

Other innovations did not change the social milieu of gaming, but helped to create new opportunities for it. The telegraph revolutionized communications in antebellum America. Along with the railroad, it represented the first faltering steps toward humanity's attempt to master time and space—by providing an instant link to a distant location, it made the nineteenth-century world smaller. It was not long, of course, before gamblers took advantage of this new technology. Instantaneous access to race results from tracks across the nation, bookmakers soon discovered, let them offer more betting. Regardless of the season, horse racing was taking place somewhere, and the telegraph let bookmakers create new places to gamble, the horse rooms or poolrooms, where customers could experience the thrill of the racetrack—for the price of an afternoon of betting.

These new betting parlors were usually hidden behind a bar or a cigar store. Though, strictly speaking, they did not advertise, successful horse room operators employed steerers who hustled bettors into the action. Sometimes, horse room steerers went to other cities to find new customers; Atlantic City horse rooms paid agents to canvass the Philadelphia train station and steer bettors down the shore.[63] These rooms often ran with the knowledge and sometimes the active cooperation of the local police, who might intimidate or even jail those who protested the decisions of the house. Accommodations in horse rooms ran the gamut from spartan to sumptuous; some were "barn-like places with rows of crude benches," while others were furnished to resemble Wall Street brokerages. Many horse rooms had two levels, literally and figuratively: fifty-cent and one-dollar bettors used the first floor, with plain benches and no frills, while women and those betting more than two dollars visited the second floor, which was often outfitted quite lavishly. Among the perks of the second floor were complimentary sandwiches and other refreshments.

All rooms had loudspeakers describing the race currently being run, using florid language with dramatic flourishes, and announcing betting information. Relay of the shifting odds in the minutes before the race added to the excitement of betting and generally stimulated play. A horse room was a bustle of frenetic activity. Clerks scampered to post odds and results on large blackboards. Bettors bought and redeemed betting slips at a cashier's cage window, modeled on that found at a legal racetrack betting station.[64] These sophisticated, well-run businesses had customers who demanded the most recent racing odds and news. The free sandwiches and lively play-by-play were nice, but few players would bet without access to breaking updates and odds information. The telegraph was the key component of these thriving operations.

Another important technological advance greatly aided the popularity of horse race betting. The pari-mutuel system, developed in France in the 1860s, pooled all bets into a single pot from which the operator took a commission and paid the winner. The amount of money bet on a horse determined its odds: the more money wagered, the lower the odds, as the operator had to distribute more cuts of the same pool. When performed manually, these calculations could be time-consuming and only roughly accurate. The pari-mutuel system failed to catch on in the United States when it was first introduced in the 1870s.[65] In 1927, however, "engineer-entrepreneur-sportsman" Harry Straus took it upon himself to devise a more efficient system. His totalisator, or tote, electronically calculated the correct odds as wagers came in.[66] This system allowed the entire horse race betting industry to be conducted in an open, auditable environment, which greatly eased its acceptance by states as a legal form of gaming in the 1930s.

But horses weren't all that Americans wagered on. A Progressive-era anti-gaming broadside quoted Chauncey Depew, "railroad president, European traveler, and well-informed man of affairs," bemoaning the growth of gambling, which he saw as perilously ubiquitous throughout the civilized world because of both social and technological changes:

> We now bet on everything. We put our money on stocks, on food products, and upon everything that enters into our markets. . . . We do the same with real estate, and we now bet in a different way upon our amusements. Our base-ball system has become a lottery, and betting grows . . . on race and at cards all over the world. The telegraph enables us to carry the betting stands of Jerome Park track to San Francisco, and there is a crowd around the blackboards in every city betting on the races.[67]

The line dividing betting and speculation was fine indeed, and the same technology that powered the growth of American industry and commerce in the late nineteenth century opened virgin land for gaming.

Similarly, developments on the broader stage of U.S. history directly altered the development of gaming in the late nineteenth century. The turn toward mechanization, which greatly accelerated during this period with the creation of recognizable structures of industrial production, produced the slot machine, an automated gaming device that, beginning in the 1890s, would change the way Americans gambled.[68] The same gaming syndicates that operated horse rooms and gambling spots often branched out into slots as well. Needless to say, the profits to be made from the machines only intensified the corrupt entente that bound gambler, politician, and police. Most states outlawed the devices, but some attempted legalization schemes; the federal government, however, enacted no laws against them.

Slot machines, which began to appear in the 1870s but exploded in popularity in the 1890s, captured the American fancy in an age of new mechanization in ways that other games didn't. A new game that appeared around the same time in which the operator would place a bill in a small casket and sell keys to bettors (the winning key opened the casket and the winner took the bill) failed, probably because it lacked the automatic play of the slot machine.[69]

Slot machines came on the scene around the same time as other coin-operated amusements and vending machines. The catalog of a Progressive Era slot manufacturer placed automatic gaming machines in the center of a cornucopia of automated devices that a saloonkeeper could install to learn "THE ART OF MAKING MONEY AUTOMATICALLY." With no irony intended, the advertisement sang the praises of the "Poor Man's Club," where the poor man could spend his time "just as pleasantly as the rich man." In such a place, patrons could do far more than guzzle watered-down booze. They could "try their luck on games of chance," exercise with a punching bag, "test their strength and prowess in various ways," watch the latest pictures and hear sound recordings, and buy candy and gum for themselves or their children.[70] Gaming machines included a mechanical roulette wheel, a "reward paying punching bag," and various early slots such as the Liberty Bell, which today's audience would recognize as the distant ancestor of the modern reel slot machine.

Over the next century, gaming technology continued to evolve. By the turn of the millennium, gaming operators had introduced several technical innovations onto casino floors throughout the United States. The development of video poker and video slots hinged upon advances in computer electronics. Bill validators allowed patrons to insert bills directly into machines and signified an increasing mechanization of the gaming floor, as human change people became largely obsolete. Automatic shufflers on table games sped up the gaming and removed another human element from the equation. Electronic and eventually digital surveillance cameras and monitors, to say nothing of biometric technology, scrutinized the casino floor far better than any hawk-eyed floorman ever could have. Marketing advanced; whereas horse rooms had once dispatched steerers to train stations to bring in patrons, casino operators like Harrah's Entertainment pushed the envelope of the use of databases for player marketing and data mining, and throughout the nation both casino managers and state regulators used a panoply of tools to better record and analyze casino performance.[71]

Clearly, gaming has never been far behind the leading edge of technical innovation. So it is really not that surprising that creative entrepreneurs eventually pushed the envelope of bookmaking by taking bets over the phone or via the Internet. Those who make a living at the business of gaming have always needed access to customers who have discretionary income, whether gaining that access meant taking phone bets from the mainland United States at an offshore sportsbook or using the Internet to accept bets from patrons worldwide. It would have been nothing short of shocking had gamblers not made the transition to telephones and, from there, to the Internet.

The Race Wire Service Emerges

One particular intersection of gaming and technology has special weight for a consideration of the Wire Act: the race wire service, the raison d'être for the law. The wire service had strictly corporate origins. Originally run by Western Union and open to any entrepreneur with a betting venue and the money to lease a ticker, the transmission of racing and wagering information evolved into a national monopoly that straddled the line between legitimate media and illegal gaming. Once considered the means by which organized crime controlled illegal gaming in America, the wire service's emergence confounded citizens who were despondent about the use of American technology to further the American appetite to gamble.

The telegraph, one antigambler noted, made it possible for both men and boys to "indulge their propensity to gamble" on more races than would otherwise be possible; it was therefore evident, to him, that "a noble discovery has been turned to base and hurtful uses."[72] Using the high tech of the era to transmit gambling information was doubly hurtful to antigamblers because it not only increased the scale of gambling but also used a supposedly benign technology to do so. Antigamblers harbored mounting fears that industrial advances would not liberate people from their vices; they would only amplify the ways that they could indulge their worst desires. Their descendants in the twenty-first century, shocked by the facility with which gamblers exploited the Internet, were singing a tired refrain.

Beginning in the 1890s, Western Union carried the racing service as a matter of course. The company was, after all, in the business of transmitting information. Specially hired employees openly cased racetracks, relayed the latest odds calculated on the tracks' pari-mutuel machines, and reported the results as they happened. Any bookmaker who leased a special ticker could subscribe to this service. It was good business. Bookmakers, who needed a constant stream of information, were good, steady customers. Leasing the telegraph lines to horse rooms was lucrative enough to cover the costs of collecting race information internally and to yield a healthy profit, something that Western Union's stockholders appreciated.

Under this arrangement, Western Union had a reliable customer base and bookmakers had a trusted source of information. It was the start of a beautiful friendship. If a trusted third party who had nothing to gain from the outcome provided information to the horse rooms, bettors could place their wagers with a fair degree of confidence that the game was on the square.[73] But not everyone was happy. Antigamblers howled that Western Union, a pillar of national strength, was abetting illegal wagering, but the company (in a line later adopted by "sports consultants" and oddsmakers) insisted that it was merely providing information; if its customers chose to use that information to break the law, the company was no more responsible than a gun manufacturer if its weapons were used to commit murder.

As time went on, though, anti-corruption reformers united with antigambling activists like John Phillip Quinn to demand that the telegraph giant stop providing racing results. For them, the sophistry of whether providing information was or wasn't abetting illegal gaming was secondary to the obvious reality that, without the service, horse rooms could not continue to provide wagering. By May 1904 they had applied enough pressure to the directors of Western Union that the company finally stopped collecting race information.[74]

But this did not stop the race wire. Services including the Metropolitan News Agency of Louisville and the Payne Telegraph Service of Cincinnati used their own networks to gather information, which they then disseminated over wires leased from Western Union. Thus, the telegraph company was officially out of the racing information business, though it continued to profit from it.[75] Payne's service quickly moved to secure a near-monopoly on the service, but in 1909 Chicago gambler and bookmaker (and local agent for Payne) Mont Tennes launched a rival enterprise, the General News Bureau, which in 1910 absorbed the Payne organization.[76]

Mont Tennes was best described by a study of Chicago organized crime as a man whose life history, if known in every detail, "would disclose practically all there is to know about syndicated gambling as a phase of organized crime in Chicago" in the first third of the twentieth century.[77] Tennes came to prominence in the first years of the century as the owner of several saloons and racehorses. As a result of his craftiness and ruthlessness, he allegedly built up a controlling interest in all gaming on the north side of Chicago before diversifying into handbooks, or small betting operations, reportedly operating hundreds of books throughout the city. Tennes used his monopoly of the race wire in the Windy City to force bookmakers to accept him as a 50 percent partner; all those who refused lost their wire service and had to cease operations.[78] Illegal gaming in Chicago was hotly contested between rival operators, and Tennes became the target of physical beatings and bomb attacks from his competitors. In 1907 a series of bombings targeted Tennes's franchise of the Payne Telegraph Service. Tennes and his organization survived and by 1909 had secured absolute dominion over Chicago racetrack and handbook wagering. Tennes established a "chain store system" of handbooks that prospered despite occasional bombings and police raids.[79]

In 1910 Tennes successfully supplanted the Payne service as the national source for racing results, despite John Payne's protests that Tennes would abuse his monopoly by overcharging handbooks and poolrooms for race information. Payne argued that he was "fighting Tennes fairly" but that Tennes was both behind police raids on Payne distributors and threatening the "renewal of the gambling war." A 1911 Interstate Commerce Commission investigation found that the transmission of race results was legal, allowing Tennes to continue his monopoly. Over the next decade and a half, Tennes warded off challenges brought through the legal system, mutiny by his lieutenants, a City Council Crime Commission investigation in 1915, and graft exposés in 1916, 1917, and 1918.[80] Continuing raids by police did little to disturb his thriving business.

But the times were changing. In June 1927 the Illinois legislature legalized pari-mutuel wagering at racetracks. Illinois officials hoped that legalization would cut into the business of Tennes's illegal handbooks and horse rooms. It may have caused some slowdown in business, but the market remained lucrative, sufficiently so to bring on more competitors. In July an upstart wire service, the Empire News Company, obtained an injunction that prevented the police (working at Tennes's bidding, allegedly) from harassing its operations.[81] Prohibition Era Chicago's organized crime, now dominated by bootleggers such as Al Capone, was far different from the turn-of-the-century enterprise that Tennes had originally dominated. Getting older and with no desire to compete with increasingly brutal contenders, Tennes chose to retire from the field.

Tennes sold his General News Bureau to Moses L. "Moe" Annenberg, who had first distinguished himself in the gratuitously violent newspaper wars of early-twentieth-century Chicago. In 1907 he moved to Milwaukee, where he parlayed a newspaper circulation agency into a network of publishing, real estate, and commercial ventures. In 1918 he moved again, this time to New York City, where he continued to explore new business opportunities. Such an opportunity presented itself in 1922 when he acquired the *Daily Racing Form*, a publication that horse bettors used to make their wagers. Annenberg transformed the struggling *Form* into the dominant publication for bettors and a supremely profitable investment, partially by providing detailed descriptions of track and race conditions and partially by pressuring news agencies into selling the *Daily Racing Form* exclusively.[82]

Annenberg, always looking to expand, jumped at the chance to acquire Tennes's wire service in 1927. He bought out the rival Nationwide News Service and restored a near-monopoly to the wire service, sending information to bookies throughout the United States and into Canada, Mexico, and the Caribbean. This monopoly provided daily service to an estimated 15,000 bookmakers nationwide and returned to Annenberg more than $2 million in profits annually. While most of the nation languished in the Depression, Annenberg worked assiduously to extend his domination of the wire service by any means necessary, including intimidation, violence, and corruption.[83]

But Annenberg's domination could not last forever. Federal authorities, doubtless spurred on by allegations of ties to corrupt city politics and his visceral attacks against Franklin Delano Roosevelt's New Deal, began investigating him intensely in the late 1930s. In 1939 Annenberg divested himself of the Nationwide News Service, and the following year he was indicted and ultimately convicted of income tax evasion. Sentenced to a four-year prison term, he served only two before being released after the discovery of a brain tumor.[84] Before he died in 1942, he turned over his remaining media empire, which was still substantial, to his son Walter Annenberg, who expanded an already impressive portfolio with publications like *TV Guide* and channeled a substantial portion of his fortune into educational and philanthropic efforts, including communications schools at the University of Pennsylvania and the University of Southern California. This apparently higher social use for the proceeds of the Annenberg monopoly on the race wire contrasted starkly with the violent fight over the remnants of his race information empire.

War Over the Wire

The departure of Moe Annenberg left a void. Mont Tennes had demonstrated that nationally as well as locally, a monopoly on the wire service could be far more lucrative than bookmaking itself. Annenberg perfected Tennes's system and continued its track record of legal and profitable operation. So it was inevitable that after Annenberg other operators would scheme to win control of the national wire service and that local ownership of the wire franchise would continue to inspire competition among rival bookmakers.

James Ragen had partnered with Annenberg in Nationwide and its distributors in Chicago and St. Louis, and he faced federal indictments on income tax charges at the same time as Annenberg.[85] When Annenberg "simply walked out" of the race wire business, Ragen turned it over to his associate Arthur McBride without any formal transaction or official sale. Under McBride, the wire service reconstituted itself as the Continental Press Service in Cleveland. Ragen reassumed control of the service in 1941, although McBride purchased a one-third interest in the service in the name of his son, Edward, who was then overseas serving in the armed forces and had absolutely no knowledge of how this intricate operation ran.[86]

Things went smoothly until 1945, when Ragen asked Hymie Levin, apparently a man of great influence among Chicago bookies, to turn the distributorship for Chicago back over to Ragen and to content himself with operating handbooks in the city. Levin took a dim view of this request, prompting Ragen to turn off his wire service.[87] Virgil Peterson of the Chicago Crime Commission firmly tied Levin's R. and H. Publishing Company to "the Capone gang," leading the Kefauver Committee to conclude that this struggle was an example of the Capone group's "muscling in" on an innocent businessman. In fact, Ragen was just as closely tied to criminal syndicates as Levin and his partners were.

In March 1946, Ragen's rivals officially launched the Trans-American Publishing and News Service, hiring away Patrick Burns of Continental as president. Ragen complained bitterly to anyone who would listen and threatened to speak with the FBI about the interesting secrets of the Chicago bookmaking community. Trans-American began to build up its business, beginning with the Chicago stronghold of R. and H. and continuing with operations in Florida (where the distributor paid both Continental and Trans-American), Nevada (where Benjamin Siegel had the Las Vegas concession), Missouri,

Iowa, and Colorado. Usually the Trans-American franchise simply took over Continental operations, but sometimes the two companies competed.[88]

On an otherwise serene June night in 1946, as Ragen was driving through the streets of Chicago, already rattled by the jousting over the wire, he stopped at a red light on State Street. Two of his six bodyguards, former police officers whom Ragen had only recently hired, trailed him closely. But they did little more than watch as a tarpaulin on a truck beside Ragen lifted and, in a hail of gunfire, unidentified gunmen (predictably linked by Peterson and Kefauver to the Capone organization), ambushed the race wire czar. But Ragen wasn't dead yet; rushed to a hospital, he was slowly mending when, two months later, he suddenly died, probably the victim of poison.[89] Though he had never impressed friends with any special precognitive abilities, Ragen had previously given a lengthy statement to the district attorney of Cook County in which he asserted that he had been threatened. He had actually named his probable killers, men associated with the Capone syndicate.

The violent deaths of Ragen and the Trans-American representative in Las Vegas, Siegel, brought tremendous amounts of negative publicity. Newspapers crowed about a looming gang war to rival that of the Prohibition era. Before a full-scale national hoodlum war over control of the wire service began, though, cooler heads seem to have prevailed. A long-standing bit of wisdom held that organized crime flourished best when it drew the least attention, as public executions tended to arouse more-fervent policing of the antigambling statutes. The war, in other words, was bad for business. With so much money at stake, it was inevitable that the two sides should reach some rapprochement, yet this happened in a singular fashion.

After Ragen's death, his former partners, David Kelly and Arthur McBride, bought his share of Continental, placing it in the name of McBride's son Edward, who was now attending law school and, when questioned about the operations of the company he ostensibly owned, had hardly a clue.[90] In June 1947 Trans-American announced its intention to disband because of insufficient funds to continue in business. Continental promptly rehired all those who had deserted it for Trans-American. Illinois Sports News, Continental's Chicago franchise, rehired both Patrick Burns and his children, all of whom had abandoned Ragen for Continental.[91] Service to franchises that had bolted for Trans-American resumed under the aegis of Continental. The Kefauver Committee later alleged that Continental had been completely taken over by "the Capone mob" in a brutal reverse acquisition. This explained, they thought, why the operators of the Kansas City franchise, who had joined the Trans-American fold, actually received better terms for their service after the reestablishment of Continental.[92] Capone's successors, they charged, used his strategies to monopolize the race wire just as they had dominated bootlegging in the Roaring Twenties. This was a lucrative national monopoly literally worth dying for.

Struggles for local distributorships often matched the 1945–47 battle for control of the monopoly. The S. & G. bookmaking syndicate of southern Florida, later made famous by a Kefauver Committee investigation, is a case in point. In 1944 five previously independent bookmakers formed a syndicate that served, like most gaming syndicates, to eliminate competition and facilitate financing. S. & G. controlled a network of more than two hundred bookmakers, whom it protected from police interference and to whom it supplied the wire service. Those who refused to submit to S. & G. found themselves the target of police harassment.[93]

In 1949 the S. & G. partnership added a member under mysterious circumstances. After the appointment of a Florida state special investigator reputedly tied to Harry Russell of Chicago (who himself was possibly a confrere of the Capone group), S. & G. bookies became the exclusive targets of police raids. Continental then shut off service to S. & G., and when the syndicate attempted to siphon information from other Florida bookmakers, the wire service placed the entire state under interdict, cutting off all wire service. After two weeks, service resumed and police raids stopped, and Russell was established as a full partner of the syndicate. The Kefauver Committee seized on the "Russell Muscle" episode as evidence of the pervasive control that Continental (and therefore the "Capone mob") had on bookmaking everywhere.[94]

In other areas, possession of the wire service franchise, though lucrative, seemed no guarantee of a leisured existence. The Kansas City distributor, for example, closed completely after the assassination of gambling power and political figure Charles Binaggio and his associate, Charles Gargotta, in a Democratic clubhouse;[95] Gargotta had been a partner in the group that controlled the Harmony Publishing Company, the Kansas City distributor; after his death, bookmakers had to get their service secondhand from operators in nearby cities.[96] In cities like St. Louis, New Orleans, Chicago, and Las Vegas, the Kefauver Committee believed it had found evidence of violence associated with alleged mob "muscling in" to local distributorships. It seems far more likely that, rather than representing hostile takeovers of legitimate businesses by organized crime, the violence associated with the distributorships was internecine warfare over particularly lucrative rackets.

At the local level, operators might struggle over who received the wire service, but at the top there were few challenges to Continental's reign after the 1946 Trans-American fight. The Continental Press Service steamrollered its way into the next decade with a virtual monopoly over the wire service. By 1950 Continental disseminated its news to a network of twenty to twenty-four ostensibly independent distributors, who sold the information to subdistributors or directly to bookmakers. In many cases, distributors paid Continental all of their receipts in excess of salary and expenses. These distributors were actually dummy companies, set up to legally shield Continental from charges that it sold directly to those in the business of illegal bookmaking.[97] Distributors muscled into bookmaking operations, however, by demanding that bookmakers pay according to a sliding scale, thus giving the distributor de facto profit sharing, in which the wire service was provided not at a fixed price but as a percentage of the bookmaking business. The *New York Daily News*, for example, paid $20 a week to Continental for service, but bookmakers paid anywhere from $40 to $350 for exactly the same service.[98] This made possession of the local franchise especially lucrative and explains the violence with which franchisees fought for their operations.

Studying the Continental Press Service in 1951, the Kefauver Committee concluded that not only did Continental monopolize the wire service and thereby control most bookmaking operations except the smallest but also that the "Capone mob" controlled Continental. Thus the profits of bookmaking went directly to one of the most notorious criminal syndicates in the nation.[99] Kefauver and his staff connected some dots that might better have been left alone, and their conclusions gave the bookmaking community, actually rather loosely organized and with few barriers to entry or exit, the appearance of an unstoppable criminal conspiracy. This view would color public perceptions during the subsequent anxious decade preceding the final passage of the Wire Act.

2 The Anxious Decade

Americans learn to fear organized crime but refuse to admit that, as gambling citizens, they are part of the problem.

Gambling has been with us for centuries, and presumably there will always be people who are willing to lose their money through games of chance.
— Captain George H. Bullen Jr., *FBI Law Enforcement Bulletin*

PROFESSIONAL GAMBLERS TAKING BETS from the public are, out of necessity, exposed to prosecution for running gambling businesses. Yet for much of American history, ostensibly illegal gaming operations thrived, beneficiaries of the mechanics of direct democracy. Politicians achieve and hold power by satisfying more interests than they offend. In the big-city machines of yesteryear, this meant accepting cash from, and doling patronage out to, an assortment of ward heelers and neighborhood big men, many of whom had more than a passing interest in gaming and other illegal enterprises.

Usually, this proved problematic only to stubborn bluenoses who sought to enforce unpopular laws against moral offenses, be it schoolgirls selling flowers on Sunday or guys laying action on the home favorite to beat the spread. Local antigambling efforts proved to be cyclical at best. When, at times, the corruption inherent in a society with an illegal popular pastime became too noisome for the mass of voters, a "reform ticket" swept control of the city, county, or state in question. After a few raids and a period of quiet, illicit gaming resumed as before.

For decades, this sine wave of wide open/reform/wide open status undulated fairly predictably. Far fewer guardians of the public trust retired in disgrace than retired rich from this arrangement, and "boss gamblers" made fortunes. Most Americans, if asked, saw nothing particularly sinister in it. But beginning in the late 1940s and intensifying into the early 1960s, American perceptions of crime — particularly gaming crimes — shifted profoundly. Once viewed in strictly local terms, gambling became linked to criminal conspiracies that were national, if not international, in scope. Americans woke up from fitful dreams of jackpots and winning long shots to the disturbing realization that all the money spent on illegal gambling actually went somewhere. The ultimate profiteers of illegal gambling, known variously as boss gamblers, racketeers, and hoodlums, took a place beside foreign and domestic spies and saboteurs in American nightmares.

A National Dilemma

Crime in America is widely considered to be a local problem. When citizens are outraged at increased lawlessness, they usually search for community solutions before turning to the federal government. The crisis over the boss gamblers, building during the late 1940s, crystallized into a truly national concern in early 1950, but not before several local groups investigated and denounced gamblers, organized crime, passive police, and acquiescent politicians. After citizens were frustrated in their attempts to root out the syndicates through local solutions, they appealed to the federal government for help.

After World War II, many Americans braced for a crime wave, and had one not appeared they would have been disappointed. President Harry S. Truman himself, using rather broad analogies, claimed that after every armed conflict the United States had faced an upswing of crime. In an idiosyncratic analysis, he expounded that after the Revolutionary War "we had almost exactly the same problem with which we are faced now"; consequently Congress passed the Alien and Sedition Acts. Most historians, of course, believe that the Federalists in fact passed the acts to stifle Jeffersonian opposition rather than to stem the tide of interstate bookmaking syndicates. Lumping together a post–Civil War increase in "banditry" and an increase in crime after World War I (which had nothing, apparently, to do with the Volstead Act and national Prohibition), Truman concluded that the problem of crime facing America in the postwar years was a historical certainty.[1]

Crime does not follow automatic patterns, swinging with a pendulum's regularity, so if Truman was not mistaken, he was certainly misinformed when he made his analogy to postwar criminal sprees. In fact, looking at the most violent (and easily discovered) of crimes, homicide, historian Eric Monkkonen found no link between postwar demobilization and a rise in murders. After World War II there was a minor increase in murder rates, then a decline, but nothing like the explosion the nation would see in the 1960s.[2] Despite popular expectations, there was no postwar crime wave.

If crime was not definitely on the rise in those years, gaming certainly was. The encroachment of legal pari-mutuel wagering across the nation — roughly half the states had on-track betting by 1950 — signaled an underlying gaming boom, much of it illegal. According to the prevailing wisdom, "loose wartime spending" fueled this boom.[3] Wagering apparently grew during the lean Depression years but positively thrived in the wartime hothouse conditions of rising wages and restricted consumer spending. Other observers believed that a general nihilism fueled gambling. According to a 1951 *Scientific Digest* summary of a *United Nations World* article, European croupiers related that "desperate gamblers" both rich and poor had become the rule and deliberate ones the exception. "The psychology of the 1950 gambler," the article reported, "was that of a desperate person with nothing to lose. Thousands of times the croupiers heard rich and poor alike say, with a bitter smile, 'What does it matter — the atomic bomb will get us anyhow!'"[4] Regardless of the psychological implications of nuclear holocaust, civic leaders concluded that if legal gaming was growing at such a precipitous rate, illegal gaming must be expanding even more quickly.

No documents conclusively prove how much illegal gaming actually took place in the years after World War II, for by its very nature, illegal gaming leaves little evidence of its true volume. But it is possible to learn what the public perception of the scale of illegal gaming was — a factor that is particularly important in determining why politicians chose to restrict gaming at the federal level in some ways but not in others. The available evidence clearly indicates that Americans believed that they gambled more in the years after the war than they had before. Pollster George Gallup reported in 1950 that 57 percent of Americans questioned admitted they had "played for stakes in some game of chance" within the past year. In a similar poll in 1945 only 45 percent of those questioned had admitted to indulging in such games.[5] These numbers must be accepted with the caveat that people were asked to admit placing illegal bets, something they may have been chary about doing, and therefore the numbers of people who actually placed bets may have been greater. Still, the numbers do indicate that Americans were gambling more — or being more forthright about their wagering — in 1950 than in 1945.

Estimates of the "take" for illegal gaming ranged from conservative guesses, which simply doubled the legal revenues at on-track pari-mutuel operations, to wildly exaggerated numbers that confused the handle (or total amount bet) with the revenue (the amount that the gaming operation actually retained). This problem was particularly acute in racing and sports betting, which traditionally have operated upon very narrow margins of profit; operators usually retain no more than 5 percent of the gross handle.

When New Orleans mayor deLesseps Morrison presented "the most conservative estimates" of the profits of illegal gaming in 1950, he gave historians a snapshot of what informed civic leaders believed. He estimated a $1
billion to $2 billion annual take for slot machines, calculating that figure
from the facts that 105,000 gaming machines had received tax stamps and
each machine averaged $10 to $15 a day. Morrison allowed that there were
probably double or triple that number of machines actually in operation. He
was sure that the Continental Press Service, over its 16,000-mile network of
leased wires, monopolized the bookmaking information service, but he offered only a vague guess that bookmaking ran at a volume of between $3
billion and $8 billion.[6] In the same year, the attorney general of the United
States estimated that "the numbers racket" yielded more than $2 billion a
year.[7]

The most plugged-in of public servants and crime fighters, then, told
Americans that the business of illegal gaming took in anywhere from $6 bil-
lion to $12 billion annually. These leaders further told the public that two ma-
jor syndicates stood behind all of this gambling. In the words of deLesseps
Morrison, "One controls the large slot-machine industry and engages in allied gambling rackets; the other dominates the race wire."[8] It would be nearly
impossible for such a volatile industry as gaming to be subject to such strict
monopoly control, but trusted leaders and respected police officials insisted
that it was so. Americans thus believed that the syndicates that organized
much of the illegal gaming earned greater profits in the years after World
War II and that the problem was only getting worse as syndicate criminals
muscled in on "legitimate" businesses.

Citizens believed that local law enforcement was not doing enough to
fight the gambling bosses. In many cities, a quasi-public institution, the local crime commission, joined the fray. Usually privately financed but staffed
by former law enforcement officials, such groups had initially appeared in
the 1920s but truly flowered in the 1940s.[9] The Chicago Crime Commission,
headed after 1942 by Virgil W. Peterson, was first among equals of postwar
crime commissions. Speaking to anyone who would listen, from civic groups
to municipal executives to newspaper reporters, Peterson energetically expounded the dangers of "criminal-political alliances" and "racketeering and
underworld elements" in general.[10] Gaining many disciples by the sheer
weight of the seemingly indisputable hurricane of facts, statistics, and minu-
tiae that he cited to support his contentions, Peterson inspired the growth of

a broad-based movement. Crime commissions were soon everywhere, seeking the truth about crime and corruption in cities across the nation.

Despite the popularity of the crime commissions, they faced the nearly Herculean task of explaining to voters how they themselves were a big part of the problem. Peterson, with unwitting irony, captured the paradox when he declared, "The citizens must understand that the principal source of revenue of the underworld is derived from those activities which prey on the weaknesses of mankind: gambling, prostitution, narcotics, and rackets of a similar nature."[11] Peterson placed himself in the unenviable position of trying to save citizens from themselves. Many of them doubtless found gaming a fun diversion; yet his task was to elucidate why gaming was, in fact, bad for the citizen and the nation.

Peterson's anti-gaming invective was quite different from that of earlier anti-gaming reformers. The first American antigamblers, those who denounced gaming from the pulpit in colonial days, castigated gamblers as unproductive, morally decrepit idlers. For them, gaming was a personal shortcoming that endangered the individual soul and only by extension the community. With the expansion of the commercial impulse in the young United States, arguments against gaming began to be couched in more secular terms: parasitic gamblers, through crooked games and lotteries, drained money from productive citizens. Yet this problem was still one that was primarily individual; should the community roust the three-card monte dealers and outlaw the lottery, the problem would go away. Through the late nineteenth century, admonitions against gaming remained virtually the same, warning that unscrupulous cheats plucked the unwary with crooked schemes. Social gaming, though not a problem in and of itself, was a menace in that it inculcated the youth with the gaming impulse. The inherently unfair odds of games run by professional gamblers made them undesirable because the player could not possibly profit by them.

But Peterson and his comrades urged a new understanding of gaming: that even "square games," which followed accepted rules and paid winners fairly, corrupted not just individuals but the state itself. By fueling dishonest political machines that were themselves rooted in the realities of American electoral politics, gaming menaced honest government:

> It is the gambling business . . . that is peculiarly adapted to the requirements of corrupt machine politics. Existing solely to prey upon

emotional weaknesses which defy all forces of logic and common sense, and operating on a percentage basis which assures huge profits, the gambling business has always appealed to the criminal classes. In recent years, the entire nation was shocked when it was revealed that professional gamblers had bribed youthful college athletes in order to fix basketball games. Generally overlooked was the fact that activities of this nature are part of the gambling business. . . . The gambling business always has been and always will be under the control of the underworld.[12]

Supported by tavern owners who needed the extra income that a gaming concession guaranteed, the ward politician who required the financial and electioneering assistance of gambling bosses, and the average citizen who placed two-dollar bets, the business of illegal gaming was an inextricable part of urban corruption. In the years during which Peterson fulminated against political-criminal alliances, social and demographic shifts were already undercutting the power of city-based political machines, but at the time Peterson's image of widespread urban corruption infecting the entire apparatus of American government played to the worst nightmares of "honest" citizens.

In addition to arguing that organized illegal gaming corrupted the political process, Peterson went to great lengths to prove that it was also a monopoly concern dominated by "the Syndicate," the organization originally built by Al Capone and, by the late 1940s, effectively administered by Tony Accardo and Jack Guzik.[13] Later sensationalized media accounts of the Syndicate (and Peterson's denunciations thereof) during the Kefauver Committee era (1950–51) tended to overestimate the centralized nature of the combine, but the earliest coverage of Peterson's efforts was a bit more accurate. A 1949 *American Mercury* article, which asserted that the "Chicago Syndicate" controlled Chicago gaming and was "striving to seize control of gambling all over the United States," described the group as all-powerful but not entirely cohesive. "The Syndicate," the *Mercury* observed, was "shorthand for a semi-organized crowd of gunmen and gamblers, lawyers and bondsmen and politicians. Strictly speaking, only the gunmen and gamblers are Syndicate men; they hire the others." While Syndicate members pooled their resources to control gambling, "each of the Syndicate men has his own private angles, sometimes legitimate."[14]

This view of syndicated crime, in contrast to later espousals by the Kefauver Committee, squares fairly well with academic analyses based on the available evidence. Claims that the Chicago group might "control" all gaming in the nation were a bit overheated. Mark Haller, in his theoretical and historical interpretation of illegal enterprises, found that within the realm of Cicero (Illinois) operations (which were likely representative of all of the group's businesses), the various enterprises of syndicate members were not subject to bureaucratic control. Rather, each was a discrete small-scale operation. Typically, "senior partners" of the organization enlisted an on-site manager as a partner. There was no hierarchy; instead, the partners involved often operated other enterprises, legal and illegal, independent of the senior partners.[15] Payoffs to police and politicians and a desire to informally regulate and suppress competition often led to a degree of coordination between illegal enterprises, but the monolithic "control" of a fragmented business like illegal gaming was impossible.

Still, Peterson and his allies drilled into the public consciousness the idea that a single coterie of evil men controlled gaming in certain cities and that an overarching Syndicate constantly sought to dominate gaming nationally. Politicians, aware that crime was a potentially explosive issue, moved to exploit it. Increasingly, they concluded that local solutions were not enough. In 1947 the California legislature authorized no fewer than five special commissions to study crime, and Governor Earl Warren called for a "general crime conference" to deal with the perceived migration of "Eastern gangsters" to the Golden State. Two murders reportedly linked to criminal syndicates, those of Nick DeJohn in San Francisco and Ben Siegel in Beverly Hills, were not isolated crimes to be solved by local police but "a double warning to Californians that their state was being regarded as fertile soil for cultivation of matters other than agrarian." A California senator warned that "gamblers, racketeers, and blackmailers" were pouring into the state, which faced a "bloody gang war" as the hoodlums struggled to divvy up the spoils of illicit businesses.[16] Local authorities had no chance of containing these gangsters, and even state commissions could do little more than make recommendations.

Elsewhere, gamblers were already entrenched. The gaming operations flourishing in Bergen County, New Jersey, directly across the Hudson River from New York City, exemplified the degree to which illegal gaming had grown. Since the 1930s, illegal casinos, like Ben Marden's Riviera, which sat just north of the New Jersey end of the George Washington Bridge, flourished. With an upswing in concern over illegal gaming, by 1951 this opulent club had ceased to operate as a gambling concern. This hardly meant an end to casinos, however; the "syndicate" simply moved to lower-profile settings. "They always took abandoned or rundown estate[s] far off a main road . . . old garages, old barns, old factories, with no nearby residential district." The syndicate refurbished the abandoned buildings, spending up to $150,000 to convert them into plush casinos, but not before ensuring that the police would not interfere. The casinos themselves were remarkably like nineteenth-century first-class houses; the New York Times reported that all through and after World War II the gaming houses, often catering to black market manipulators, offered "free steak dinners, rare wines and faultless service and surroundings."[17] Such houses attracted primarily New Yorkers, who continued to gamble even after Fiorello LaGuardia's campaign against gaming in the city. This seemed to demonstrate the ineffectiveness of strictly local solutions to illegal gaming; gamblers who were denied one district would simply relocate to the next.

The steady chorus of journalists and crime commissions promoting gaming as a growing problem that, combined with the seeming inability of local and state police to shatter the invidious syndicates lurking behind gaming operations, set the stage for the elevation of syndicated crime to the federal arena. At the 1949 meeting of the American Municipal Association, held in Cleveland from November 30 through December 2, the problem of criminal syndicates emerged as the major theme.

In his keynote address to the association, which was composed of the mayors of the towns and cities of America, the redoubtable Virgil Peterson stressed the menace that syndicates posed to public citizens and the necessity of reforming local law enforcement agencies into "efficient, virile, and incorruptible crime-fighting bodies." This was to be accomplished by creating intelligence divisions within police departments to develop and record information on suspected criminal syndicate members, their background, affiliations, and activities. Peterson did not call, at this time, for any federal action against the syndicates, stating that since the syndicates primarily broke state laws, "the brunt of the battle lies with local governments."[18] The greatest danger to these governments was the tendency of syndicates to corrupt and acquire political power, not as an end in itself but to protect their lucrative enterprises. If the cities remained vigilant against this development, they would be up to the task of defeating the racketeers.

Startled into action by Peterson's hard-hitting diatribe, which "named names and sketched some of the activities of organized crime . . . in various cities," the mayors and municipal executives of the association felt they had to take some kind of action. The purpose of the conference was not solely to discuss crime, however; other issues on the agenda included street and highway financing, urban redevelopment, use of new tax revenues, and the role of municipalities in reducing unemployment and promoting urban stability. Despite all of the animated discussion, the conference yielded few real deliverables. The mayors produced a policy statement on the relations between municipal, state, and federal governments, which made no overt reference to criminal syndicates, but they did little else. Attendees did not initially request any special federal aid, but, recognizing that the problem was national in scope, they requested that the board of trustees develop a program through which cities could pool information and resources.[19]

Originally this program was to be no more than an information service whereby each city could "keep track of the techniques and plans of criminal syndicates throughout the country."[20] But local solutions, it seemed, would be of little use against an apparently national criminal confederation. Arresting the proprietor of the local franchise of the wire service, to say nothing of an individual bookie, would hardly stop the flow of gaming information via the Continental Press Service network. Rousting a slot machine parlor, and even physically destroying one-armed bandits, would, in the big picture, not halt the importation of slot machines into a city. In order to truly wage war against a national enemy, civic and law enforcement leaders came to believe, the battle must be taken to the federal level.

The Attorney General's Conference

In an elective democracy with a federal division of powers and responsibilities, blame, it seems, migrates upward. In the case of illegal gaming businesses, local politicians confronted a local problem that simply would not go away. Frequently, local police involved themselves in gaming operations by accepting graft, thus rendering any real attempt to squelch gaming merely academic, but even cities renowned for their law-and-order mayors, like New Orleans, Portland, and Los Angeles, made little headway in eradicating gamblers. Certainly, efforts to close illegal casinos and slot machine operations often proved successful. The efforts of Mayor Fletcher Bowron and his administration succeeded in torpedoing the gaming cruises that had serviced Los Angeles in the 1930s (and, indirectly, promoted the growth of Las Vegas as a gaming center by pushing gaming entrepreneurs toward the Southwest's oasis of legal casinos). But many mayors charged that as diligent as they might be in wiping any trace of gambling from within their city limits, operations in the next county or state continued to prey on citizens unabated. And it was impossible for any district attorney, no matter how resourceful, to stop the flow of gaming information over the race wire services.

It made much sense for mayors to call for a concerted federal action against gaming. In an ideal world, this would consist of a superagency through which municipal law enforcement might share information and access to data compiled by the FBI. As mayors of large cities, though, these officials were keenly aware that they did not live in an ideal world. Not willing to cede dominion over local gamblers to federal authorities, cities and states appealed, nonetheless, for federal aid in fighting the gaming menace. On September 20, 1949, the American Municipal Association petitioned Attorney General Howard McGrath for just this: federal "coordination and cooperation with local agencies" in battling the "growing menace of organized Nation-wide gambling syndicates."[21]

In his sometimes strident requests for federal assistance, Mayor Morrison sounded the familiar tropes of overburdened municipal executives. Speaking for the AMA, Morrison denied that he wanted the federal government to "take over" the task but decried the impossibility of a war fought by only local powers against "nationally organized underworld elements whose supply lines, communications, and general operations cut across municipal, county, State, and even national lines."[22] At the same time, local officials were often in the dark about the actual nature of criminal activities; federal agencies did not share information about the race wire service or slot machines with other federal departments, let alone municipal officials. For example:

> A few days ago we learned of an extensive report on racing wire services compiled several years ago by the Federal Bureau of Investigation. Yet, when our police superintendent asked for a copy he was told that none was available in New Orleans. And, even if there were, the FBI said, it could not permit us to see such a confidential document.[23]

Such departmental secrecy, known as smokestacking, still flourished in federal intelligence fifty years later, when post-9/11 reports excoriated the FBI, the CIA, and the NSA for precisely this failure to share vital information while terrorists plotted to successfully launch well-planned, coordinated attacks from within the United States itself.

While Morrison interpreted the FBI's failure to share the wire services report as arrogant administrative snobbery, there were undoubtedly good reasons for the bureau not to turn over all of its information to municipal officials. First, as the anti-crime lobby had clearly established, illegal gaming operators by nature bought the cooperation of local law enforcement officials with graft; federal authorities could be given no guarantees that corrupt members of the local police might not leak the documents to the very subjects under investigation. Second, the information contained in FBI reports was frequently obtained by the use of wiretaps, confidential informants, and other sensitive methods. Even sixty years later, FBI files obtained under the Freedom of Information Act have extensive redactions that hide sources for legal or security purposes. Finally, many of the reports, at least those made available to the public, seem to be cobbled together from hearsay, wiretaps, and rumors. Since the release of many FBI files under the Freedom of Information Act, it has become abundantly clear that much of the FBI's vaunted trove of information was of spurious value. What value would the Los Angeles police have found, for example, in knowing that, while discussing an unfavorable report possibly leaked to the press by the FBI, Ben Siegel had referred to Director J. Edgar Hoover by a ten-letter word that later got Lenny Bruce indicted for obscenity?[24]

But the mayors and the anti-crime lobby made an end run around the FBI and successfully planted the idea that the agency was indifferent, or even apathetic, about criminal syndicates. FBI disinterest in pursuing organized-crime investigations has been attributed to several factors. The director officially stated that since criminal syndicates were essentially local operations, they should be fought at the local level and the FBI did not have jurisdiction over them. Observers who pointed out that even local criminal syndicates' activities crossed state lines posited that there were other motivations for Hoover's lack of interest. Some believe this was for administrative and political reasons. Hoover demurred on committing assets to developing organized-crime investigations, which were time-consuming and resource-intensive, in favor of the "quick hit" violent and property crimes that generated impressive statistics that could justify his budget.[25] Those with a conspiratorial mind-set have alleged that Hoover, a known casual horse bettor, was somehow influenced by illegal gaming syndicates or that crime bosses had incriminating photos or information with which they blackmailed the FBI director. Whatever the reason, in the early 1950s the FBI made it clear that it would not pursue investigations of gaming operations.

With the Justice Department's big guns at the FBI making no public moves against gaming syndicates, the onus of action again migrated up, this time to the attorney general himself. Facing the political embarrassment of potentially ignoring what seemed to be a grassroots campaign for federal intervention into "the crime problem," Attorney General Howard McGrath, formerly the chair of the Democratic National Committee, settled on a cautious initiative. He tacked on an extra day to the annual conference of U.S. attorneys, which was slated to run February 13 and 14, invited representatives from the National Association of Attorneys General, the American Municipal Association (of which the outspoken deLesseps Morrison was immediate past president), the United States Conference of Mayors, the National Institute of Municipal Law Officers, along with a smattering of officials from Justice, Treasury, the U.S. Post Office, and the Federal Communications Commission, and labeled it "the Attorney General's Conference on Organized Crime."

Thus, on February 15, 1950, delegates from around the nation, including the media and interested citizens who just happened to wander in, like Senator Estes Kefauver (already maneuvering to become the Senate leader in the war on organized crime), met in the Great Hall of the Department of Justice in Washington, D.C. Those attending the conference understood that they would discuss four major items: the interstate transportation of slot machines, the "effect of gambling with reference to organized crime," the Fugitive Felon Act and extradition of fugitives, and "more effective means of cooperation" among federal, state, and local law enforcement.[26]

To underscore his administration's commitment to giving full faith and credit to the crime-fighting enterprise, President Harry S. Truman delivered the opening address. In a relatively brief statement, he thanked those in attendance for their efforts and then offered his thoughts on the historical pattern of postwar crime waves. He further reminded delegates that "the fundamental basis of this Nation's law was given to Moses on the Mount" and that without "the fundamental moral background, we will finally end up with a totalitarian government which does not believe in rights for anybody except the state." Truman then singled out equality of opportunity as the greatest of all anti-crime initiatives, denounced corruption, praised idealism, and exhorted the delegates to follow the due process of law.

The emphasis on due process, rather than on results, seems to signal that Truman considered gambling crime a low priority. His closing remarks underscored the need to respect the law, even to the detriment of political efficacy or personal convenience. In a final, bizarre admission, he reminded delegates that though he had "the greatest position that could come to any man on earth," he never forgot that he was "the servant of the people," subject to follow the law with even more exactitude than the average citizen:

> I believe that as President, it is even more necessary for me than for any other person to be careful in obeying the laws. I never infringe a traffic rule. I never exercise the prerogatives which I sometimes have of going through red lights. I never exercise the prerogative of taking advantage of my position as President of the United States because I believe that I am, first, a citizen, and that as a citizen I ought to obey the laws first and foremost.[27]

Contemporary readers, inured by allegations of presidential misdeeds from criminal conspiracy to perjury that seem to be an inevitable part of a modern administration, might take from these words only the caveat not to get stuck behind Truman when running late for work. But he undoubtedly meant to send a message to delegates to avoid the twin temptations facing those charged with policing illegal gaming: graft and zealous overreaction. He then thanked the assembly and left, presumably stopping at all traffic lights, to attend to more serious matters of state.

In the morning's major address, Attorney General McGrath reminded delegates of the successful work of past attorney general's conferences in 1929, 1934, 1940, and 1946 before getting to the meat of his message: The problem they all faced was unprecedented in its organization. This was "a new phase of the old problem," as "the mobsters of the 1930s," though not entirely eliminated, found themselves supplanted by a new leadership that "combines the worst features of big business manipulations with violence and corruption to clamp . . . monopolies on the illegal businesses of book-making, slot machines . . . the numbers game, and other forms of commercialized gambling." The gaming rackets, whose cost to the public he estimated in the billions, threatened respectable local self-government and may have had ties to prostitution and narcotics, even darker crimes of the underworld.[28]

Organized gambling, according to McGrath, was "the biggest illicit traffic since Prohibition." What was more, he argued, even though states licensed or didn't license gaming according to the dictates of the electorate, the universal ban against lotteries, given federal assistance in 1890, 1895, and 1934 through statutes barring the interstate traffic of lottery tickets or information, constituted a basic public policy against gaming. Despite his admission that about half of all states had legalized on-track pari-mutuel wagering and that a "very few" states had gone even further in allowing various legalized gaming schemes, McGrath insisted that he was justified in taking the view that the national public policy condemned organized gambling and made its activities illegal unless otherwise specified.[29]

McGrath further advised delegates to consider "reexamining and modernizing" local codes before passing new federal laws against gaming and to always remain cognizant of public support of the anti-crime effort. He cautioned those in attendance to stand fast against both intimidation by gaming interests and "well-meaning but misguided appeasers, who believe that since the desire to gamble is found in many persons, it must be a virtue which should be legalized and permitted to flourish commercially." Having said his piece, McGrath turned the conference over to temporary presiding officer Mayor Quigg Newton of Denver, Colorado,[30] and the meeting then began in earnest.

The various officials in attendance brought disparate agendas to the working executive session, which followed the opening niceties. Alan Bible, attorney general of Nevada, for example, allowed that organized gambling presented a problem to law enforcement but also cautioned that "what some States permit, other States prohibit." With this in mind, states should look to strengthening their own laws rather than asking for federal assistance.[31] New York City corporation counsel John McGrath, on the other hand, noted the interstate nature of "organized gambling," particularly with reference to the slot machine trade and the wire services, and recommended "a more perfect system of cooperation" between all levels of government, possibly capped by pending congressional legislation banning the interstate transport of slots and authorizing a congressional investigation into interstate gambling. De-Lesseps Morrison asked for even more direct intervention, including congressional legislation outlawing the race wire, tightening of tax regulations that required the licensure of slot machines, stepped-up tax investigations of suggested racketeers, and in short, a "coordinated master plan" led by a "Federal effort or agency through which the cities and States can work."[32]

Most other speakers seemed content to report the situation in their own jurisdiction, sometimes exaggerating the presence of gaming interests and sometimes comically understating it. Otto Kerner, U.S. attorney for the Northern District of Illinois, which included Cook County and Chicago, protested that some had suggested Chicago was a bad place to live. Kerner insisted that having lived there all his life, he knew personally that Chicago authorities immediately raided any location they suspected of harboring slot machines or bookmaking activities. Flying in the face of the Chicago Crime Commission's lurid tales of all-pervasive syndicate influence in the Windy City, Kerner asserted that both Chicago and Cook County were "100 percent free of the slot machines which . . . are manufactured but not in use in Chicago." Punchboards, too, were made but never used in the city, and "the Chicago police have been doing a spectacular job in tracking down all the professional bookies. . . . There is no organized gambling in the city of Chicago to my knowledge."[33] The other delegates, having imbibed the visions of hoodlum-dominated Chicago circulating through the press but not wishing to embarrass their colleague, politely ignored his impassioned speech.

The main work of the conference took place in the Resolutions Committee, which resolved to appoint the Executive Continuing Committee, composed of members from the bodies represented at the conference. This group in turn selected the members of the Legislative Committee, which was to appoint subcommittees to discuss federal legislation, state laws, municipal ordinances, and cooperation with the Conference on Organized Crime. Delegates from the floor forwarded several proposals for the Legislative Committee to study. These topics constituted a laundry list of actions that could be taken to suppress crime, some bordering on violations of individual rights. They included:

1. federal legislation to prohibit the interstate shipment of gambling devices, as well as federal registration of the devices where they were legal
2. a uniform firearms licensing law requiring all sellers and users of guns to register them, and the creation of a national central bureau where all firearms registration information would be maintained
3. mandatory fingerprinting for all applicants for Social Security numbers, and compulsory cooperation between the Social Security Agency and all law enforcement officers in providing fingerprint records on request
4. a federal law outlawing the interstate use of the telegraph, telephone, or radio to disseminate horse race results for illegal gambling purposes

5. broadening the fugitive felon law to include all felonies
6. cooperation with any and all congressional committees (particularly Kefauver's embryonic crime committee) investigating crime and gaming.[34]

Following the conference, Mayor Newton chaired a press conference at which he disseminated the conference's continuing agenda to the public. Notices in the press the next day provided generally positive assessments of the conference and took the claims of the more energetic speakers, particularly Morrison and John McGrath, at face value. The *New York Times* gave tremendous weight to the speeches at the open morning session by the president, the attorney general, Mayor Morrison, and corporation counsel McGrath, providing faithful summations of their remarks (and the complete text of the presidential address) and also noting that the conference was "largely preliminary." In a note of foreshadowing, the *Times* account mentioned that Senator Estes Kefauver "spent considerable time in the meeting," with little idea that his subcommittee would, within the year, recast the "gambling problem" as a national fascination. [35]

Two Bills Enter, One Bill Leaves

By April 1, 1950, the legislative committee that grew out of McGrath's conference had assembled two bills, which the attorney general presented to Congress. The first, less ballyhooed measure, s. 3357, sought to halt the shipment of slot machines to states where they were illegal. The second, more important (in the opinion of contemporary writers) one, s. 3358, proposed to ban interstate transmission of gambling information for horse racing and sports events, striking at the core of the network of wires and bookmakers that, according to most of the speakers at the conference, was pouring dollars into the coffers of criminal syndicates.[36] Ultimately, the second bill, recognizable as an early iteration of the Wire Act, would be defeated in the Eighty-first Congress, though it would pass eleven years later and be written into the United States Code as Section 1084 of Title 18. It would take Robert Kennedy's stewardship, and all of the political pressure he could bring to bear, to usher that bill into law. The first bill, though, skated through the Senate, passed with amendments — and reservations — and after a bicameral conference was passed by both houses, becoming law by the end of the year. The respective fates of both bills, which shared strong endorsements from the attorney general, the president, and the anti-crime lobby, reveal much about the political realities of 1950 and the unique force that Kennedy applied to get his bill passed in 1961.

The legislative group of the Attorney General's Conference on Organized Crime had quite a few proposals to deal with, some of dubious constitutionality. Even though the resolutions might have been of assistance in fighting crime, a few of them were clearly beyond the scope of the conference. The question of whether to create a central database of fingerprint records of all tax-paying citizens, for example, involves issues of the fundamental privacy rights of Americans rather than criminal jurisprudence. Since the two most germane proposals for fighting crime — bans on the interstate transmission of betting information and the traffic of slot machines — approached the issue from the aspect of interstate commerce rather than criminal justice, it made sense to forward the bills to the Commerce Committee of the U.S. Senate.

On April 4, the committee's chair, Edwin C. Johnson, introduced both bills. Attorney General McGrath submitted a brief to Congress that outlined his belief that Congress had the power to enact the legislation. In it he cited several precedents for the use of federal power to support state policies. Federal laws against the interstate transmission of alcohol to a state banning intoxicating liquors, the interstate transmission of prison-made goods to states banning them, and the shipment of birds and game illegally killed demonstrated the right of Congress to pass laws that allowed federal assistance to state police powers. In addition, he cited the 1902 Supreme Court case *Champion* v. *Ames*, which reaffirmed the right of Congress to supplement the actions of states in protecting citizens from illegal sales of lottery tickets.[37]

The first proposal, s. 3357, ran through the Senate quickly, being reported by committee after no formal hearings on April 12 and passed by the full Senate on April 19.[38] This version of the bill required slot manufacturers and dealers to provide monthly reports to the federal tax authorities that detailed the names of purchasers and the number of machines they purchased. Each machine would bear a serial number, and if a slot machine was seized in a state that prohibited them, the owner of record would be traced and prosecuted, facing fines of up to $2,000 and/or one year's imprisonment. States that allowed slots (at the time Nevada statewide and Maryland on local county option) would still be permitted to have slot machines, but only after the state's governor certified to the federal government that machines were legal in that state.[39] In a major point, the bill defined a slot machine rather vaguely as "any machine . . . adapted for gambling or any use by which the user as the result of the application of any element of chance may become entitled to receive . . . anything of value."[40]

The bill then headed to the House of Representatives and its Interstate and Foreign Commerce Committee, chaired by Ohio Democrat Robert Crosser. As he had with Johnson of the Senate, Attorney General McGrath sent Crosser a message of concern, declaring that the bill was of vital importance and deserved "prompt consideration." Crosser, unlike Johnson, held hearings on the bill before putting it to a committee vote. Representatives of the Coin Machine Institute (which represented manufacturers of non-gaming machines) and the Justice Department recommended that the bill pass as it was. Speakers from other groups representing vendors and manufacturers of amusement devices asked that the bill's definition of a slot machine be made more specific; according to the bill passed by the Senate, a variety of amusement devices and games, including pinball machines, which gave free games to high scorers, could be considered slot machines. A representative of the American Coin Machine Manufacturers Association, which included slot machine makers, argued that the bill would invade states' rights and not be of any help in law enforcement.[41]

The committee then amended the bill, liberalizing it in some ways but tightening it in others. One amendment defined slot machines in three paragraphs, the crux of the definition being that the gambling devices prohibited by the bill were "any so-called 'slot machine' or any other machine . . . an essential part of which is a drum or reel with insignia thereon," which delivered as the result of chance, "any money or property."[42] Other amendments required manufacturers to register with the Justice Department rather than the Internal Revenue Board, stiffened penalties for violators, and required states permitting slot machines to pass a new bill that would exempt them from the law. With these changes, the committee approved the bill on July 27.[43]

While the bill was under consideration by the full House, its supporters turned aside three challenges. One, from Pat Sutton, a Tennessee Democrat, would have permitted slot machines on armed forces installations. Sutton's arguments that the profits from the machines went to the soldiers themselves, not to "gamblers," failed to persuade Congress to make an exception. Nevada Democrat Walter Baring made two abortive efforts to deflate the bill. He attempted to eliminate the provisions of the bill that required states to pass new laws reauthorizing the use of slot machines and prohibiting shipment of machines to states that manufactured them but banned their use. The latter provision was particularly galling to Baring because Nevada slot machines were made — and repaired — in Illinois, a state to which, under the House bill, it was illegal to ship slot machines. A final effort by Baring to send the bill for recommittal failed as well, and the House passed the measure by voice vote.[44]

A House-Senate conference convened to work out the differences between the two bills reported on September 19, recommending that the Senate accept the House amendments. The Senate took up the conference recommendation the next day but was blocked by Nevada Republican George Malone's filibuster, which at ten hours and fifteen minutes was one of the longest on record. Much of Malone's pointedly rambling talk concerned matters not even nearly on topic, including foreign policy and socialism, but he did manage to elucidate his objections to the bill, namely that the provisions Baring had sought to strike violated states' rights and, specifically, threatened Nevada's legal slot machines. On September 21 Malone again filibustered, and the bill was tabled until December 18. Malone, suffering from a sore throat, still delayed passage of the conference report for a day. The House passed the report on December 20, sending the bill to President Truman, who signed it into law on January 2, 1951.[45]

Johnson was able to successfully deliver the slot machine ban to McGrath because the slot manufacturers and operators had, apparently, little real influence. The lobbying efforts of the American Coin Machine Manufacturers Association, the only group to strongly oppose the bill in the House hearings, had no real impact. The rival Coin Machine Institute, representing only non-gaming vending machines, supported the measure. Other groups, like the National Association of Amusement Parks, Pools, and Beaches and the Toy Manufacturers of the U.S.A., successfully persuaded the House to tighten the definition of a gambling device to exclude their amusement machines. With this done, they too approved the bill. The Nevada delegation's failure to defeat the bill did not augur well for that state's legal casino industry, and it symbolically showed the importance of federal law, even in an area such as gaming regulation, which had traditionally been reserved to the states.

The biggest beneficiaries of slot operations, illegal gaming operators and the politicians and police whom they corrupted, could hardly be expected to formally lobby against s. 3357 or any anti-slot legislation. So, without any real opposition other than the procedural prevent defense of Baring in the House and Malone in the Senate, the bill to ban the shipment of slot machines across state lines easily became law. It was a good year for anti-slot measures. Congress that year also flexed its anti-gaming muscles by raising the federal excise tax on slot machines from $100 to $150 per machine.[46] Slots made an easy target.

The second bill that Johnson introduced in April at the behest of the attorney general, S. 3358 (Ban on Gaming Data), fared much differently, meeting eventual defeat in the face of a determined opposition. As originally introduced, S. 3358 prohibited "the use of or the leasing, furnishing, or maintaining of any communication facility for the transmission of gambling information in interstate commerce." While it permitted the transmission of sports and race information for news publication and television and radio broadcast, it placed the burden of proof on the supplier of the information to demonstrate that the news being disseminated was not, in fact, used to facilitate gambling. The bill also imposed a blackout on radio and television coverage of gambling information (defined as entries, scratches, jockey information, horse information, track conditions, odds, and prices) until one hour after the end of the race in question and banned the broadcast of more than one race a day by any single station.[47]

S. 3358 also required anyone who used communication facilities "operated for or in connection with the transmission of news or other information pertaining to sporting events or contests" to file a statement with the carrier of the transmission (i.e., the telegraph or telephone company) affirming that the information was used for legitimate news reporting. The carriers were then to turn the statements over to state or federal law enforcement for investigation. Failure to file such a statement "shall create a presumption" that the service was being used to circumvent the act. The common carriers were also required to maintain lists of the addresses of receiving and sending points for sports information and to make these lists available to state and federal law enforcement. The Federal Communications Commission was responsible for the enforcement of these provisions.[48]

Like the slot machine bill, the ban on gambling information was intended to aid state efforts "to cope with the growing evil of organized gambling and bookmaking activities," in this case by "denying the use of interstate communications for such activities."[49] As the bill was only designed to lend federal aid to state law enforcement, it called for FCC rather than Justice Department action. Attorney General Howard McGrath, the driving force behind both anti-gaming bills, played rather obvious politics here. Just as the original Senate version of S. 3357 required the Internal Revenue Board and not the Justice Department to oversee enforcement, this bill would give Mc-Grath a claim to have done his job in fighting for stronger controls on the race wire service without involving his department in the tedious business of actually doing so.

The Internal Revenue Board, under a 1942 act requiring a federal tax on gambling devices, already issued tax stamps for slot machines, so pumping up its enforcement responsibilities was not initially perceived as particularly onerous. Congress did not accept McGrath's views, however, and though the bill passed the Senate without any real hearings, Congress ultimately did pass enforcement to the Justice Department; Internal Revenue must have lobbied persuasively in caucus.

The McFarland Committee

The other anti-gaming bill, s. 3358, attracted immediate attention upon its introduction, and it would not cakewalk through the Senate as its companion bill had. Before permitting a committee vote, Senator Johnson acceded to demands that he hold public hearings on the bill by appointing a subcommittee to do so. The question of how to solve the "organized gambling" problem would again migrate upward.

The subcommittee chosen to hold hearings on s. 3358 first met on April 17, 1950. Johnson tapped Ernest McFarland, an Arizona Democrat, to chair the group. Perhaps mindful of Estes Kefauver's ongoing politicking for an investigation into organized crime, McFarland noted right after taking his seat that his subcommittee was hearing testimony on only the bill at hand and not on any other investigations into "crime syndicates or murders or narcotics traffic, or other rackets." First his committee was to learn the pattern of interstate gambling, and then it would decide if the specific measure before it would "meet the problem." Believing that waiting for Kefauver's proposed investigation would result only in killing any chance of enacting the bill during that session, McFarland promised to hold prompt hearings, which would rely on the expertise of the Justice Department and selected witnesses to determine the "pattern of operations."[50]

Attorney General McGrath, whose testimony opened the hearings, reiterated that the bill was intended only to help states enforce their own laws against gaming through the exercise of the federal regulatory power, an area in which the power of Congress was "complete."[51] In a lengthy statement, he summarized the results of his February conference, noted the surfeit of federal anti-gaming enforcement power, and sketched out the operations of "modern bookmaking."[52] McGrath's conception of off-track betting, which the committee accepted as substantively accurate, bears examination.

According to McGrath, about twenty major racetracks throughout the nation provided the action, and a national service that transmitted race information and results profited tremendously. Bookmakers profited from the small bets placed by generating sheer volume, which required bettors to place wagers on entire cards of daily races held by more than one track. This was possible only if bettors knew the actual races being run, the odds, and various related information on the conditions of the jockeys, horses, and tracks. Some of this information could be found in racing scratch sheets and the *Daily Racing Form*, but both the bookmaker and his clientele needed up-to-date information that was provided only by electronic communication: telegraph tickers, telephones, or radio signals. In addition to receiving race and wager information, bookmakers needed to be able to communicate with other bookmakers in order to lay off bets.[53]

McGrath further stated that a central service collected race information, sometimes with the permission of the tracks and sometimes not. The central service then sent this information out to six distributors, which in turn forwarded it to thirty-six subdistributors, which furnished the information to bookmakers. The central service (the Continental Press Service by name) thus insulated itself from charges that it abetted illegal gambling. Without this service and access to a telephone, the small-time bookmaker would quickly fail.[54]

McGrath called attention to the pains the bill took to safeguard the freedom of the press and to prevent setting up a new era of "Prohibition," in which the federal government took up the policing and prosecution of gamblers (a state of affairs that would have given responsibility for enforcement to his Justice Department). As he explained, the Federal Communications Commission already exercised authority over communications carriers by requiring them to submit and adhere to tariffs. The proposed bill would extend this power by requiring the FCC to authorize carriers to refuse service to people who used their services unlawfully. This was, McGrath argued, the best possible solution:

> The federal experience with the Federal Trade Commission Act, with the Civil Aeronautics Act, and even with civil suits under the antitrust laws, has demonstrated how more effective [sic] the civil proce-

dures can be than criminal penalties in dealing with intricate regulatory problems. The problem here is intricate.[55]

This intricate problem required little more than the strengthening of regulatory statutes. Just as Al Capone was ultimately convicted not for bootlegging or murder but for tax evasion, the operators of the central race news service could be brought down by FCC regulations.

FCC chairman Wayne Coy had a quite different perspective and offered a much different solution. Appearing before the committee on April 24, Coy complained that McGrath's proposal defined "gambling information" so vaguely that it would lead to the probable "failure of the law to achieve its objectives."[56] Rather, he thought, the bill should criminalize the use of interstate communications to actually place bets or wagers. Limiting the ban to actual odds or wager information allowed the free exchange of all but these crucial data, without which the track conditions and other items of news were worthless to gamblers. In addition, this crime should not be policed by the FCC, which had "neither the manpower nor a reasonable expectation of getting sufficient funds for the needed manpower" to enforce the law; it should be handled by local police. Coy thus politely rebuffed the McGrath proposal. Though he insisted that he was "not trying to avoid all responsibility for the problem," it was clearly not the FCC's battle to fight. S. 3357 had not enjoined the Civil Aeronautics Board to inspect airplanes for illicit slot machines, and this bill had no right to force the FCC into a parallel situation.[57]

Showing a true spirit of cooperation, Coy then submitted an alternate proposal that he and his colleagues at the FCC had written. This version maintained much of the original S. 3358 but limited the definition of "gambling information" to bets, odds, and prices paid. In addition to prohibiting such a transmission, it made a crime punishable by a $1,000 fine and a year's imprisonment, the penalty already in the Criminal Code for the broadcasting of lottery information. While the proposal kept the requirement that those leasing communications facilities register, it eliminated the provision of the bill that directed the FCC to enforce the prohibition.[58] Just as the Justice Department and the Treasury had each tried to duck enforcement of the Volstead Act in 1920 (Justice won, sticking the rival agency with the thankless task of enforcing an unenforceable law), Justice and the FCC each insisted that the other was the perfect agency for the job.

With the public demanding action, Kefauver gearing up to launch a special investigation, and the potential enforcement agencies pointedly evading

responsibility, one wonders exactly what McFarland was supposed to do. Mc-
Farland read into the record his frustrations when thanking Coy for taking
the time to address the committee — and drop off his exculpatory version of
the bill:

> We certainly appreciate your coming here and giving your version
> of how the problem can best be met. This committee is going to study
> all of these proposals, and it may well be that when we get through, we
> will recommend legislation that will be a combination.
>
> I can readily understand why you do not want the responsibility and
> I can readily understand why the Attorney General does not want the
> responsibility, after the experience in the enforcement of the prohibi-
> tion laws, and what grew out of the lack of enforcement of those laws
> and the rackets that grew out of them. So our committee appreciates
> your coming here and giving us these recommendations.[59]

McFarland had little help from his senatorial colleagues. None of the committee members had any special knowledge of crime or, for that matter,
gambling. Committee member Homer Capehart, after suggesting that the
Congress ban all pari-mutuel wagering, received indignant telegrams from
members of the legal pari-mutuel industry and was the subject of a satirical
article in the *Washington Daily News* titled "Close the Tracks and Shoot the
Nags, Senator Capehart," which he perversely insisted on reading into the
record, much to McFarland's chagrin.[60]

Complicating matters, the committee heard a great deal of testimony
about the extent of bookmaking operations that reads like a cinematic
trailer for the later hearings held by the Kefauver Committee. A New York
City delegation headed by John McGrath provided charts, graphs, and an explanation of how the wire service made millions of dollars a year.[61] Bookmakers like James Carroll of St. Louis and Frank Erickson of New York, both of
whom downplayed the importance of the wire service, willingly spoke to the
committee. Erickson insisted that a bookmaker needed no up-to-the-minute
news service, only a racing form, "a little money, [and] a few customers."[62]

Although some witnesses, including New York police commissioner William O'Brien and Attorney General McGrath, disavowed any knowledge of
a national criminal syndicate, others, like anti-gaming stalwarts deLesseps
Morrison of New Orleans and Fletcher Bowron of Los Angeles, brought witnesses who described the hoodlum menace. Captain Lynn White of the LAPD

described interstate relations between gangsters and racketeers as a "loose confederation," not yielding to the more alarmist notions of a single, unified national crime syndicate.[63] The media, already sniffing a story, began giving front-page coverage to the committee, something that McFarland bemoaned aloud. "These hearings have been confused, more or less, with the expected hearings that would take place if a crime investigation is launched by the Senate. . . . We are not interested in a crime probe as such."[64]

After hearing a barrage of testimony from all quarters, and aware that Kefauver had gotten his special investigation, the committee rewrote the bill, incorporating elements of the Justice and FCC proposals. It defined gaming information as both bets, odds, and prices and horse, jockey, and track information. The bill prohibited transmitting this information before or during a race, but after the race it could be disseminated. Radio and television broadcasters could air races, provided they did not broadcast any gambling information.[65]

Its work done, the subcommittee disbanded. The full Commerce Committee favorably reported the legislation soon after, on May 26, but the Senate took no further action on the bill.[66] Butting heads with executive agencies over jurisdiction, wary of passing a law that violated freedom of speech, and paralyzed by the unfolding drama that would soon begin with Estes Kefauver's criminal road show, most of the Senate had had its fill of bookmakers and crime. But the public had just whet its appetite.

Kefauver Goes on the Air

Even before the McFarland Committee met, preparations for a full-bore senatorial investigation into gaming had begun. As early as January 5, 1950, Democratic senator Estes Kefauver of Tennessee had introduced a bill calling for a national investigation into organized crime. Kefauver had originally appeared on the national scene in the early 1940s as an anti-boss opponent of the Crump-McKellar Memphis political machine and a stalwart champion of the Tennessee Valley Authority. During his ten years in the House of Representatives, which began in 1939, he developed a reputation as a Southern liberal who supported the New Deal and opposed the poll tax but gave his unqualified endorsement to Jim Crow and balked at even the most moderate proposals to end public segregation.[67]

In 1945, Representative Kefauver chaired a House Judiciary subcommittee that investigated judicial corruption in Pennsylvania. Kefauver later claimed that this experience had impressed upon him "the full import of what rotten-ness in public life can do to [the United States] and ultimately inspired [his] work against crime in the Senate.[68] Certainly his fight against Boss Crump in Memphis gave him an appreciation of the scope of criminal/political cor-ruption. Historian William Moore takes a more cynical view of Kefauver's at-tention to postwar crime; he asserts that the contacts Kefauver made during the investigation, including several crime reporters and Justice Department prosecutors Max Goldschein and Boris Kostelanetz, kept Kefauver abreast of developments in crime, which he exploited for political purposes. According to Moore, Kefauver's interest in crime became even more acute in 1949, when Phillip L. Graham and J. Russell Wiggins of the *Washington Post* directed him to the reports of the California Crime Commission, which indicated that a national criminal syndicate was indeed a threat.[69]

After introducing his proposal, Kefauver championed it wherever possi-ble, making appearances at the attorney general's crime conference and sit-ting in on the McFarland Committee's hearings. He was not alone in believing crime to be a hot issue; Edwin Johnson, chair of the Commerce Committee, jumped at the chance to ally with Attorney General McGrath and present the two anti-crime bills to Congress, and he proposed that his committee un-dertake an investigation similar to that proposed by Kefauver. Given that any legislative proposals would logically pass through his Commerce Commit-tee, Johnson argued that he, not Kefauver, should lead the investigation.[70]

Ultimately, Senate Democrats chose to merge the two investigations. Intra- and interparty wrangling continued through April and into May, as both pro-cedural and partisan sniping sought to control what was bound to be a politi-cally sensitive investigation in an election year. Finally, on May 3, the Senate accepted a compromise plan that called for a five-member committee with two Republicans and three Democrats.[71] Vice President Alben Barkley then selected the committee, officially known as the Special Committee to Investi-gate Organized Crime in Interstate Commerce, choosing Kefauver to chair it, with Herbert O'Conor of Maryland and Lester Hunt of Wyoming occupying the Democratic seats and Charles Tobey of New Hampshire and Alexander Wiley of Wisconsin representing the Republicans.[72]

After creating a staff and handling administrative details, the committee began hearings in Miami, where it eagerly investigated the morass of South Florida's gaming scene. Over the next year the committee traveled the na-tion, holding open and closed hearings in fourteen cities: Washington, D.C., Tampa, Miami, New York, Cleveland, St. Louis, Kansas City, New Orleans,

Detroit, Chicago, Philadelphia, Las Vegas, Los Angeles, and San Francisco. During the course of these hearings, the committee heard the testimony of more than six hundred witnesses, ranging from U.S. narcotics commissioner H. J. Anslinger to alleged Mafia head Paul "the Waiter" Ricca of Chicago.[73]

Throughout 1950 the hearings entered a great deal of information into the public record about gaming and crime, some of it helpful, much of it not. Comparison with the McFarland Committee is instructive. Whereas McFarland had been interested in a single, unbending, utilitarian end — to determine if the legislation before his group would help fight crime — Kefauver seemed more interested in a sprawling, open-ended investigation into crime and corruption everywhere and anywhere. McFarland had a far more grounded approach, taking officials like Attorney General McGrath and New York police commissioner William O'Brien at their word when they refused to confirm the existence of an organized national criminal syndicate, though he and Homer Capehart asked such witnesses whether, if such an organization did exist, the proposed legislation would successfully combat it.[74] Kefauver, on the other hand, encouraged law enforcement witnesses who claimed that an all-powerful national syndicate tightly controlled crime. When the parade of suspected criminals failed to confirm this hypothesis, he concluded only that it was further proof of the conspiracy.

Still, the committee received an avalanche of publicity, most of it favorable. In early 1951, local and then, with the New York hearings, national television coverage of the hearings brought the committee into millions of American homes. At the peak of the New York testimony, between 20 and 30 million viewers watched daily broadcasts and nightly rebroadcasts of the stream of politicians, police, and suspected racketeers that the committee's general counsel, Rudolph Haley, produced.[75]

For all of its televised mayhem, the committee ultimately produced rather slender results: seventeen general conclusions about crime in interstate commerce, twenty-two federal recommendations, including proposed legislation, and seven suggestions for action by state and local governments. Among its seventeen findings of apparent fact, the committee concluded that organized criminal gangs were "firmly entrenched in our large cities" and made "tremendous" profits from a variety of rackets. Rather than the loose confederation that many astute police felt they could prove to exist, the committee stated that organized criminal activities were a virtual monopoly concern, that the Accardo-Guzik-Fischetti syndicate of Chicago (AKA the former Capone syndicate) and the Costello-Adonis-Lansky syndicate, based in New

York, controlled operations in cities throughout the country. The committee also popularized the idea of the "sinister criminal organization known as the Mafia," a descendant of a Sicilian crime group that also called itself the Unione Siciliano and the Black Hand.[76] According to the committee, the criminals who operated rackets often did their business unmolested because they consistently bribed politicians and police.[77]

With specific regard to gaming, the committee found that "gambling profits are the principal support of big-time racketeers and gangsterism."[78] It enlarged upon the dual-syndicate theme of the attorney general's conference: the Accardo-Guzik-Fischetti syndicate controlled the Continental Press Service, which provided the rapid transmission of racing and gaming information, while Frank Costello's New York group ran slots throughout the nation. Both syndicates were linked together as part of a single axis of evil, the transnational mafia. In conducting illegal businesses, syndicate members were given aid and comfort by a range of members of the otherwise law-abiding business and civic community, from corrupt public officials permitting "wide-open towns" and from the Western Union Telegraph Company, whose leased wires were essential to Continental's service. In sum, criminal syndicates, operating across state lines, infiltrated legitimate businesses and defrauded the U.S. Treasury of "huge sums of money" in the form of unpaid taxes.[79]

The recommendations of the committee, none of which became law, suggested a broad range of solutions. One proposal invited the committee itself to continue to "scrutinize the efforts of Federal agencies to suppress interstate criminal operations." Further legislation would set up an independent Federal Crime Commission, which would continue to study crime, make reports to the Senate committee, suggest legislation, coordinate state and federal efforts, and serve as an information clearinghouse. Special "racket squads" within Justice and Internal Revenue would supplement this commission and complete the federalization of the fight against interstate crime.[80]

The committee also suggested several pieces of legislation to restrict interstate gaming operations. It supported the idea of s. 3358, which by the time of the committee's final recommendations had already died, that the transmission of gambling information should be suppressed, and it believed that the transmission of bets and wagers by any facility of interstate commerce whatsoever should be prohibited. The committee also endorsed enlarging the Johnson Slot Machine Act by including other gambling devices like roulette wheels and punchboards.[81]

In the final analysis, all of the televised hearings and suggestions of the committee came to nothing, or next to nothing. The only action Congress actually took in 1952 was to adopt a measure that Kefauver had opposed, the Wagering Tax Act. This law levied a 10 percent excise tax on bookmakers and required them to register and pay a special occupational tax of $50 per year. Originally passed with the promise of bringing in tremendous revenues and opening bookmakers to police prosecution, the law did neither, triggering only about one thousand federal cases, registration fees of about $500,000, and collections of around $5 million annually — pocket change compared to the billions that Kefauver and his allies had insisted that bookmakers saw.[82] In what may have been an unintended consequence, this levy drove legal Nevada casinos out of the horse and sports betting business, but besides that the bookmakers' tax changed little.

Ultimately, the committee did little to change the federal government's basic approach to interstate crime, though it did spark a wave of harassment by local and state police against illegal gaming that would profoundly change urban gambling. Local crime commissions, taking their cues from Virgil Peterson's Chicago group, took up the anti-crime banner and successfully disrupted illegal gaming operations throughout the nation. Reformers combated gaming even in "wide open" towns like Galveston, Texas, which boasted an estimated one thousand slot machines and the Balinese Room, a nightspot that catered to the Texas wealthy and had reported annual revenues of more than $4 million. In 1951, using a new state law that made possession of a slot machine a felony, the investigations of the "Texas Kefauver committee" and the local reform newspaper, a grand jury issued the first indictments against gambling in decades.[83] The flourishing illegal casinos of Bergen County, New Jersey, began to wilt under the spotlight provided by Kefauver; a group of local businesses and clergy formed a Citizens Crime Committee and moved strenuously to fight the gamblers.[84] Such local solutions proved eminently successful at quieting the public outcry against racketeers. Even the federal government was goaded into action as both the Justice Department and the Treasury Department briefly stepped up investigations and prosecutions of "racketeers."[85]

Once the committee disbanded in 1951, Americans let the problem of "gangsterism" slip from the forefront of public consciousness. The war in Korea, Joseph McCarthy's charges of widespread Communist conspiracies within the government itself, and growing ferment over long-standing racial inequities displaced rackets in the news. Still, the public vaguely remembered that Kefauver had argued that a national criminal syndicate known as the mafia existed — though he had not proved it. Although none of Kefauver's suggested legislation came close to being passed, the general spirit that he advocated, one of vigilance against racketeers and a general mistrust of gamblers, became part of the public consciousness. By the end of the decade, a new maelstrom of allegations about organized crime would bring the matter before yet another congressional committee and set the stage for the passage of the Wire Act.

Finding the Enemy Within

Americans could be forgiven for losing sight of the fight against gambling racketeers. After local law enforcement proved to be an effective mechanism for driving the most visible forms of clandestine gaming — illegal casinos, slot machine operations, and horse rooms — out of the cities, there was little reason to expect much more in the way of public outcry. Still, the idea of a mafia remained tantalizingly on the edge of public consciousness. But with no proof of such a tremendous criminal conspiracy, to take action against it seemed fruitless.

Despite (or perhaps because of) the successes of local and state crime commissions in uncovering illegal gaming and political corruption, the federal government took very little further action. Attention shifted somewhat to the problem of narcotics. In 1951 Kefauver had thrown into his hopper of recommended legislation an anti-narcotics act, an almost desultory stab at an issue the committee ranked far lower than gaming on the scale of national evils. But in 1956, while the rest of his suggestions were already being forgotten, Congress passed the Narcotics Control Act, which stiffened penalties for trafficking in illegal drugs.

In January 1957, the Senate Permanent Subcommittee on Investigations, at the urging of its chief counsel, Robert Kennedy, launched another congressional investigation into organized crime. This one, chaired by John Mc-Clellan of Arkansas, drew its members from the Labor Committee and Investigations and brushed aside queries about the persistence of illegal gaming to focus on labor racketeering. The Senate Select Committee on Improper Activities in the Labor or Management Field, as it was officially known, included Barry Goldwater, the Arizona Republican who had, ironically, ousted Ernest McFarland from the Senate; Joseph McCarthy, already near death and sliding into political obscurity; and John F. Kennedy, a freshman senator from Massachusetts and, of course, the brother of the chief counsel.

The McClellan Committee's investigations focused on corruption within labor unions and more specifically the Teamsters, where the committee, at Kennedy's urging, targeted union president Dave Beck. After it sent Beck to prison for larceny and income tax evasion, the committee doggedly pursued his successor, James Hoffa.[86] The committee stayed far away from gaming, but unfolding events brought the connections between gaming and organized crime as a national conspiracy before the public once more. Americans began to suspect that a single common thread — organized crime's grip on gaming — linked a chain of events in Las Vegas, New York City, and south central New York State.

The story begins on the Las Vegas Strip, where the Tropicana casino resort opened in April 1957. A typically lavish resort of the period, it cost more than $15 million to build. "Miami hotelier" Ben Jaffe served as its primary paper investor, although according to scandal-minded reporters, he was actually a beard for Frank Costello, famous as the crux of the New York syndicate, leader of what the Kefauver Committee had identified as one of two groups that controlled gaming throughout America. In the early 1950s, Jaffe bought land on the Strip and affiliated himself with Phil Kastel, a partner of Costello in Louisiana. This partnership inspired rumors of Jaffe's fronting for Costello, and Kastel had difficulty in obtaining a license from the newly powerful Nevada State Gaming Control Board because of his own close connections to Costello. While Kastel's public role in the operation was diminished, he remained active in the hotel's financing.[87]

On May 2, 1957, less than a month after the opening of the Tropicana, an assailant shot Frank Costello in the lobby of his Manhattan apartment building. Costello survived the would-be assassin's bullet to the head and was rushed to Manhattan's Roosevelt Hospital. As the police waited to query him about the identity of the shooter (which he adamantly refused to reveal), they conducted a peremptory search of his discarded clothing and discovered a slip of paper on which were written figures for "gross casino wins," "slot wins," "markers," and what appeared to be payments to four investors.[88]

Authorities in New York and Nevada soon discovered that the figures matched the Tropicana's first-month take to the dollar. To exacerbate the situation, the handwriting on the note matched that of Louis Lederer, the treasurer-secretary of the syndicate that owned the Tropicana. This revelation confirmed what many had suspected — that Costello had anted up the real money behind the Tropicana — and seemed to substantiate the claims of Kefauver et al. that a powerful criminal syndicate controlled gaming throughout the nation. How else to explain a New York gambler and alleged crime boss holding the detailed financial records of a state-licensed casino 2,500 miles away?

Experts on organized crime later theorized that the shooting of Costello was no random act of violence or even an individual crime of vengeance but part of an underworld coup. Costello himself "got the message," forswore revenge for the attack, and reportedly abandoned his reputed mob leadership. The October murder of Albert Anastasia, leader of another family, preceded by that of Frank Scalise, his underboss, completed the uprising and paved the way for the elevation of Vito Genovese as undisputed leader of New York organized crime.[89]

Partly to discuss the new underworld order, organized-crime watchers believe, mob leaders convened a meeting on November 14, 1957, at the Apalachin, New York, estate of Joseph Barbara, owner of a beverage-distributing business and suspected organized-crime figure. Townspeople might have noticed something out of the ordinary when a flood of late-model Lincolns and Cadillacs arrived in the small rural town en route to the Barbara estate. A New York State Police sergeant who had long suspected Barbara of malfeasance, Edgar Croswell, with another trooper and two Treasury agents, drove onto Barbara's property and copied down license plate numbers before retreating to a point about half a mile from the estate and setting up a roadblock.[90]

At this point, several of the attendees, suspecting that a raid was imminent, panicked and fled, some on foot and some by automobile. Officers stopped a total of sixty-three well-dressed men fleeing the Barbara estate. Ironically, had the men stayed on Barbara's property (as did approximately forty other visitors), they would not have been subject to any immediate danger, because Croswell had no warrant and they broke no laws by merely gathering there. Once they abandoned the house for the public road, however, officers could stop them and demand identification.[91]

Most of those stopped hailed from New York, New Jersey, and Pennsylvania, but some came from as far as California, Colorado, and Florida. Most of those who remained inside the house, it was later alleged, were from the Chicago area. Those stopped by police were primarily involved in the bar and restaurant, garment manufacturing, trucking, importing, vending, and construction industries. When asked why they were gathered in Apalachin, those who answered at all claimed to have come to visit a sick friend, to discuss personal business, or to attend a party—answers that did not satisfy law enforcement officers.

Following the arrests, the New York state legislature and a state investigations committee began probing the meeting, and in the summer of 1958 Sergeant Croswell testified before the McClellan Committee, where a steady procession of Apalachin attendees subsequently asserted their Fifth Amendment rights and refused to speak. The attorney general then appointed a special investigating group that gathered intelligence and actually got twenty of the attendees convicted for conspiracy to obstruct justice for reportedly agreeing with each other not to disclose the true reason of the meeting; these convictions were then reversed by an appellate court, which ruled that prosecutors had not proven that a specific crime had taken place. Ultimately, except for those who went to jail for civil contempt for refusing to tell why they were at the Barbara estate after having been given immunity and directed by the court to testify, none of the Apalachin attendees served time for the meeting itself, though many found themselves the subjects of stepped-up investigations by local and federal authorities.[92]

The Apalachin meeting, though, reminded Americans that for more than a decade crime commissions, prosecutors, and journalists had been insisting that a national criminal syndicate controlled a variety of rackets, chief among them gaming. The abortive gathering and the investigations that followed reawakened many citizens to fears of this criminal syndicate and scuttled purely local explanations of illegal gaming enforcement. If criminals could pool their resources for collective national action, the argument went, so must law enforcement. So legislators began to appreciate again the political expediency, if nothing else, of enacting federal laws against illegal operations that crossed state lines.

The McClellan Committee now found itself with new wind in its sails. The enduring refusal of those arrested at Apalachin to reveal the purpose of their meeting only seemed to confirm that secret cabals of gangsters and racketeers had ominous designs. The committee's investigations into the labor world furthered the public conception that organized crime was a growing menace, a threat to the American economy and to American democracy itself.

More important for the immediate legislative future, the ambitious and dedicated chief counsel of the committee, Robert Kennedy, would find in

Teamsters boss James Hoffa a worthy adversary and a pesky defendant who stubbornly refused to be convicted. Once Kennedy tired of the Hoffa feud, he easily transferred his enmity to organized crime in the abstract. Disturbed that J. Edgar Hoover and the Federal Bureau of Investigation had apparently little intelligence on organized-crime figures, Kennedy found reliable sources in the Bureau of Narcotics who had long suggested that an offshoot of the Sicilian Mafia dominated traffic in illegal drugs.[93]

Kennedy acquired his new zeal at the perfect historical moment. The expanded character of gaming as it existed at the middle of the century demanded a stronger national solution. Local crime commissions and honest police officials vehemently argued that since supra-local syndicates controlled gaming, local efforts to roust it were futile. To fight against national gaming syndicates, one needed a national law enforcement imperative. Though there was much debate over this issue of gaming, the revelation that gaming was an inseparable part of organized crime did little to truly stop American appetites for gaming. In many cities, newly vigilant enforcement of the anti-gaming laws shuttered illegal slot operations, horse rooms, and gaming houses. For well-off Americans who wanted the option of gambling, Las Vegas emerged as a national resort, with plentiful gaming for those who could afford the vacation.

On the federal level, the desired action never materialized. The Johnson Slot Machine Act was partially effective, but for the most part bills that might have attacked organized crime's gaming interests languished in Congress, which was soon occupied with more pressing matters. It would take the election of a new president and the installation of his determined brother as a powerful attorney general to force a bolder federal response to organized crime and gaming.

In 1959 Robert Kennedy began to transfer his energies to the election plans of his brother, and in September of that year he resigned as chief counsel of the McClellan Committee. He penned a book detailing his investigations into organized crime and the labor movement called *The Enemy Within*, a title that perfectly captured the chilling realization that the United States faced a subversive presence sponsored not by Moscow or Beijing but by suit-wearing, cigar-smoking Americans intent on subverting honest government to enrich themselves. These gamblers grossly parodied American business and civics, enriching themselves and fearing little from the police. After his brother won the presidency and appointed him attorney general, Robert Kennedy was ready to begin the fight against organized crime in earnest.

With the investigation of labor unions behind him, Kennedy sought to strike the organized-crime menace at the root of its power — its money. Following a decade of expert testimony, grand jury indictments, and mayoral proclamations, Kennedy — and most other Americans — believed that profits from gaming operations, above all other "rackets," sustained organized crime. It would be a natural move to attack the perceived organized-crime monopoly grip on illegal gaming as the first step in a war on organized crime. Surveying his domain as the most powerful attorney general in history, Kennedy, in 1961, would do just that.

3 Camelot Strikes Back

The forceful attorney general gets his tools to fight organized crime and is able to accomplish in 1961 what Kefauver could not in 1950.

It should be clear that the Federal Government is not undertaking the almost impossible task of dealing with all the many forms of casual or social wagering which so often may be effected over communications. It is not intended that the act should prevent a social wager between friends by telephone. This legislation can be a most effective weapon in dealing with one of the major factors of organized crime in this country without invading the privacy of the home or outraging the sensibilities of our people in matters of personal inclinations and morals.

—Robert F. Kennedy, 1961

THE ATTORNEY GENERAL OF THE UNITED STATES, under any circumstances, is an incredibly powerful citizen. The nation's "top cop," he or she sits at the head of the Justice Department, commanding an army of lawyers, investigators, and officials. Charged with representing the legal interests of the United States, the attorney general is the lead partner in the world's largest law firm and directs agencies like the Federal Bureau of Investigation, the Bureau of Alcohol, Tobacco, and Firearms, the Drug Enforcement Agency, and the Bureau of Prisons. A determined attorney general has an abundance of available resources within easy reach. When the newly elected John F. Kennedy nominated his brother to fill that office in December 1960, common sense held that, with the infinite fraternal support of the president, Robert F. Kennedy might become the most powerful attorney general in U.S. history.

Most accounts of Robert Kennedy's tenure as attorney general emphasize his position as his brother's sounding board and resident heavy, his seemingly personal vendetta against Teamsters president James R. Hoffa, or his role in the civil rights struggle. There are comparatively few analyses of his fight against gambling and organized crime. This is perplexing, for upon assuming the office Kennedy identified organized crime—and in particular its perceived monopoly control of gaming—as a top priority and took immediate action to fight it. His first press conference as attorney general saw him unveil his anti-crime legislative agenda, signaling its import.[1] While he was content merely to uphold existing civil rights laws, he demanded immediate coordination of the Federal Bureau of Investigation, the Immigration Service, the Internal Revenue Service's Intelligence Division, narcotics agents from the Treasury Department, the Secret Service, and the Bureau of Alcohol, Tobacco, and Firearms. He insisted that federal law enforcement immediately target the top one hundred names in organized crime; once selected, those individuals were to have "the full weight" of the various investigatory agencies thrown against them.[2] Within weeks, he had outlined an entire legislative program to better fight organized crime. Clearly, Kennedy felt that organized crime was a major problem.

Most analysts of Kennedy's legacy feel that he abandoned organized crime as a major issue at some point in 1962. There were certainly great challenges before the attorney general in that year and the next, particularly Cuba, which bedeviled his brother's administration, and the intensifying fight to secure civil rights for African Americans in the South. Yet the Kennedys did not drive Castro from Cuba, and comprehensive civil rights legislation passed Congress only during the administration of Lyndon Johnson, the elder Kennedy's successor. As attorney general, Robert Kennedy took office with the pledge to fight organized crime, and in 1961 he secured passage of several statutes to help him in this fight. Legislatively, that achievement may be his most enduring legacy. A relatively unheralded item in this pack of new legislation, the Wire Act, would eventually come to define federal gaming policy in the Internet age, a development that would have shocked its chief advocate as much as anyone.

"Get Organized Crime"

Robert Kennedy was a complex, driven man, full of passion and determination. In 1968 he captivated the nation—and has dazzled historians since then—with his boundless energy and seemingly magic potential to take on the problems then facing America, the most important of which, by the time of his political maturation into a major national figure in his own right, were the conduct of the Vietnam War and civil rights. But much of his public career was spent chasing those defined as "un-American" and prosecuting those who violated the law. His first job after graduating law school was as an attorney in the Criminal Division of the Justice Department, which he soon left to run his brother's campaign for the Senate.[3]

Kennedy's first high-level position came as assistant counsel on the Senate Investigations Committee, better known as the McCarthy Committee after its notorious chairman, the Red-hunting Joseph McCarthy. Kennedy hagiographers have taken pains to distance him from the aggressive Red-baiting tactics of the committee. Yet Kennedy at first expressed no reservations about the committee's work, and he angled for a position as staff director, though he was outmaneuvered by Roy Cohn, who became chief counsel and the driving force behind the committee's investigation. After a series of disagreements with Cohn (the two reportedly came to the brink of public fisticuffs on one occasion), Kennedy resigned as assistant counsel, but returned to the committee within months as Democratic counsel.[4]

In his role as minority counsel, Kennedy grew to distance himself from the progressively more outrageous charges of conspiracy formulated by Roy Cohn and expressed by McCarthy. Careful never to publicly criticize McCarthy, Kennedy still seethed at Cohn; their mutual antagonism, according to Cohn, drove Kennedy to return to the committee on the side of the Democrats "to get that little son of a bitch Roy Cohn." When the committee and its chairman publicly disintegrated with the ill-fated investigation of Communist infiltration into the armed forces, Kennedy found himself able to walk away from the wreckage with little of the stigma that attached to McCarthy and Cohn.[5]

After dabbling in the hunt for subversives, Kennedy showed an interest in criminal justice that spanned most of his adult life, and he was at his most acute when pursuing those who, in his estimation, made a mockery of American institutions by corrupting them. He awakened to his passionate zeal for uncovering corruption in his role as chief counsel to the Senate Permanent Committee on Investigations, which he began in 1955 as a fresh-faced twenty-nine-year-old. Originally pursuing prosaic investigations into government procurement fraud, Kennedy became increasingly interested in both organized crime and trade union corruption.[6] At his urging, a subcommittee known as the Select Committee on Improper Activities in the Labor or Management Field began investigations that spotlighted Kennedy as an aggressive—some said ruthless—investigator.

Toppling Dave Beck and doggedly pursuing Jimmy Hoffa at the helm of the Teamsters, Kennedy established a reputation as someone who, thanks to his work with McClellan, had developed "unrivaled knowledge" of organized crime and its inner workings.[7] Kennedy was far from bashful about his work on the committee (unlike his service with McCarthy, at whose funeral he pointedly asked reporters not to photograph him), publishing an account of his fight against labor racketeers in The Enemy Within. Though civil libertarians charged him with evincing a deliberate carelessness with the rights of some of the committee's witnesses, the general public accepted his new image as "scourge of the labor racketeers."[8] If, when drafted as attorney general, Kennedy needed a platform, his earlier work with the McClellan Committee gave him one: organized crime.

The fight against organized crime was more than an abstract struggle against corruption; for Kennedy, it had a decidedly personal dimension. Though he was initiated into the urban demimonde of prostitution, narcotics, and gambling—and the political corruption that made it possible— only by riding along with "flying squads" of New York Police Department detectives in his McClellan Committee days, Kennedy found himself matched against men who had dealt with or lived within the criminal element for most of their adult lives. He had three major public adversaries from the late 1950s until his death. Two of these had direct stakes in his decision to strike at organized crime. Jimmy Hoffa, the outspoken leader of the Teamsters Union, rose to his ultimate position of power only after Kennedy's work on the McClellan Committee helped to send his predecessor, Dave Beck, to prison, thus clearing a path for him to assume the presidency of the Teamsters. J. Edgar Hoover, the longtime director of the Federal Bureau of Investigation, had for decades insisted that there was no national criminal syndicate. In seeking to smash organized crime, as well as for a range of political and personal reasons, Kennedy earned the sullen hatred of Hoover. Kennedy's third big-time rivalry, with Lyndon Johnson, best analyzed in Jeff Sheshol's *Mutual Contempt*, was a fascinating struggle between two men with competing visions of America—and personal political ambitions—that has only tangential bearing on the Kennedy drive against organized crime.[9]

The feud between Kennedy and Hoffa quickly assumed a pronounced personal cast, with each ridiculously trying to outdo the other in "toughness"; they publicly argued over who could do more push-ups.[10] Kennedy regarded Hoffa as brutal, corrupt, cynical, and not, despite his bravado, a truly tough man; in *The Enemy Within* he mused that after hearing Hoffa declaim on his toughness, "if a person was truly tough . . . he need not brag and boast of it to prove it. When a grown man sat for an evening and talked continuously about his toughness, I could only conclude that he was a bully hiding behind a façade."[11] Kennedy could thus rationalize that the diminutive Hoffa, who had risen from a loading dock to the presidency of the nation's largest union only by the sheer, terrible force of his will, had no more claim on virile manhood than did the ambassador's son, who lunched daily on broiled lamb chops and chocolate ice cream delivered by his butler.[12]

For his part, Hoffa despised Kennedy just as fervently. He felt that the "ruthless little monster" was little more than a dilettante dabbling in crime fighting. As a "young, dim-witted, curly-headed smart aleck," Kennedy was beneath Hoffa's contempt.[13] The Teamster boss was the hero of the working man, and Kennedy was the spoiled persecutor of an underdog. Hoffa contested Kennedy's manhood no less vehemently than the racket buster challenged his own, charging that he had a weak handshake—a sure sign of a pantywaist—and, even worse, "he's a touch-football player."[14]

Hoffa could not doubt Kennedy's resolve, though; upon taking office as attorney general, Kennedy installed Walter Sheridan, a former McClellan investigator who shared Kennedy's obsession with the Teamsters president, at the head of the "get Hoffa squad." This unit consisted of sixteen attorneys, thirty FBI agents, and support staff, and had no other purpose than to prosecute Hoffa.[15] The anti-Hoffa drive was so formidable that in some quarters it effectively turned the union leader into a sympathetic victim of a personal vendetta promoted by an attorney general with no care for civil liberties.

Hoffa bedeviled Kennedy's efforts to remove him from the helm of the Teamsters. If anything, his hold on power grew stronger despite Kennedy's opposition, as he signed a national master freight agreement in 1964 that incorporated nearly all over-the-road truckers under a single collective bargaining umbrella. After a series of trials in the late 1950s and early 1960s, Hoffa remained out of prison; it was not until 1967 that he was convicted of a crime. Found guilty of bribing a juror, he was sentenced to fifteen years in prison. The personal rivalry between Kennedy and Hoffa, and Hoffa's catlike ability to avoid conviction for his crimes, strengthened Kennedy's certainty that organized crime was the nation's chief law enforcement problem. Unable to strike Hoffa down, Kennedy would discover a coterie of criminals from labor racketeers to bookmakers against whom he hurled the ample resources of the Justice Department.

Kennedy's other rival, FBI director J. Edgar Hoover, was no less resilient than Hoffa and had a similarly indirect role in shaping Kennedy's campaign against organized crime. Hoover commanded the federal government's chief crime-fighting organization, yet for decades he insisted that there was no national crime syndicate and that local, not federal, resources were best used against crimes like bookmaking. Kennedy, taking up the Kefauver banner, proposed a countervailing view: Organized crime was indeed a national conspiracy and a deadly "enemy within" that could be crushed only by concerted federal action. In addition to their differing views of the crisis, Kennedy and Hoover were divided by Hoover's need to protect his power base in the bureau from Kennedy's perceived and real encroachments on it. Hoover sought to keep both the attorney general and his brother in check by dutifully maintaining a file on the president's continuing sexual liaisons. The tension between lead G-man and top cop led to daily mundane annoyances, as Hoover frustrated Kennedy's attempts to use the sunlamp at the Justice Department gym and Kennedy insisted on bringing his dog Brumus, who boasted a surly incontinence, into the Justice Department, to Hoover's exasperation.[16] His personal animosity against Hoover may have served only to harden Kennedy's resolve to fight organized crime; it doubtless inspired him to posture as the relentless prosecutor of organized crime who could succeed where Hoover's FBI had apparently failed. Most important, it probably pushed him to give priority to drafting laws that would unmistakably federalize anti-organized-crime efforts.

Despite Kennedy's focus on labor/management racketeering while with the McClellan Committee, he was keenly aware that gaming was likely the preeminent organized-crime industry. Kennedy adopted the Kefauver orthodoxy of organized crime's structure: It was a national conspiracy whose chief source of revenue, gaming, enabled it to advance into other fields. He said so plainly before Congress in May 1961: "Organized crime is nourished by a number of activities, but the primary source of its growth is illicit gambling. From huge gambling profits flow the funds to bankroll the other illegal activities . . . including the bribery of local officials."[17] Prosecutors might fight organized-crime infiltration at the union hall and pursue narcotics smugglers and leaders of prostitution rings, but to truly smash organized crime involved taking the battle to its heartland—organized gambling, which by the late 1950s was understood to mean primarily the numbers and bookmaking, although illegal casinos remained an important subsidiary operation.

To face the enemy within, Kennedy overhauled and substantially enlarged the organized-crime section of the Justice Department's Criminal Division. When he took office, the unit's seventeen lawyers primarily reviewed cases and screened investigations. Kennedy proposed to immediately get fifty Justice Department lawyers to take the fight against organized crime into the courtroom. With his constant support, the organized-crime unit would become a major force. In the first two years of the Kennedy Justice Department, indictments against organized crime rose from zero to 683, and the section, which had no convictions in 1960, had successfully prosecuted 619 defendants by 1963.[18]

To head the organized-crime section, Kennedy chose Edward Silberling, special prosecutor in Suffolk County, New York. Kennedy eased William Hundley, the holdover section chief, into an assistant's chair from which he was to coordinate the crime-fighting efforts of different government agencies.[19] Silberling, who had been appointed by New York's Republican administration to investigate political corruption on Long Island, was a Democrat and a leader of the local pro-Kennedy effort in 1960. When political considerations precluded him from accepting Kennedy's offer of a U.S. attorney's position, he eagerly accepted the post as coordinator of Kennedy's flagship program.[20]

Initially, the organized-crime section used approximately the same methods as the anti-Hoffa squad: Identify leaders of organized crime, collect all outstanding information about them, and initiate further investigations, which would hopefully generate enough evidence of criminal wrongdoing to secure indictments and, ultimately, convictions. In the words of one attorney, the process was to "investigate the guy up to his eyeballs," using the resources of the FBI, the IRS, and other federal agencies.[21] Since organized-crime leaders made their livings from illegal activities, Kennedy and Silberling were certain that such an intense investigation would bear fruit. Frustratingly, this often meant that bosses were not prosecuted for major crimes, such as murder, drug smuggling, extortion, or prostitution—they had too many layers of insulation between themselves and the actual commission of the criminal acts for that—but for tax-related and procedural violations, such as income tax fraud and perjury. Given the enormity of the crimes that Kennedy had traced to his "enemy within," devoting Justice Department resources to prosecutions for tax evasion often seemed petty and somewhat incongruous.

Kennedy therefore recognized early on the need for new statutes that would help to indict suspected organized-crime bosses as the leaders of an interstate conspiracy to profit from violating the law. Surveying the landscape of existing and proposed legislation, Kennedy and his advisors dusted off old proposals and crafted a few new ones, then quickly set to getting these ideas made into law. With new weapons to match their zeal against organized crime, they hoped, they could truly meet the challenge.

A Hesitant Legacy

Fighting a war on organized crime was, in 1961, nothing new. American anxieties—and American betting volume—had increased in the years after World War II, and politicians since Estes Kefauver had found gambling and organized crime to be a powerful push-button issue. The McClellan Committee's digressions into labor racketeering had somewhat blunted the message that organized crime was primarily a gaming business, but the public still believed that gaming provided a major source of funds for organized crime and that organized crime was an increasing threat. The problem for those charged with enforcing the law was how to go about disrupting gaming operations and jailing those who ran them.

Organized crime as such had first become a major issue during the term of Howard McGrath as attorney general, which fell during the frenzy of anti-gambling sentiment that crested in the Kefauver Committee. Yet McGrath would not tilt at windmills. Though he hosted the first Justice Department symposium on organized crime in 1950, he demurred from accepting the responsibility of fighting organized gambling. Citing limited resources before the McFarland Committee, he pointedly did not elaborate except to say that if Congress enacted a federal ban on the transmission of interstate gambling information, the federal government was not equipped to enforce it.[22] Had he really wanted to champion the fight against organized crime, he might have laid out a detailed program and requested funds to realize it. Instead, he rather lamely suggested that the government could best fight interstate gambling by enforcing existing regulations.

Attorney General Kennedy might have been familiar with Estes Kefauver's attempts to get a law banning the interstate transmission of race and betting information, but he also might have been surprised to know that half a century earlier such a proposal had been introduced, debated, and ultimately rejected. Senator Elmer Burkett, a Republican from Nebraska, first introduced a bill to "prevent the nullification of state anti-gambling laws by international or interstate transmission of race-gambling bets or racing odds" by banning such transmissions in the Sixtieth Congress, which met in 1907–8. Burkett has a footnote's mention in the annals of the Congress for another bill he sponsored in his freshman session that would create a national holiday to celebrate the mothers of America on the second Sunday in May. Although the Senate demurred on memorializing motherhood when Burkett first proposed the bill, citing it as superfluous and possibly unconstitutional ("Every day with me is a mother's day," declared one senator, while another rued the day that such trivia came before the Congress), it ultimately passed in 1914, thanks to the support of the World Sunday School Association.[23]

Burkett, who had been put up to the Mother's Day bill by the Young Men's Christian Association, apparently felt that in addition to honoring their mothers, young American men needed protection from the evils of race gambling. He therefore introduced the anti-betting bill. It failed to gain any traction in the Sixtieth Congress, but Thetus Sims, a Tennessee Democrat, presented the same bill as H.R. 2160 to the House in the next session. Introduced in March 1909, it was referred to the Committee on Interstate and Foreign Commerce. Commerce coupled the bet ban bill with a measure to ban the interstate transmission of pictures or descriptions of prizefights (H.R. 25825) and held hearings on May 17, 1910.

To weigh the impact of the proposed banning of interstate betting, the committee elicited testimony from two speakers who had become regular advocates of the proposal, appearing like clockwork before Congress to plead for a ban whenever this bill appeared on the docket. They made an odd but effective pair: the Reverend Wilbur Crafts, superintendent of the International Reform Bureau, and Harry Brolaski, who after twenty-one years as a gambler, poolroom proprietor, and bookmaker, had found the cause of antigambling. Crafts himself estimated that he spoke at nearly seventy hearings concerning "moral legislation," a testament to his persistence, if not his effectiveness.[24]

Year after year, Crafts laid out the problem for committee after committee. In 1910 he reported that although forty-one states had passed laws prohibiting gambling on horse races, "seven backward states and Mexico and Canada" continued to permit it.[25] Telegraphy allowed these rogue jurisdictions to export their gaming to the enlightened states. The interstate commerce clause of the Constitution, intended to restrict states from imposing restrictions on each other, was being perverted:

> Under new constructions of this interstate commerce clause the people of Maryland may do in Pennsylvania what Pennsylvanians themselves cannot do. Under the shield of interstate commerce they can come into a state that has recently turned down the gambling proposition and secure a larger profit for Maryland races out of Pennsylvania than out of Maryland itself. Nine-tenths of the profits of the races are

derived from telegraph business, by which the backward states, seven of them, rob and demoralize the more progressive states.[26]

In an era when Americans were increasingly asking the government for protection, be it against alcohol, monopolies, child labor, or the interstate transportation of women for illicit purposes, demands that Congress pass an act to criminalize interstate betting were understandable. Antigambling is a protean movement that melds itself to the spirit of the times. In the 1950s, when Communist subversion seemed to lurk in every shadow, antigamblers asked that Congress ban interstate betting so as to throttle a national criminal conspiracy. In the Progressive Era, they begged for the protection of the citizens of "progressive states" against backsliders that still permitted race gambling.

After describing the nature of the problem, Crafts introduced Mr. Brolaski, whose integrity he defended resolutely (perhaps too resolutely; by protesting that after a year of testing, he had never made a misstatement, he could not help but put the thought into listeners' heads that Brolaski was prone to embellishment). Brolaski then described the nuts and bolts of race gambling, and his additional statements provided exact figures on the numbers of poolrooms and handbooks operating in major American cities.[27]

The 1910 hearings provide ample evidence as to why the bill foundered in committee. Although Crafts and Margaret Ellis, a representative of the National Women's Christian Temperance Union, both spoke of the importance of such a "moral bill," and Brolaski detailed how such a bill could curtail race gambling throughout the nation, the bulk of the Commerce Committee remained unconvinced that the bill would solve any problem. Ellis praised the committee for having passed the "white slave traffic bill," which protected "womanhood," and asked the committee to pass the current measure, which would extend protection "for our boys and our young men."[28] But the committee was not so easily goaded by flattery. Representatives Charles Bartlett and William Richardson disputed Brolaski's contention that local law enforcement was ineffective against handbook operators in Georgia and Alabama, respectively.[29] That two Southern congressmen emphasized the primacy of states' rights and local solutions to local problems is hardly surprising, given that the South had invoked—and would continue to invoke—states' rights as a defense for segregation and the denial of civil rights to African Americans.

Others wondered what business the federal government had in trying to block gaming-related messages. Representative Charles Kennedy of Iowa openly doubted whether the bill would "accomplish anything like the good you anticipate," noting that "some things have to be relegated to the school, the church, and the home, and moral suasion."[30] Citing Blackstone, he also noted that laws that cannot be enforced should not be on the statute books in the first place. Furthermore, he suspected that severing access to one form of gaming would only lead to the proliferation of another. Though he acknowledged that federal action had effectively smashed the Louisiana lottery, he offered that there had likely not been "any less gambling of some other kind."[31] Even at the height of the Progressive antigambling movement, some recognized an innate American predilection toward gaming and wished to err on the side of toleration.

Despite Congress's rebuff, Crafts and his legislative allies continued the fight. On the state level they had considerably more success than in the federal arena. While seven "backward" states permitted race gambling in 1910, Crafts reported in 1917 that only two states, Maryland and Kentucky, still allowed it. When the antigambling bill appeared before Congress in that year, it had seemingly brighter prospects, and went a bit further than previous attempts. The House version, sponsored by Thetus Sims, was favorably reported out of committee to the House and placed on the calendar.[32] With the tide of reform cresting behind them (the national campaign against alcohol was sweeping forward), antigamblers had reason to be jubilant. But the measure failed to pass either the full House or the Senate, and it did not appear before either body again until 1950, when the McFarland Committee considered it. The first historical moment for a national law against the transmission of race gambling information had passed.

Thirty years later the measure reappeared. No longer couched in the language of protection, it now sought to give the federal government a tool to dismember national gaming syndicates. When initially proposed during the 1950 antigambling fervor, the bill died because of mutual sidestepping by Justice and the FCC. If an antigambling bill could not pass with the public imagination consumed by the hearings then spiraling before the Kefauver Committee, one might assume that it could never pass. But its backers would not consign it to oblivion; they brought it back repeatedly. In 1953 the Senate Interstate and Foreign Commerce Committee favorably reported a bill to "prohibit transmission of certain gambling information in interstate commerce by communications facilities," substantially the same bill that had originally been the subject of the McFarland Committee.

By that year, the bill's champion, Charles Tobey, could rattle off an impressive list of endorsees: representatives of the Justice Department, mayors of some of America's largest cities, police chiefs, and nearly half of the states' attorneys general.[33] This was more than a mere clamoring for law-and-order legislation and a chance to stifle gambling; as opposed to the 1907–17 period, now the majority of states had a direct and growing interest in where the public spent its gambling money. By 1953 twenty-seven states had legalized, regulated, and taxed pari-mutuel betting at racetracks.[34] Every dollar wagered at poolrooms or with bookies was presumably lost to the public treasury. States, wishing to protect their rights to prosecute bandit bootleggers, now asked for federal assistance in stopping the cross-country dissemination of gambling information.

As in 1950, the bill to ban interstate gambling transmissions had its opponents. Major boss gamblers and betting commissioners like Frank Costello, Frank Erickson, and James Carroll professed indifference at the prospect of the bill's passing; race gambling would continue with or without it. But the bill's sponsors felt that these representatives of the gambling fraternity were being disingenuous. If the race wire were so trifling a concern, they wondered, why did some bookmakers pay more than $6,000 a week for it?[35] Obviously, those with something at stake did not wish to tip their hand.

But others, perhaps with even more at stake, spoke against proposals to cut the interstate betting wires. Representatives of the nation's telecommunications industry, chiefly Western Union and AT&T, press associations for print and radio media, and publishers of racing newspapers and scratch sheets like the *Daily Racing Form*, denounced the measure as violating the First Amendment.[36] The "common carriers," i.e., telephone and telegraph companies, worried that they could be subject to criminal action for merely allowing the public to transmit gaming information over their wires. As a palliative for their concerns, the bill's sponsors added a clause that made a common carrier liable for prosecution only if it ignored written notification from a law enforcement agency that its facilities were being used to transmit or receive gambling information. Should the carrier then fail to discontinue service, it would be penalized, but it was under no obligation to conduct any kind of preemptory surveillance of its wires to guard against gambling information.[37] Likewise, the bill made concessions to the legitimate media: Only the transmission of information *before* the beginning of a race was circumscribed; after the contest had begun, it was no longer gambling information, and anyone was free to transmit, receive, or publish it without fear of prosecution.[38] Despite these concessions the bill fared no better in 1953 than it had previously, and it did not pass into law.

The next year, an even broader bill found its way before a subcommittee of the House Judiciary Committee. This measure would have imposed fines and prison terms upon anyone who imported, transported, or mailed a number of gambling and lottery materials, including tickets, punchboards, shares in a gambling enterprise, and even newspapers or magazines with advertisements or solicitations "for any gambling enterprise." Those receiving materials were subject to less-severe penalties, as was any postal agent who knowingly sent by mail or delivered gambling materials. Likewise, the bill prohibited information about or advertising for a gambling enterprise over the radio, though it contained statutory exemptions for fishing contests, state-regulated track racing, and foreign newspapers or publications that were bona fide media for news from abroad.[39]

This bill's author, Kenneth Keating of New York, wished to extend the prohibitions on interstate solicitation of bets, already expressed in the 1895 anti-lottery act, to other gambling enterprises. While Keating, in his testimony in favor of the bill, made amply clear his respect for "the legitimate economy of Nevada" and emphasized that he did not wish to bring federal laws into conflict with state laws, the language of the bill as originally proposed could not help but do so.[40] According to the letter of the law, Nevada's licensed casinos would no longer be able to advertise in any publication that might be sent through the mails; it was even possible that they might be prohibited from placing orders for non-gaming supplies with manufacturers in other states. Accordingly, Charles Russell, the state's governor, and Representative Clifton Young spoke against the bill. Keating then asked the committee to amend the bill to include "any licensed enterprise" in the list of exemptions.[41] But the bill, like others before it, never made it to a vote on the House floor.

During the anxious decade, gaming and organized crime never quite passed from the public's agenda, though more pressing concerns, particularly the Cold War, pushed it from the top. President Dwight Eisenhower made no memorable statements against organized crime or gaming. Philosophically, he seemed to place more emphasis on the protection of personal liberty than on the extension of the government's power to prosecute criminals. In a 1964 speech he warned against the development of a powerful, paternalistic government, which would put him on the opposite side of the increased powers that Robert Kennedy had sought to fight organized crime.[42]

Still, as the public's anxieties about organized crime increased, federal law enforcement continued to seek new weapons to fight it. Eisenhower's attorney general from 1957 to 1961, William Pierce Rogers, offered five proposals to Congress, three of which directly addressed the problem of interstate gaming. One of these included the interstate bet ban, specifically defined to include telephone and telegraph wires, while others placed prohibitions on the interstate transportation of betting slips and new gambling devices, such as pinball machines and roulette wheels, that currently fell under exemptions in the 1951 Johnson Slot Machine Act. The final two proposals grew out of the McClellan Committee investigations (thus partly the work of Rogers's successor, committee counsel Kennedy) and sought to broaden the list of crimes covered by the Fugitive Felon Act and to grant immunity and impel testimony from those called as witnesses in labor-management racketeering cases.[43]

The public shock of the abortive Apalachin meeting inspired a revival of the 1950 anti-organized-crime agenda with more focus and more immediacy. Organized crime was no longer Frank Costello wringing his hands before the Kefauver Committee, or a series of witnesses denying that any criminal conspiracy existed; it suddenly had shape and form. Still, until John F. Kennedy installed his brother as attorney general, no one seemingly cared enough about the problem to make it a priority or had sufficient legislative muscle to see it passed.

Kennedy's response to the challenge of organized crime was nothing if not energetic and immediate. Not content to merely authorize the investigative carpet bombing of suspected major criminals that saw the federal government throw all of its resources into sprawling, nonspecific hunts for any wrongdoing from jaywalking to criminal contempt, Kennedy almost immediately had his aides begin drafting new legislation that was most nearly analogous to the relief and recovery improvisation of Franklin Delano Roosevelt's first term. Though Kennedy had rather definite ideas of the scope of the menace, he could not suggest a single key to unlock the problem. Instead, he favored an expansive program that would effectively federalize organized-crime prosecutions.

By April, Kennedy had forwarded to Congress eight proposed measures to help fight organized crime. Five of them were revised or unchanged versions of the Rogers proposals, including the bans on interstate bet transmission and on the transport of betting paraphernalia across state lines. Kennedy's innovations included a measure to prohibit interstate or international travel that advanced illegal business activities, an enlargement of the class of ex-convicts prohibited to send or receive firearms across state lines, and an act that made illegal the intimidation of witnesses in preliminary government investigations.[44]

In seeking to get these bills through Congress, Kennedy faced the same obstacles as his predecessors had. While few sitting representatives of Congress or lobbyists could argue against measures that, most agreed, would fight crime, the basic fact that had prevented the passage of a ban against interstate bet transmission—that the actual gambling took place within a state and that the state's police power gave it sufficient means to stop the gambling if need be—that opponents had raised in the bill's first go-round in the early part of the century remained true. The telecommunications "common carriers" were still wary lest they be saddled with the responsibility of policing wire transmissions for gaming content. In addition, the civil liberties lobby, already put on notice by Kennedy's putative disregard for the niceties of due process while he had served as McClellan Committee counsel, could be expected to raise objections to the new slate of proposals. From one corner, the odds on Kennedy's receiving his new weapons against organized crime seemed long.

On the opposite side of the ring, though, supporters of the bills had reason to cheer. With the unraveling of the conspiracy behind the Apalachin incident and the McClellan Committee's ongoing (if sometimes unfruitful) investigations into labor racketeering, the public perceived organized crime, and by extension illegal gaming, to be a larger problem than in previous years. Antigamblers now had a supremely powerful champion. Robert Kennedy, unlike earlier attorneys general, had the unequivocal backing of the president. Kennedy also had the conviction, forged in his investigations of labor-management racketeering, that organized crime was a terrible menace to his brother's New Frontier. Kennedy did not merely push papers across his desk in a perfunctory attempt to quiet a muckraking congressional committee; he sincerely believed (if his public pronouncements are taken at face value) that organized crime was a threat.

Robert Kennedy's emotional antagonism toward organized crime is often overlooked. His eventual transformation into the antiwar, pro-social justice candidate of 1968 outshines his attempts at ethical leadership in the early years of his brother's presidency. His public statements, even then, carried a starkly moralistic tone. Organized crime, juvenile delinquency, antitrust abuses, and civil rights violations, to the Kennedy of 1961, were all symptoms of a larger predicament: Americans' greed. All of those problems, he said in a June speech to a meeting of state attorneys general in New York, flourished because the public was more devoted to material things than to the national interest. Preoccupied with "making an extra buck" and buying bigger cars and televisions, the public had lost its resolve in the fight to stamp out crime and corruption.[45]

Kennedy's seething against greed was his interpretation of his brother's inaugural message that Americans should ask not what their country could do for them but what they could do for their country. The younger Kennedy was right: America needed—and needs now—more team players and less self-interest, though some questioned the propriety of a man born into wealth and privilege denouncing others for trying to make "an extra buck." Greed for material possessions was only part of the problem, according to Kennedy. Scandals surrounding television quiz shows and college basketball betting served as shocking exemplars of selfishness that betrayed the public trust, but Kennedy also rapped state and local officials who neglected to enforce federal civil rights laws and, by extension, local authorities that permitted wide-open gambling in defiance of anti-gaming statutes. Whether the officials liked the existing laws or not, Kennedy felt, they had a duty to impose them as interpreted by the courts.[46] If other Americans agreed with Kennedy's assessment that a moral decay underlay most of the nation's problems is less important than the fact that a supremely powerful attorney general felt that fighting the symptoms of this moral decline—illegal gaming and organized crime paramount among them—was his mission. Applying the right amounts of force to the necessary political pressure points, he would ultimately get Congress to yield to him, among other treasures, what it had denied to others for more than half a century—a ban on the transmission of interstate gambling information.

A New Deal Against the Rackets

So for Robert Kennedy, the Wire Act was more than a statute to curtail betting. It struck aggressively at organized crime and by extension at the moral decay that threatened America just as much as foreign aggression. To fight the enemy within, America would have to federalize criminal statutes previously enforced by states. Along the way, this would mean prosecution of those who shipped gambling devices, traveled to advance their illegal enterprises, and transmitted betting information across state lines. The final provision, the Wire Act, was not the centerpiece of the new anti-crime initiative but one of its supporting measures. It is also important to note that Kennedy never suggested that interstate gambling transmissions themselves were the problem; they were undesirable chiefly because they were used by hoodlums.

The keystone of the Kennedy program was the ambitious proposal to prohibit interstate travel that advanced certain illegal business activities. Kennedy promoted this measure as the centerpiece of the anti-crime drive because it would take down "the bankrollers and kingpins of the rackets," men who had thus far been able to elude prosecution. These men personified Kennedy's fear of a creeping moral decay within America; though they looked like productive, prosperous citizens, they actually drew sustenance from illegal enterprises. Kennedy often expressed his contempt for men who "live luxurious, apparently respectable lives in one state but return periodically to another state to collect from the rackets they run by remote control."[47]

This certainly was a new twist on the problem of interstate crime that Kefauver had first brought to the public's attention. Kennedy vividly described racketeers living in stately, staid comfort, seemingly pillars of the community, yet furtively stealing away and crossing state lines to pick up the fruits of their remote-control crime firsthand. In his testimony before the House Judiciary Committee on May 17, Kennedy explained that he hardly expected high-ranking racketeers to act as their own bagmen, personally collecting the drop after a day's betting was done; the kingpins would be prosecuted under aiding and abetting statutes, assuming that those actually charged with the crime cooperated in the prosecutions of their bosses—not the most realistic expectation.[48] On its surface, the law seemed to willfully ignore what Kefauver and a decade of anti-crime muckrakers had tried to establish (and what Mario Puzo would indelibly etch into the American consciousness with *The Godfather*): that the leaders of the rackets built layers of insulation between themselves and any overt criminal act. In the absence of a turncoat within, it could never be proven that they had masterminded anything.

In retrospect, particularly in comparison with 1970's RICO statute, the Kennedy anti-crime program seems to be a clumsy patchwork of past legislative burnouts and grandiose new proposals. Certainly the Wire Act idea had been gestating long enough—the initial proponents of the Burkett Bill and its successors were long dead, and their arguments over the need for the bill likely forgotten. But this amalgam succeeded where previous efforts had failed, becoming law within six months of its first presentation to Congress. Where Wilbur Crafts and Harry Brolaski had to bear the frustration of returning year after year to querulously argue for a ban on the nullification of state antigambling laws by interstate telegraphy, Kennedy confidently bent Congress to his will, getting all of his proposals, with the exception of a wire-tapping measure, written into law.

Kennedy's success came not because he provided a better answer to the problem of state jurisdiction over gaming operators or to the importance of preserving individual liberty against a possibly authoritarian federal government. Instead, he changed the question. Picking up the banner of the Kefauver conspiracists and steeled by an increased public apprehension about organized crime in the wake of Apalachin and the McClellan Committee hearings, he presented Congress with a plan—the only plan—that could defeat the menace of racketeers. As he wrote in his message to Congress of April 6, which accompanied his legislative proposal:

> Over the years an ever-increasing portion of our national resources has been diverted into illicit channels. Because many rackets are conducted by highly organized syndicates whose influence extends over State and National borders, the Federal Government should come to the aid of local law enforcement in an effort to stem such activity.[49]

Prosecuting those who violated state laws against gaming and prostitution or smugglers of alcohol was no longer the mission. The goal now was to smash the interstate rackets. Local law enforcement, which might or might not be willing to roust the local bookmaker, was not equal to this task. Only an empowered federal strike force under the command of the attorney general could be trusted to achieve success.

Congress warmly received the package of bills and began grinding them through the legislative process posthaste. The House Judiciary Committee scheduled hearings on the proposals for May, its Senate counterpart for June. The hearings before the Senate were especially poignant for Estes Kefauver, who as a member of the Judiciary was able to see many of his suggested reforms finally reach the cusp of passage. But he did more than gloat; he actively questioned witnesses, often drawing on his experience as chair of the original congressional foray into crime investigation. Sometimes, though, he seemed fairly clueless. When Richard Marsh, attorney for the United States

Independent Telephone Association, a trade group of non-Bell service and equipment providers, presented his association's opposition to s. 1656 (the Wire Act), Kefauver objected rather vaguely:

> I remember during the time in the early fifties when we had the Senate Crime Investigating Committee, a number of people representing telephone companies, and I suppose they represented the Bell System or AT&T, said that they would welcome some law along the line contemplated by s. 1656, because they were helpless to do anything about the situation where a bookie or a gambler applied for a telephone, even though they might know what the telephone was going to be used for. They cited instances of where people would apply for 15 to 20 telephones in a small place next to a racetrack. They knew quite well what they were going to be used for, but they couldn't do anything about it, and were regretful that they could not do something about it.[50]

Despite Marsh's prepared statements, which emphasized the narrow profit margin of independent telephone companies and the undue burden that enforcing the statute as proposed would place on them, Kefauver insisted that a decade earlier "the telephone companies said they would be quite happy if we placed the burden on them to stop the service."[51] This was the unfortunate sum of his contributions to the discussion; he made a rather poor showing as an elder statesman of the anti-crime lobby.

Attorney General Kennedy provided much more direct and effective advocacy for the new bills. Having honed his animus toward organized crime in *The Enemy Within* and pooled all available intelligence about the scope and operations of criminal syndicates, he proposed a forthright agenda and supplied a bounty of evidence to prove its need. Before the House, Kennedy delineated the need and benefit for each of the bills separately, but along the way he pounded home three themes: racketeering was a large and growing danger; it prospered through interstate commerce; and because "the modern criminal has become more sophisticated in the planning and perpetration of his activities," state and local police needed federal assistance.[52] The attorney general, needing both the political support and the enforcement cooperation of local police and public officials, did not flatly accuse them of being on the take, but he implied as much when he prefaced his presentation of the bills by declaring that the hoodlums and racketeers he wished to prosecute had "become so rich and powerful that they have outgrown local authorities."[53]

Kennedy offered quite specific, but tantalizingly anonymous, examples of illegal operations that the new bills would frustrate. "Some notorious individuals, whose names you would immediately recognize," he began one account of an illegal numbers bank operated across state lines, and this was his typical approach.[54] Kennedy concentrated on bookmaking (dominated by horse race betting and wire transmission of the same) and numbers games, though he mentioned illegal casinos in Newport and Covington (Kentucky) as a minor related problem.[55] Throughout his remarks on the bills covering travel, transmission of wagers, and transmission of betting paraphernalia, Kennedy wove the thread of the interstate wire through the fabric of organized crime. "It is quite evident that modern, organized, commercial gambling operations are so completely intertwined with the Nation's communications systems that denial of their use to the gambling fraternity would be a mortal blow to their operations," he said plainly at the climax of his discussion of the Wire Act.[56]

For Kennedy's purposes, the network of bookmakers using phones and telegraphs to coordinate betting information and layoff wagers represented the ideal crime: By its very nature, the race wire permeated jurisdictional borders and demanded a federal solution. If one took the position that local police were helpless to stop out-of-state bookmakers from wiring betting information into their communities, making a crime of interstate bet transmission was manifestly sensible. But Kennedy and his legislative allies left unsaid a deeper truth, perhaps for fear of embarrassing local authorities: that no bookmaking business can operate in complete secrecy, and that competent local policing could certainly be used to disrupt the poolrooms and handbook makers that disseminated betting information at the street level. This unspoken possibility, of course, would have undercut the very foundations of Kennedy's federal war on organized crime.

From the attorney general's office, the war on organized crime was paramount, overriding any semblance of concern for the general public's access to gambling. Proponents of the bills to ban the interstate transmission of wagering information in the Progressive Era had emphasized the deleterious effects of gambling on both the republic and the individual. In a 1916 editorial pleading for Congress to adopt the Sims-Kenyon version of the bill, the *New York Globe* decried the ruinous impact of gambling, which was "sapping American manhood, destroying countless homes, wrecking countless lives," and ultimately "playing havoc with the breed of men."[57] But Kennedy, though he could offer case piled upon case of the corrupting influence of organized crime, had few cautionary words against gaming per se. In fact, if one reads between the lines of his testimony, gaming was not so bad on its own; it was bad only insofar as it fueled organized crime and corruption.

Reflecting the mores of a nation that had rejected gambling prohibition outright and was in the process of being seduced by public-interest gaming, Kennedy took pains to emphasize that his bill would not target people who gambled for fun but only those who illicitly profited from the business of gambling. He claimed that the bill would help suppress *organized* gambling, adding:

> The word "organized" is italicized because it should be clear that the Federal Government is not undertaking the almost impossible task of dealing with all the many forms of casual or social wagering which so often may be effected over communications. It is not intended that the act should prevent a social wager between friends by telephone. This legislation can be a most effective weapon in dealing with one of the major factors of organized crime in this country without invading the privacy of the home or outraging the sensibilities of our people in matters of personal inclinations and morals.[58]

In this brief paragraph, Kennedy encapsulated the fractured approach to the control of gambling of the Wire Act. American citizens were apparently free to gamble as much as their consciences permitted; this was a matter of "personal inclinations and morals." Kennedy himself admitted that the public's hunger for gambling was anything but moderate, asserting that gambling was a $7 billion business with seventy thousand employees nationwide. Yet those who served that appetite were guilty of "organized" gambling, and hence organized crime, and therefore subject to prosecution.

Before the Senate, Kennedy sounded many of the same themes as he had before the House: Hoodlums and racketeers had become rich and powerful and were a growing menace; only the federal government could effectively combat organized crime; and finally, a point that he seemed to make a bit too fussily, the Justice Department did not "seek to preempt" local law enforcement but only to help it. Citing the successes, real or imagined, that federal law enforcement had achieved in fighting narcotics, auto theft, and prostitution (incidence of these crimes continued to rise during the 1960s, in fact), the attorney general declared that since organized crime was "so well organized and entrenched on a multistate basis," the local police were powerless to act against it without the aid and assistance of the federal government.[59]

For each of the eight bills presented to Judiciary, Kennedy prepared a brief statement of the Justice Department's intended uses. For s. 1656 (the Wire Act), the attorney general noted the exceptions already carved out of the bill—the bill was careful not to interfere with print, radio, or television reporting of sports events, and wireless communication was entirely exempted on the grounds that the Federal Communications Commission already had sufficient authority to discipline misuse of the airwaves.[60]

Although he left radio and television out of the new bill, Kennedy insisted on maintaining sanctions against common carriers who provided service used for illegal gambling purposes. Representatives of the telecommunications industry objected that this provision would force them to police the telephone and telegraph lines, but Kennedy insisted that if they did not intentionally supply or maintain facilities used to disseminate gambling information, they "would not be hampered or burdened by this measure."[61] The attorney general suggested that prosecutions would by nature be selective: "The people who will be affected are the bookmakers and layoff men, who need incoming and outgoing wire communications to operate."[62] Kennedy did not elucidate how police would prosecute gamblers using wire services and bypass the technicians and operators who physically maintained the offending wire communications facilities, but he implied that prosecutors would target only those who, in their judgment, were the true offenders.

With regard to the untutored mass of "social wagerers," Kennedy openly declared that since the law would be used selectively, they had nothing to fear. His language was instructive, as he torturously explained that in order for the bill to be effective it would not have any formal exemptions for casual bettors, though as a matter of course prosecutors would be instructed to ignore the letter of the law and let social wagers take place without fear of molestation:

> Law enforcement is not interested in the casual dissemination of information with respect to football, baseball, or other sporting events between acquaintances. That is not the purpose of this legislation. However, it would not make sense for Congress to pass this bill and permit the professional gambler to frustrate any prosecution by saying, as one of the largest layoff bettors in the country has said, "I just like to bet. I just make social wagers." This man, incidentally, makes

a profit in excess of a half million dollars a year from layoff betting. Therefore, there is a broad prohibition in the bill against the use of wire communications for gambling purposes.[63]

Kennedy continued to justify this seemingly unjustifiable position by remarking that, since social bettors and professional ones used the same facilities—the telephone system—to place wagers, there was no statutory distinction between social and professional wagers. In the bill as presented, a professional could not claim to have accepted noncriminal wagers. No matter how friendly the call, both parties were still liable to prosecution, though Kennedy assured the assembled senators that only professionals would actually face it.[64]

James Carroll and Frank Erickson, bookmakers who had faced the ire of the Kefauver Committee a decade earlier, might have blanched at Kennedy's next qualification: "We did not feel it would be wise to differentiate between the type of wagers being made without implicitly authorizing or condoning the conduct of the nonprofessional."[65] Though Kennedy pledged that the Justice Department would never bring criminal cases against nonprofessionals, he reasoned that the department "could not in good conscience" use language that "might be construed as condoning gambling."[66] Gaming would go on, he reasoned, and that was not necessarily a bad thing; but profiting from gaming was unbearable. Kennedy's statement in favor of the Wire Act ranks as a noteworthy case study of measured ambiguity toward gaming: tolerable as a "friendly" diversion but intolerable as a professional enterprise.

No one seems to have taken issue with Kennedy's hypocrisy, which made criminals of those who catered to Americans' unchallenged gambling propensities. Interestingly, Lawrence Speiser, the director of the Washington office of the American Civil Liberties Union, declared that s. 1656 was entirely unobjectionable and imposed no significant restrictions on Americans' constitutional freedoms.[67] In the hearings and in the newspapers, no one raised significant opposition against the need to pass a law criminalizing the transmission of gaming information on the grounds that it violated civil liberties or privacy rights.

But opponents to s. 1656 could have pointed to Kennedy's successes in fighting "organized gambling" without the proposed law. In June, after Kennedy had insisted before both houses that Congress must give him his new legislation or let organized gambling run rampant, a federal grand jury effectively broke up a national betting network by indicting thirteen of those involved for tax evasion and theft of service from AT&T. The investigation, conducted under the supervision of the attorney general via Edward Silberling's organized-crime task force, focused on New Orleans and revealed that the indicted men had bribed telephone company employees to provide them with illegal phone hookups that let them make toll-free calls. This illicit system linked twenty cities throughout the nation in a network that, the grand jury charged, permitted the exchange of layoff bets from major cities like New York, Chicago, and Los Angeles to betting emporiums like Biloxi, Newport, and New Orleans, where most of the indicted men lived and where the indictment was delivered.[68]

The New Orleans investigation had originated when IRS agents discovered the activities of Benjamin and Robert Lasoff of Cincinnati. These brothers had been operating a race wire information and betting network using stolen phone service. Because they did not pay for their phone calls, they also neglected to remit the necessary excise tax on the calls. Under earlier attorneys general, the investigation would have stopped with the collection of delinquent taxes by the IRS. But Kennedy insisted that the Treasury Department continue to probe and eventually induced the FBI to join the investigation.[69] The new legislation, including s. 1656, would allow this sort of prosecution to take place without the constant prodding of a hyperaware attorney general.

In all likelihood, Congress and its constituents accepted Attorney General Kennedy's assertion that while federal prosecutions for tax evasion were fine interim weapons against organized crime, true progress in the war would be made only when interstate betting itself became a crime. Many Americans had qualms over the use of the IRS as a law enforcement agency; while its investigations could uncover criminal wrongdoing, its chief mission was ostensibly to collect revenue and not to serve as a national police corps.

The senators accepted this contention, and the debate over s. 1656 seems to have been restricted to the question of the degree of liability that the telecommunications industry would bear. Herbert Miller, assistant attorney general for the Criminal Division of the Justice Department, fielded additional questions concerning the disparity between the intent and actual language of s. 1656. Senator Kefauver, belying his earlier fogginess, raised valid questions about the need to hold telephone companies liable, noting that s. 1657 (which prohibited the transportation of gambling materials across state lines) indemnified common carriers, while s. 1656 did not. Still, he marred his questions by tending to lapse into extended verbal reveries about his 1951 investigations. Kefauver also queried Miller about the definition of a sporting contest—though Miller had originally stated that wrestling matches were to be considered contests, he then recanted and allowed that though he was not in the habit of watching them on television, the performers involved were "more actors than wrestlers"; thus it would not fall under the scope of the statute.[70] Unfortunately, the panel did not call on Gorilla Monsoon or Classy Freddie Blassie to clarify the status of professional wrestlers. Here ended the committee's scrutiny of the measure.

Though debate finished quickly, behind the scenes the committee made extensive revisions to the bill. Through skillful maneuvering, the telecommunications lobby effectively bought itself a measure of protection. Not content with Kennedy's word that telephone companies had nothing to fear, they and Western Union presented an amendment that required law enforcement to notify common carriers in writing that a wire communications facility was being used in violation of the statute before they were required to terminate service. This provision allowed them to indemnify themselves from prosecution (unless they chose to violate a written notification) and neatly placed the burden of investigating wired bookmakers on the shoulders of the police.[71] Because of the telecommunications companies' strenuous efforts, the Wire Act read the way they wanted.

After being favorably reported by the Judiciary, on July 28 the full Senate passed s. 1656 along with five other bills that Kennedy had recommended. The only measures that did not pass on that day were the law tightening the firearms restrictions for felons, which had passed earlier, and the enlargement of the Fugitive Felon Act, an amended version of which was approved after the House took action.[72] The Senate acted on the bills that did pass together, approving them by voice vote and with no opposition.[73]

In the House of Representatives, the bills faced stiffer opposition. The slot machine measure, the labor racketeering immunity provision, and the anti-obstruction bill all failed to pass, though Robert Kennedy would continue to fight for them and a wiretapping law in the following year. The other five measures—the laws against transmitting gaming information, using interstate travel to conduct an illegal enterprise, transporting betting materials across state lines, and those that broadened firearms restrictions and the Fugitive Felon Act—passed the House, and therefore passed the full Congress. From there, the bills headed to the Oval Office for the president's signature or veto.

Since the bills had been proposed by Kennedy's brother, his own approval was a foregone conclusion. The president signed the bills into law in an almost anticlimactic ceremony. As his own brother had strenuously lobbied for the bills as the legislative crux of his flagship program to demolish organized crime, this in and of itself was unsurprising. Kennedy put his signature on S. 1653 (travel), S. 1656 (gaming information), and S. 1657 (gaming paraphernalia) on September 13, 1961, giving them a brief vanilla endorsement:

> It is a pleasure to sign these three important bills which we hope will aid the United States Government and the people of this country in the fight against organized crime.
>
> These pieces of legislation are the culmination, in these three areas, of years of effort by the Federal Government and by the Congress to place more effective tools in the hands of local, State, and national police.
>
> It is therefore a pleasure to sign them, and in the presence of the representative of the Justice Department, Mr. Hoover—and Members of the Congress of both parties who have given this legislation strong bipartisan support—most particularly Senator McClellan whose recent hearings indicate great need for this kind of legislation.[74]

Robert Kennedy tactfully stepped aside to permit J. Edgar Hoover to stand for the Justice Department; after all, his bills were now law, and his prosecutors would be leading the fight against the racketeers. There apparently was glory enough to go around, though perceptive observers might have asked why Hoover, with four decades' experience in fighting interstate crime and no stranger to Congress, had never testified in favor of the bills. Kennedy's singling out McClellan for praise was both a sop to Congress and an indirect attribution to his brother, who had made his public reputation as the driving force behind the McClellan Committee.

With that brief ceremony in September, S. 1656 became law. Originally proposed in the Progressive Era, revived by Kefauver, and debated for a decade, the "Attorney General within" made a bet ban the law before he had been in office three hundred days. Still denied some of his requested legislation—he frequently complained that he urgently needed the wiretapping measure—Kennedy was nevertheless now empowered to skillfully direct the resources of the federal government to assist the states in fighting organized crime. Now the only obstacle to disassembling the network of illegal gaming that permeated the United States was the wavering resolution of its citizens that gambling was, in fact, a crime.

A Moment's Victory

Even with his new statutes, Attorney General Kennedy continued to press Congress to take further action against organized crime. The legislative victory only emboldened congressional champions of the fight against the racketeers, as Kennedy, in alliance with his former boss McClellan, continued to vigorously advocate new laws to throttle the rackets. Pressing the advantage, Kennedy eventually benefited from a fortuitous turn of events that delivered into the hands of an eager McClellan Committee the ultimate instrument with which to prove the seriousness of the organized threat: the Valachi hearings, in which an authentic mafia turncoat was willing to break his vow of silence and reveal, in open session before the world, the inner workings of the national criminal syndicate.

Even before this triumphant revelation, Kennedy could celebrate some success in the fight against the rackets. As early as November 1961, federal agents used the new federal statute prohibiting the transportation of betting paraphernalia to arrest six men in a Brooklyn raid that, according to the Justice Department, resulted in the disruption of a "large scale" numbers operation.[75] The following year, President Kennedy himself declared that the drive against organized crime was one of his administration's "most effective though least known" efforts. The president declared that the race wire service had been almost completely disrupted and that sports betting had declined by 10 percent. Organized-crime convictions, he proudly stated, had increased eightfold since he had taken office. He also related the tale of a patriotic "Las Vegas gambler" who reportedly hoped that the administration would "be as tough on Berlin as [it's] been on Las Vegas." A smiling Kennedy assured the nation, "We intend to be."[76] That this gambler's offhand remark was likely overheard on an unauthorized federal wiretap, if reported, would have foreshadowed coming problems for the federal assault on organized crime.

With this encouragement, the first brother's "pet project" continued apace. In western Pennsylvania, federal agents raided a dice game that had long operated with the connivance of the local police, sending the message that enforcement of gaming statutes was no longer on local option. In the eastern part of that state, they fared even better, seizing 120 gamblers and more than $50,000 in cash in a major bust. Significantly, this game was an interstate enterprise, as "luggers" imported customers from New Jersey; out-of-state loan sharks happily tended to any financial reverses suffered by players.[77]

Though the Justice Department could not discover that enterprise's hidden operators, it considered the gambling crackdown in Newport, Kentucky, to be an unqualified success. For nearly thirty years, Newport had been a notorious gambling center. Citizens who had pled for reform had been told that to close the city's thriving gambling and prostitution rackets would be tantamount to economic euthanasia for the one-horse town. A reform candidate for sheriff, in a bizarre chain of events not truly explained even after two federal trials, was apparently drugged, placed in a compromising situation with a stripper, and thrust into the spotlight after police inexplicably chose that moment to raid his hotel room.[78] For those profiting from gaming in Newport, this embarrassing (for reformers) episode hopefully augured the end of a reform candidacy and the continuation of business as usual.

But corruption in Newport, thanks to Kennedy's devoting significant resources to fighting it, became a national story. Kentucky's governor ordered the ouster of Newport police officials who had not enforced the vice laws, and federal agencies began investigating with renewed vigor.[79] Kennedy made Newport a focus of his congressional testimony in support of his legislative package. Unable to withstand the heat, most Newport gaming operations folded. In early 1962 the *New York Times* declared, "Newport . . . is dead as a gambling center."[80] The next year Kennedy himself reported sanguinely that "the fight is not over in Newport, but organized gambling and prostitution have been eliminated." As proof that his anti-racketeering convictions ultimately made good business sense, he further declared that the Newport economy, which had previously been thought inextricably tied to illegal gaming, "has had a sharp upturn," though he did not quantify the statement.[81] With its new legislative tools, the Justice Department took the lead in smashing interstate gambling rings in New Orleans and the Southwest and an international narcotics smuggling operation.[82] Still, Kennedy declared, there was more work to be done.

With this success came appeals for more information and even stricter legislation. The McClellan Committee investigated gambling and organized crime in 1962, focusing attention on the race wire and sports gambling. The subcommittee assigned to report on the topic, noting the dependence of horse betting bookmakers on the race wire and sports bookmakers on handicap services that dispensed the line, recommended amending the Wire Act—which had become Public Law 87-216 the previous September, to tighten it and account for advances in technology, including Wide-Area Tele-communications Service (WATS) and wide-area data service. The committee also suggested legislation to outlaw the interstate distribution of crooked gambling equipment and to further study the corruption of athletes by pro-fessional gamblers through bribery.[83]

Congress, perhaps content to have finally passed a prohibition on inter-state wagering transmissions after more than half a century of consideration, declined to take up the issue again. Still, that Congress felt compelled to up-date the Wire Act because of technological innovations may suggest that the authors intended it to have a narrow definition—and that current arguments that the Wire Act should not apply to the Internet, as that technology had not been in use in 1961, may carry more weight than most legal scholars assume. When the Wire Act returned to public prominence with its use as an anti-Internet prosecutorial tool in 1998, no one explored the fact that Congress's reconsidering the Wire Act only a year after its passage meant that it was in-tended to be read narrowly rather than as an expansive ban against gambling transmissions.

Congress continued to consider anti-crime measures. A related "anti-crime" act fared a bit better, but not by much. The Senate Judiciary Commit-tee considered an act to make illegal the use of interstate transportation or communication in connection with attempts or conspiracy to influence the outcome of sporting events through bribery. This measure passed the Senate by voice vote, but since the House took no action, it failed to advance, likely because the bribery of sports figures, though noisome, was hardly of press-ing concern to the federal law enforcement community.[84]

Attorney General Kennedy's proposal to broaden the 1951 Johnson Slot Machine Act successfully ran the congressional gauntlet and became law. This law expanded the ban on interstate shipment of gambling devices to in-clude roulette wheels and any other machine that was manufactured primar-ily for gambling and that had the potential of giving a player money or prop-erty as the result of the application of an element of chance.[85] The original slot ban had specified traditional reel slots, and crafty gamblers had circum-vented the ban by altering the designs of their machines. This law closed that loophole, though it contained exemptions for shipments to states in which the device was, by statute, legal, and for pinball machines and "claw, crane, and digger machines" used at carnivals and fairs. The amended statute also required manufacturers, distributors, buyers, and sellers to register with the attorney general's office annually. Legislators hoped the law would cut into crime syndicate profits and help the states better enforce their own statutes against gambling devices.[86]

All along, Kennedy had insisted that the most valuable lesson in the war on the rackets was intelligence, defined as "the most detailed information available on the background and activities of suspected criminals." He argued that good intelligence was particularly important in the fight against racketeers. When convicted heroin trafficker Joseph Valachi, fearing a plot by alleged mob kingpin and cell mate Vito Genovese to kill him, decided to reveal to the authorities his knowledge of the inner workings of organized crime, Kennedy felt he had scored the ultimate intelligence coup. In a series of debriefings with Justice Department attorneys and FBI agents, and in televised testimony before the McClellan Committee, Valachi exposed the organization and rituals of a national organized crime syndicate that he called "La Cosa Nostra," Italian for "this thing of ours."[87] Eagerly anticipated, Valachi's intelligence ostensibly proved what federal authorities had labored to demonstrate since the days of the Kefauver Committee: that a national crime syndicate did exist and that it sponsored extensive gambling, prostitution, extortion, and narcotics operations throughout the nation.

Valachi's revelations fueled Kennedy's mounting desire to stamp out organized crime, and the broadcast of "the Valachi show" was a calculated attempt by the attorney general to gain public support for the final planks of his legislative platform. The bill to make criminal any attempts to obstruct justice by injuring, threatening, or intimidating witnesses had stalled in the House after being approved by the Senate the year before, and, in Kennedy's mind, two final, vital pieces of legislation remained to be passed. The first, the immunity provision, was needed to compel witnesses to testify about organized-crime operations. Kennedy requested the second, the wiretapping law, for two reasons: It would legitimate the use of wiretapping by law enforcement, and it would protect individual privacy rights by restricting use of wiretaps to the police. Though Supreme Court decisions had left the legality of wiretaps to the discretion of states, the wording of the decisions and existing federal statutes held out the possibility that police officials might be guilty of illegally wiretapping even if their state laws specifically permitted the practice.[88] As the law stood, Kennedy argued, it did not prevent anyone from tapping phones, while it failed to recognize the legitimate need of law enforcement to do so.[89]

Both the general public and Congress intensely debated this measure. While some argued that law enforcement needed the most sophisticated tools available to fight organized crime, espionage, and other threats, others felt no less strongly that wiretapping represented an unwonted invasion of privacy and that its legitimization would turn the nation into a police state. In four days of congressional hearings, police chiefs, district attorneys, and members of the Justice Department spoke in favor of the measure; Americans for Democratic Action, the American Civil Liberties Union, and other groups spoke against. The Senate Judiciary Constitutional Rights Subcommittee considered four bills that would have legalized wiretapping regimes of varying severity but recommended none to the full Senate. The measure stalled there and remained a dead letter two years later.[90]

A quixotic tilt at Nevada's legal casinos had proven to Kennedy the need for a stronger wiretapping law and the insidious lengths to which organized crime had infiltrated the legitimate world. This also brought Kennedy's crusade against organized crime into open conflict with the regulated casino industry—and the state government—of Nevada. Despite his tolerance for social betting and poker, even among his own attorneys, Kennedy had no affection for legal, state-regulated gaming, opposing legalized off-track betting and lotteries and deriding Nevada's "so-called legal gambling" as rife with skimming, or the concealment of gaming income from state authorities.[91]

Under the direction of Earl Johnson, a special assistant U.S. attorney for Nevada dispatched by Kennedy specifically to lead the fight against racketeers, the IRS and the FBI conducted extensive surveillance and audits of Nevada's casinos and their operators. Johnson believed that the IRS had uncovered massive skimming operations totaling millions of dollars in unreported annual income at individual casinos.[92] Undeniably, several Nevada operators skimmed cash from their winnings, but at a far lower order of magnitude than Johnson described. Casinos simply did not make enough money to support the level of undeclared revenue that Johnson posited. Nevada's Gaming Control Board, charged with policing the industry, remained skeptical of Johnson's claims. Ed Olsen, chair of the Gaming Control Board, felt that many federal agents assigned to the Las Vegas strike force displayed a fundamental ignorance toward both gaming operations and organized crime.[93]

At one point, Kennedy sought to have a small army of federal agents be deputized as assistants to the Nevada attorney general and conduct surprise raids on the major Strip casinos, thus closing the "bank of America's organized crime." Officials in Nevada, faced with certain economic disaster if this attack on its main industry proved successful, immediately panicked. Nevada governor Grant Sawyer promptly flew to Washington and, pledging state cooperation against organized crime in Nevada, persuaded Kennedy not to go through with the raid.[94]

But the federal strike force continued its investigations; certain that skimming was widespread in Nevada, and equally sure that legal casinos were little more than fronts for racketeers in other states, they pursued a variety of means to gather intelligence. Clandestine wiretapping yielded a trove of what the strike force believed to be helpful information. In May 1963 the FBI turned over to the Justice Department a two-volume report on skimming, compiled using the wiretaps, that delineated the colossal scale of casino skimming. Wiretapping, however, was illegal in the state of Nevada, and the "evidence" thus gathered illegally was inadmissible in court.[95] The entire operation had been futile.

Moreover, the federal charges about skimming were probably not accurate. The Nevada Gaming Control Board, to counter the federal assertion that it had little control over gaming, launched its own audit. This four-year study disproved the allegations that millions of dollars had gone unreported each year. Its estimates of unreported income, according to Olsen, were statistically insignificant; at worst, it was "less of a loss than Woolworth's sustains" in the course of that retailer's presumably non-hoodlum-affiliated operation.[96]

The drive against Nevada's legal casinos was, by most estimates, a complete debacle. The federal government won only one skimming case when in 1973 Morris Lansburgh and others pled guilty to concealing Meyer Lansky's interest in the Flamingo from 1960 to 1967.[97] In the final analysis, the increasing capital demands of the industry and the aging out of the cohort of former bootleggers that had moved into Nevada casinos in the 1950s, not Kennedy's strike force, drove organized crime out of the gaming industry.[98]

Robert Kennedy's abortive move against Nevada's legal casinos did not inhibit his Justice Department's drive against illegal gaming in other jurisdictions, which often proved successful. Some of Kennedy's anti-crime efforts bore immediate fruit; he trumpeted statistics demonstrating that more racketeers were being indicted and convicted of major crimes. Other initiatives took longer to develop but yielded impressive results nonetheless. Supporters of his fight against the rackets could point with pride to bookmaking rings and numbers operations that federal investigations had uncovered and unraveled. Indictments increased sharply—while only 49 had been charged with organized criminal activities in 1960, more than 600 were indicted in 1963. More indictments translated into more successful prosecutions; in 1963 the Justice Department obtained 288 convictions against those charged with racketeering, compared with 45 in 1960, 73 in 1961, and 138 in 1962.[99] Fighting the rackets seemed to be a growth business.

The crime fight promised even greater returns to come. By 1963, a special intelligence unit with nearly sixty lawyers in the field worked to coordinate data from twenty-six federal agencies on a list of "major rackets figures" that had swelled to more than three thousand. According to attorney and author Ronald Goldfarb, who as a lawyer with the organized-crime section had an intimate knowledge of Kennedy's war on the rackets, Internal Revenue Service raids and increasing use of the new anti-racketeering statutes had led to a "veritable revolution" in the fight against illegal gaming. In New York City, the Catskills, Atlantic City, Louisville, Pittsburgh, Detroit, and elsewhere throughout the country, federal raids had arrested suspects, seized assets, and disrupted operations. As an unexpected bonus, the fines, penalties, and property confiscations of this program actually brought in more money than its administration and investigations cost.[100] The prosecutions more than paid for themselves. Fighting crime was good business.

Kennedy had come into the office of the attorney general with a reputation as a crime buster and little more. Historians and his contemporaries have shared a consensus that the attorney general gradually abandoned the fight against organized crime for more interesting targets, including civil rights. Uncharitable minds might say that Kennedy, like a spoiled child bored with an overused toy, simply became enamored of other, more interesting pursuits and tired of the fight against the rackets. As both attorney general and "the brother within," he certainly had a great many distractions. In addition to supervising the machinery of the Justice Department and determining federal policy toward emerging problems, civil rights violations paramount among them, he also served as his brother's omnibus advisor. Thus, while receiving progress reports about the state of anti-racketeering investigations in Newport, Kentucky, he was also determining how his department should respond to anti-desegregation riots in Oxford, Mississippi, and advising the president as he and the Soviets tiptoed near the brink of nuclear war over the issue of missiles in Cuba. This agenda would tax even the most energetic of attorneys general.

Publicly, Kennedy began to speak about more than simple law-and-order issues relatively early in his term as attorney general. Most credit his concerns over civil rights and urban poverty to a tardy—and politically opportune—conversion to liberalism circa 1965, but as early as November 1961 he identified the nation's worst unsolved problems as unemployment, slum clearance, overcrowding in the nation's classrooms, highway traffic, pollution, racial discrimination, organized crime, and juvenile delinquency.[101] Most of these (with the exception of traffic) were tremendously large social problems, and not nearly the sorts of things expected to keep a head-busting law-and-order attorney general awake at night. But Kennedy, quite early on, adopted expansive, wide-ranging concerns for the difficulties facing the United States.

This does not mean, however, that he abandoned organized crime in order to tackle the problems of slum clearance or that he shunted racketeering investigations aside while helping shape his brother's Vietnam policy or, for that matter, to begin directing his brother's campaign for presidential reelection. In October 1963 the *New York Times* published an extended commentary written by Robert Kennedy on the continuing menace posed by the "private government of organized crime." The threat was perhaps larger than originally foreseen; the original list of one hundred "major racketeers" targeted for prosecutorial blitzkriegs in the early days of his administration had swollen to more than eleven hundred. Still, Kennedy hailed the progress that had been made, citing dramatic increases in the federal prosecution of racketeers in terms of indictments and the time spent by Criminal Division attorneys in the field and in court, as well as outstanding work by local police in Los Angeles, Cincinnati, and New York.[102]

Gaming was still the racketeers' chief province, Kennedy argued, and he emphasized that organized crime must be "the urgent and active concern of every citizen" if efforts to quell it were to succeed. This concern did not necessarily translate into Americans' abjuring their gambling habit—something Kennedy did not, implicitly or explicitly, request—but instead meant a heightened vigilance of racketeer efforts to "bore into legitimate business" and an acquiescence to Kennedy's continuing mission to combat organized crime. At this time Kennedy was still insisting on two final weapons for his arsenal against the rackets: the immunity bill and a "reform and revision" to the wiretapping law. With these elements, Kennedy believed that he could lead the federal government and the people of the United States to victory over the hoodlums wearing gray flannel suits and secretly profiting through terror and corruption.[103] This war was winnable.

The attorney general's optimism was misplaced. The assassin's bullets that took the life of President Kennedy on November 22, 1963, did more than end the Kennedy presidency—they effectively ended his brother's drive against organized crime. Robert Kennedy suffered both the emotional agony of his brother's death and the political catastrophe of the sudden loss of his power base; he could no longer use his administrative heft to demand inter-agency cooperation or to bring Hoover at the FBI to heel. Hoover, no longer handcuffed by the president, was unrestrained in his contempt for the attor-ney general, and he swiftly removed Kennedy from the chain of command, communicating directly with the Oval Office, whose new occupant, Lyndon Johnson, had an even fiercer personal animosity toward the younger Ken-nedy.[104]

The rank-and-file attorneys of the Criminal Division immediately realized that their fight against organized crime was, for all practical purposes, over. Their chief's earlier promises that after winning the 1964 election, "we're going to finish this" were now dead letters.[105] The FBI diverted its resources to the Warren Commission investigation, and organized crime, which had never been a pet project of Hoover's, sank low among its priorities. Many of the organized-crime section's zealous attorneys left for private practice or transferred to the Civil Rights Division, which had become the new Jus-tice hot spot. The impressive gains the attorney general had cited in October 1963—more time spent in the field and in court, more indictments—fell victim to "organizational malaise," and the statistics in those areas dropped precipitously.[106]

Despite its anticlimactic termination, the Kennedy war on organized crime was, by some measures, a success. With the help of the McClellan Committee and, in particular, Joseph Valachi's testimony, Robert Kennedy succeeded in raising the public's consciousness of organized crime. Benefit-ing from a perfect storm of political opportunity, Kennedy pushed a major legislative package through Congress. As its proponents had hoped since the first decade of the century, transmitting betting information across state lines—with some exceptions—was now undeniably a crime. Though Ken-nedy's personal crusade had ended, future crime fighters might use his legis-lative platform to launch a comprehensive crackdown on interstate gambling and organized crime.

But the public was apparently less horrified at the revelations concerning the "private government" of organized crime than Kennedy would have hoped. Thanks in part to Mario Puzo's graphic fictionalization of the racketeer life conjured in part from Valachi's testimony and the biography of Frank Costello, the American public would, ironically, find a new hero in The Godfather. Puzo's novel and Francis Ford Coppola's cinematic adaptations of it would have given Kennedy fits, as they portrayed organized-crime families as vicious but honorable and police as corrupt, venal, and inept. This romantic portrayal was a first step toward organized crime's capture of the "hearts and minds" of Americans. The enemy within could be identified, but not driven out.

Partly because of the public's continuing love for gaming, Kennedy was unable to sear his own image of the racketeer into its consciousness—"that of the gambler operating the roulette wheel which is not only illegal, but fixed."[107] As the state governments of the United States increasingly encroached upon organized crime's monopoly in gaming, particularly lottery games (widely held to have the worst odds and the fewest redemptive qualities of any gaming), Kennedy's implication that gaming was inherently crooked seemed less persuasive. Tolerated by the framers of the Wire Act, Americans' penchant for betting would, within a few decades, form the foundation of several states' fiscal structures. As it did, state and federal prosecutions of illegal gaming became less a crusade to protect an unwitting public and more a drive to liquidate potential competitors.

After the sound and fury of the Kennedy presidency had passed, the elements of Attorney General Kennedy's legislative package that had passed into law remained. This, more than the impressive figures on indictments and convictions served in 1962 and 1963, stands as one of Kennedy's legacies as attorney general. Robert Morgenthau, who served as U.S. attorney under Kennedy, later credited Kennedy with ending the "free run" organized crime had enjoyed from the end of Prohibition to 1960.[108] However, Kennedy never sufficiently aroused the public to stop gambling, which would have effectively undercut these operations and significantly hurt criminal syndicates.

In his final years, Kennedy would venture far from the racketeering battlefield, taking up the standard of social justice and thrusting himself into the 1968 presidential campaign. Biographers have amply discussed many intriguing episodes in his life; from the McCarthy Committee to the inner circles of his brother's presidency, he was an energetic participant in several defining events for nearly two decades in America's history. When compared with his fractious fight against Jimmy Hoffa and his influential role during the Cuban Missile Crisis, to say nothing of tabloid tales of dalliances with Marilyn Monroe and mafia double crosses, Kennedy's legislative legacy seems a bit pale. But this legislation, used to push federal anti-gaming efforts onto the Internet, would in some ways be his most durable achievement.

4 Booking the Bookies

The fight against organized crime shifts to new ground as the continuing struggle against illegal gaming makes use of the Wire Act.

Because of the low priority placed on gambling regulation at the federal level, state and local law enforcement officers must pick up the investigations.
—Kevin Kinnee, criminal investigator, 1992

THE WIRE ACT BECAME LAW AS PART OF Robert Kennedy's war on organized crime, a program with very specific goals. But though the Kennedy attorney generalship ended within three years of the act's passage, the Wire Act
remained on the books even as the landscape changed. The directors of the
federal war against organized crime found new and better legislative tools
with which to fight the enemy. At the same time, the race wire system that the
Wire Act had been intended to disrupt effectively vanished. Crime fighters
soon began prosecuting organized-crime figures for their mere involvement
in racketeering organizations rather than for the specific crime of transmitting interstate bets.

New strategies in the fight against organized crime hardly meant that the
Wire Act had outlived its usefulness, however. While sports betting did not
require the use of a dedicated information-dissemination system à la the race
wire, elements of it were conducted across state lines. Federal authorities
therefore found that though the Wire Act might have been superseded by
RICO as an anti–organized crime statute, it still had a definite purpose: It
could be used against sports betting, which remained illegal.

The race wire service suffered an ironic death. Robert Kennedy finally got
a federal ban on the interstate transmission of wagering material in 1961. For
more than fifty years, members of Congress had advocated such a measure
as the only way to break the malicious hold of long-distance race betting on
the American public. When Congress finally passed the measure, that public was already moving away from the practice; the Wire Act and Kennedy's
increased pressure on race wire distributors hastened its demise, but sports
betting had clearly been on the rise since the 1930s. The Wire Act's original proponents would, however, have been gratified to know that this measure could be used with equal utility against the proliferation of the semi-

independent sports bookmakers that sprouted up in the wire service's absence.

Spreading the Action

Former gambler Harry Brolaski, who testified before Congress in the first two decades of the twentieth century, focused his second career on exposing the pernicious influence of the race wire. Having survived monopolization by Mont Tennes and Moses Annenberg and the race wire war of the 1940s, this information network was already in its death throes before Robert Kennedy delivered the killing blow with the Wire Act. It may be no coincidence that as race gambling became less popular, Western Union suddenly abandoned its opposition to a ban on the transmission of race wagering. Though Western Union had left the direct business of providing race information as early as 1905, it continued to profit from the trafficking in wagering information, as it carried thousands of messages to and from poolrooms and betting drops throughout the nation daily.

In the initial tumult over the Kefauver investigation in 1950, Western Union at first insisted that it forbade the acceptance or delivery of wager telegrams or money orders where such transactions were explicitly illegal but, as a common carrier, could not prevent such transmissions in states that did not officially ban them.[1] Within two years, though, the company had changed its stance, formally requesting that the Federal Communications Commission allow it to bar use of its facilities for transmission of racing information by anyone except licensed members of the media.[2] When the Senate held hearings on s. 1656, the Wire Act, in 1961, a Western Union representative reminded the committee that Western Union telegraph service tariffs already banned most wagering transmissions and that "today all subscribers to such service are engaged in legitimate business." With the exception of a few semantic distinctions over whether those who unwittingly assisted in the transmission of wagering information would be liable to prosecution, differences papered over with simple amendments to two sentences, Western Union wholeheartedly endorsed s. 1656.[3] After nearly seventy years, the company was completely out of the business of wagering information. The remnants of the race wire might try to continue their service by hacking into telephone lines (an increasing problem in the late 1950s), but the old network was crumbling.

Action-hungry bettors were not totally bereft. Public tastes, perhaps not coincidentally, were already shifting. "Never bet on anything that talks," ran a gambler's old saw, but millions of American gamblers have obviously felt otherwise. Even as the race wire diminished and betting on horses lost traction with the public, many Americans became increasingly drawn to an exciting and usually illegal form of wagering—betting on professional and amateur team sports. Sports betting often straddled the line dividing social recreation from "serious" gaming. Most sports bettors are content to put $20 down on their hometown favorite or their alma mater, possibly upping the ante a bit during the play-offs or rivalry week. But some enthusiasts eat, drink, and sleep little else but the endless morass of odds, conditions, and statistics that the smart bettor must juggle. The smallest minority of this group actually makes a living from full-time betting on sports. If team sports, particularly football, is a civic religion in the United States, betting on sports is one of its most important sacraments.

Betting on team sports, beginning with baseball, was a fixture as early as the Gilded Age, but it seriously began to rival horse race betting in the 1930s. While racing's popularity expanded in that decade, the appeal of sports betting increased at an even faster pace. With the popularity of football pool cards, which gave the bettor the chance to pick five winning teams without a loser from a list of nine, sports betting became more accessible. Bets as small as a quarter per card were common in working-class neighborhoods and on college campuses.[4] Betting remained a popular activity throughout the Depression and mobilization for war, though the decline in team sports caused by wartime exigencies necessarily diminished the excitement of sports betting.

The problem with betting on single sporting contests is that teams are rarely evenly matched. Those taking odds on horse racing mitigated this obstacle at first by adding weights to favored horses, effectively "handicapping" them, and later by offering odds. A favored horse might pay even money (a dollar won for a dollar bet) but a long shot would pay higher odds (seven to one, for example), encouraging betting on those less likely to win. With Harry Straus's invention of the electric tote, or totalisator, came the development of electronic pari-mutuel wagering systems that allowed bookmakers to automatically compute "correct" odds based on the respective levels of betting on race entrants.[5] Those accepting bets on sporting events clumsily mirrored this system by giving odds for teams to win, but this practice was generally unworkable. If a team was favored, the bookmaker would be besieged by those placing bets on it. It would be difficult to offer attractive odds to encourage betting on the other team to "balance the book," and the bookmaker would, in effect, become a gambler himself. Even if the bookmaker could accurately compute the correct odds and balance his book for a given game, during football season he accepted bets on about sixty professional and college games each week. Keeping track of shifting odds and bets for all of these contests would be a nightmare. To generate the kind of mass handle that would make his small profit margin a livable stipend, the bookmaker needed a system that would allow him to neatly breed nearly even amounts of "action" on either side of the ball.

In hindsight, the solution to the bookie's quandary seems obvious: Handicap the best teams, just as the original handicapper had affixed weights to speedy equines. Obviously, this would be unworkable in the literal sense; few star wide receivers would assent to being hobbled in order to level the playing field. But the point spread allowed bookmakers to assign handicaps to teams. Simply stated, the point spread handicaps games not by assigning odds to each team (i.e., three to one to win) but by giving the team that is judged to be inferior a point spread. If a bookie favors Philadelphia by eight points against Dallas, for example, the team must win by at least nine points for those betting on it to win. Dallas bettors can win their bet if their team loses by less than eight points. Bookmakers post these odds as negative and positive numbers: Philadelphia (-8), Dallas (+8). To avoid ties, in which case the bookmaker must return all wagers and in effect eats the cost of conducting his business, he usually sets the line on a fraction: Philadelphia (-7.5). The development of the spread greatly increased betting interest in otherwise noncompetitive games, particularly in football and basketball.

Informally, bettors used impromptu point-spread betting as early as 1909, as evidenced by Josiah Leeds's account of the action on the Penn-Yale gridiron classic.[6] More systematic spread betting may have emerged as early as the 1920s, but it became popularized in the 1940s.[7] One origin myth credits Charles McNeil, a math teacher and securities analyst with a master's degree from the University of Chicago, with pioneering the spread in the 1930s. McNeil had devised a point system that enabled him to successfully pick winners at traditional odds betting. When asked by the bookmakers why he was so consistently successful, he explained his point system to them. Presumably, they then switched to this system for wagering, not prognostication.[8] Even in the 1940s, as the line was gaining popularity, no one could agree on just who had formulated it. A 1947 *Collier's* magazine article identified Bill Hecht, a Minneapolis bookmaker, as the man who "evolved" the "point system of betting."[9] Whatever the true genesis of the spread, it was an established fact by the end of World War II.

The mere idea of handicapping teams according to the expected point differential is one thing; perfecting a system that will allow a bookmaker to quickly and accurately handicap upwards of sixty games a week in a way that gives him a balanced book with fairly even betting on each side of each game is entirely another. A bookmaker would have to weigh a variety of factors, including team performance, weather conditions, and assorted intangibles, to accurately develop the point spread, better known as the line. Charles McNeil refused to divulge his secret recipe for handicapping, which he reportedly kept sealed in a safe-deposit vault in a city whose name he also declined to reveal. Though hardly loquacious, he was not without a sense of drama. The more garrulous Jimmy "the Greek" Snyder used no fewer than eleven characteristics for his own personal handicapping formula. For a single person to accurately analyze any given matchup could conceivably take several hours and require access to voluminous files of data on past performances and current conditions.[10]

It was obviously impossible for a street-level bookmaker to spend hours handicapping each of the sixty games his bettors might want action on each week, so most bookmakers subscribed to a service that disseminated the line to subscribers. From the 1940s, the best-known source of the line was a Minneapolis associate of Hecht's, Leo Hirschfeld, who operated Athletic Publications, Inc., a "strictly legal" business that catered primarily to lawbreaking clients. For a fee of $15 a week, Hirschfeld wired his odds to bookmakers around the nation; for $20, he phoned them to a client. Bookmakers swore by his lines. According to Hirschfeld, more than eight thousand of them, as well as the *New York Times*, *Time* magazine, and the Associated Press and United Press International wire services, subscribed to his services in the late 1940s.[11]

Hirschfeld and his editors set his lines after consulting an intimidatingly comprehensive coverage and filing system, which in 1947 had "exhaustive files on every college football and college basketball team" nationwide. Hirschfeld sent his publications to colleges for free and in exchange received a steady flow of information about player injuries and illnesses, hot and cold streaks, weather conditions—anything that might conceivably affect the outcome of a game. A staff of ten handicappers, under Hirschfeld's direction, arrived at collective decisions on the odds, which Hirschfeld then disseminated through his publications and services. With a constantly sputtering ticker spilling the latest sports news, subscriptions to daily and campus newspapers throughout the nation, and a staff blessed with acute memories, Hirschfeld was an information broker par excellence.[12]

Nothing if not versatile, Hirschfeld was more than a bookmaker's salvation. He also distributed a magazine for children and religious tracts. Though he operated his business in consultation with Hecht, a "renowned bookmaker" who had been the subject of government investigations, he skated past charges that he abetted criminal betting operations by virtue of the fact that he did not take bets, or even advocate betting. "What's wrong with that?" he rhetorically asked a reporter. "Everybody bets and we just let them know the right odds."[13] He was capable of even more torturously obtuse justifications for the legality of his service, often stating that it was no business of Hirschfeld what his clients actually did with the line, and further arguing, "If I were to sell you a car, do you think I'd ask you if you planned to use it to rob a bank?"[14] He willfully ignored the patently obvious fact that while automobiles had many potential uses, of which armed robbery was a statistically insignificant one, the only practical use for the information that he disseminated for years was in the business of illegal betting.

The 1961 passage of the Wire Act prompted Hirschfeld to retire; with the line unambiguously classified as wagering information, sending it across state lines was now clearly illegal. Hirschfeld would take no chances by pleading his automobile analogy before a court. Proving the truism that nature abhors a vacuum, Las Vegas–based oddsmakers stepped into the void left by Hirschfeld's retirement; as betting was state-sanctioned there, the legal status of the oddsmaker was secure, though accepting or facilitating out-of-state bets was illegal. Jimmy "the Greek" Snyder emerged as a leading line-setter, but a 1962 charge of violating the Wire Act—to which he pled no contest and paid a $10,000 fine—as well as his burgeoning interest in a more public role as a prognosticator and promoter of gambling, meant that others superseded him as serious line-setters. Snyder's lasting contribution to the genre lay more in the fact that, thanks to a syndicated newspaper column and a high-profile job as a commentator for CBS television, he brought the point spread to a wider public audience.[15]

Bob Martin, a Brooklyn native who began setting lines in Las Vegas in 1967, succeeded Snyder as the nation's arbiter of the spread. A 1983 conviction for violating the Wire Act led to a thirteen-month prison sentence and, ultimately, to his retirement. After Martin's departure, Las Vegas Sports Consultants, a corporation headed by Michael "Roxy" Roxborough, took setting the line into the digital age.[16] CBS Sportsline, a online media and sports content company that developed Web sites for the NFL, THE NCAA, and the PGA, acquired Roxborough's company and later sold it in 2003 to "focus on its core business" of sports Web sites.[17] Still, LVSC remained more or less above reproach. It would be hard to tie a publicly traded corporation like CBS Sportsline to the racketeering underworld that Kennedy had alleged controlled organized gambling, and the sanitization of the line-setters certainly speaks to the increasing separation between betting as a crime and the legal, licensed, and taxed industry of betting that began in Nevada.

Changes in how the line was set and disseminated forced law enforcement to alter its view of the interstate connections between bookmakers. Organized crime had maintained its stranglehold on illegal race bookies, Kefauver had charged, through its aggressive monopolization of race information. With Hirschfeld and his successors apparently charging only a small subscription fee for their information services, bookmakers were free from the extortive control that the race wire syndicate once wielded over poolroom and handbook operators. In theory, this might mean that they could act as relatively independent agents. In 1985 a deputy chief of the Organized Crime and Racketeering Section of the Criminal Division of the Justice Department, Michael DeFeo, estimated that, as of the 1970s, organized crime dominated only 42 percent of illegal betting. More than half of the illegal gambling was "independent, non-LCN [La Cosa Nostra] controlled."[18]

Still, nearly half of bookmaking retained ties to organized crime, just as the nature of sports betting often required bookmakers to maintain links with larger operators. Invariably, no matter how well forecast the line was, a bookmaker would find himself with more bets on one side of the action than the other. In this case he might stand to lose mightily and would become more a gambler than a bookmaker. To mitigate this possibility, he purchased insurance through the practice of layoff betting.

An FBI expert on illegal gambling defined a layoff as a bet made by one bookmaker with another "in an effort to achieve what the bookmaker feels is a desirable balance or ratio of wagering."[19] Most commonly, bookies laid off action to simply balance their books, much as insurance companies might purchase reinsurance to avoid undue exposure to risk. But bookmakers could also play "anticipation layoff" bets when they believed that their customers would overbet one side. More audacious bookmakers, feeling secure in their own conviction that a given team would beat the spread, might lay off to deliberately achieve an imbalance in betting.[20]

Layoff betting frequently crossed state lines. Theoretically, this could be done on a purely friendly basis, in the name of enlightened self-interest and mutual need. In a hypothetical Philadelphia-Dallas matchup, for example, bettors in Philadelphia would most likely favor their home team and dispro-portionately bet on it to beat the spread, leaving a Philadelphia book pre-cariously unbalanced. By exchanging a mutual layoff bet with an oppositely unbalanced book in Texas, the Philadelphian could achieve a harmonious convergence of interstate betting equilibrium and enjoy the Sunday game se-cure in the assurance that, barring a tie, he would safely collect his 4.45 per-cent vigorish (the amount that the bookie keeps) without exposure to cata-strophic loss.

After World War II sports betting positively boomed. The "race wire war" had dominated illegal horse racing, but even as "hoodlums" shot at and bombed each other to grab or protect the lucrative race wire franchise, shift-ing tastes were making the race wire obsolete. Much of the postwar anti-gaming movement focused on a trio of illegal gaming venues: slot machines, numbers rackets, and the trafficking in horse race information.[21] Sports bet-ting thrived under the radar, benefiting from the Kefauver Committee's em-phasis on the race wire, which put pressure on a competing wagering form.

By 1952 the shift in the structure of American bookmaking was near-ly complete. From the 1930s until World War II, large-scale illegal book-making organizations with close ties to corrupt police and politicians dom-inated large-scale betting on horses and the relatively smaller market of sports betting. Through its monopoly on the race information so critical to profitable bookmaking, organized crime maintained a stranglehold on race wagering. Buying protection and willful apathy from local authorities, crimi-nal syndicates remained secure. But with rising standards (and pay) for po-lice officers and the decline of machine politics, the community of interest that made the clandestine race wire system possible collapsed. That Ameri-cans began favoring sports betting over horses was the coup de grâce. Like a mastodon struggling through a suddenly balmy stretch of the Holocene landscape, the monolithic race wire was doomed.

Throughout the nation, old-fashioned bookmakers found themselves on the defensive. A single case that crowded New York City headlines from 1949 to 1952 signified the end of the old understandings between police and book-makers that had permitted race betting rooms to thrive. As a local manifesta-tion of the national anti-gaming movement, it was, for many New Yorkers, the most familiar face of the Kefauver war on gambling. Brooklyn's Harry

Gross had built a prodigiously huge bookmaking business during the 1940s by not only paying police protection but also actively enlisting the police as partners in his operation. Gross recruited New York detective James Reardon to serve as his "chief executive officer"; Reardon actually ran Gross's operations while Gross was out of town, and when Gross himself ran up gambling debts (successful as a bookie, he was apparently a compulsive gambler as well), Reardon arranged their financing. The Brooklyn district attorney arrested Gross and Reardon in 1950 and charged them both with running an illegal bookmaking organization. After his conviction, Gross eventually identified those on the police force with whom he had worked, and his information resulted in a massive departmental shake-up that led to fifty detectives' outright firing, the resignation or retirement of an additional four hundred officers, and a complete overhaul of the city's detective corps.[22]

The Gross case stands as a great symbolic juncture for a change already under way as bettors shifted from horse betting to sports betting. In addition to the bookmakers' adaptation of the point spread, the technological advance of television opened up new vistas for gamblers. Television and radio allowed for the immediate transmission of sports-related information and results, obviating the need for any kind of wire information network. Television also broadcast games to a national audience, allowing bettors in Florida a stake in a New York–Boston matchup.

The chronology of scandals associated with sports betting provides ample evidence of its popularity and of the pernicious influence it potentially exercised over sports. The first serious sports betting outrage involved a round of allegations of point shaving that included college basketball players from several schools, among them City College of New York, Long Island University, Seton Hall, Kentucky, and Bradley, to "fix" the outcome of games from 1949 to 1951. The players involved did not "throw" games, as a jockey might deliberately lose a race, but rather missed key shots to win by less than the point spread. Thus, the gamblers who had corrupted them argued, they had not really hurt their team; they merely made themselves richer.[23]

The "scandals of '51" were a bellwether. Between 1959 and 1961, thirty-seven players from twenty-two schools were implicated in betting scandals.[24] After a relatively quiet two decades during which there were no public disclosures of point shaving, Boston College brought the problem back onto the public stage in 1981 with a new round of improprieties. It is unlikely that college basketball was free of corruption until then, but both sides evidently exercised enough discretion to remain undetected. The Boston College operation, reportedly masterminded by gambler Richard Perry and organized-crime figure Henry Hill of *Goodfellas* fame, unraveled after Hill turned state's evidence to avoid prosecution.[25]

The ten-year prison sentence (of which he served two and a half years) handed to BC forward Rick Kuhn, who brought his teammates into the scheme, hardly stopped the tide of corruption, even at Boston. Fifteen years later, Boston College suspended thirteen football players after an investigation into point-shaving during the 1996 season.[26] In the twenty years after the Boston College basketball scandal, no fewer than nine schools suspended players after investigations into student betting and point-shaving.[27] The persistence of betting scandals in college sports is perverse proof of the enduring popularity of betting on games, and of the susceptibility of the games to fixing allegations. It also spurred law enforcement to maintain pressure on illegal bookmaking, even after the practice had lost cachet as a major element of organized crime.

Bookmaking had, in fact, changed greatly from the days of betting commissioners and boss gamblers. The bookies who moved to take action on sports bets were not as well organized as their predecessors in the realm of equine betting, and this was often an advantage. These bookies need no horse room, or even street corner, from which to operate, waiting to take action on almost any game. Many of them worked from their own homes. A sociological study of illegal bookmakers conducted in the early 1980s described the betting operation of "Mack." Mack was, to outward appearances, an average middle-class citizen who just happened to run a bookmaking operation out of his den. Like many other bookmakers, Mack migrated into part-time bookmaking, at first supplementing the wages from his civil service job and eventually using his bookmaking income to augment his retirement benefits.[28]

Bookmakers like Mack took advantage of the expansion of sports broadcasting in the 1970s. Following the success of *Monday Night Football* and the increasing television coverage of college and professional football and basketball, major league baseball, and professional hockey, Americans enjoyed an abundant diet of games to watch and bet on. With extended seasons and play-off schedules, Americans could bet on at least two professional sports at any given time. In the glorious month of October, all four major professional sports and college football were live. Horse racing, which accounted for only 10 to 15 percent of illegal bookmaking in the mid-1970s, had become a year-round proposition even in the North; despite its decline, racing remained a supplemental business for bookies. Those who had never before filled out a parlay card or scanned the newswire for last-minute injury reports became increasingly attracted to sports betting, as television seemed to create new bettors. A licensed Las Vegas bookmaker reported that in 1973 he saw a 20 percent increase in business. Once thought to be the solace of men and the creator of "football widows," sports betting began to appeal increasingly to women. The Las Vegas bookie claimed that most of his new business came from women and that he expected the trend to accelerate.[29]

The pattern established in the 1950s, that of the quasi-independent operator, remained a blueprint for illegal bookmaking into the twenty-first century, as the field became a truly entrepreneurial one. After some dislocation in the wake of the Wire Act's passage, bookmakers quickly recovered. A 1972 report commissioned by the Fund for New York City cited two estimates of the scope of illegal sports gambling in Gotham, each of them impressive. Police estimated that bookmakers accepted approximately $1 billion a year in sports betting wagers. Another survey estimated that New York residents bet around $428 million a year on football, basketball, and baseball (assuming a 5 percent profit, this meant bookies earned around $21.5 million a year). This survey found that sports bettors were more likely to be white and upper income than the population as a whole, but it provided few other identifiers. Betting frequently began in the realm of social entertainment and then crossed into illegal wagering as friends placed many bets with each other and bookmakers handled bets too large for friendly arrangements.[30]

These bookmakers were far removed from the "hip-pocket" bookies of the 1930s, who literally had offices on street corners and kept records in their hip pockets. In a 2003 study, economist Koleman Strumpf analyzed the records of six New York City–area illegal bookmakers. He concluded that economic self-interest was the primary determinant in bookmaker organization. Though they could not use legally binding contracts, the bookies Strumpf studied employed a typical firm structure, with executives overseeing layers of employees. Larger bookmakers had virtually no direct contact with their customers, instead hiring sheetholders who recruited and serviced new accounts. Smaller bookmakers, though, continued to operate on a neighborhood basis, as these operators had close interaction with their customers, who usually lived near them and who remained loyal.[31]

Strumpf described quite sophisticated operations. The owner/managers of the enterprises he studied were white males of Irish and Italian extraction in their forties and fifties. Each had been previously arrested but, attesting to the relatively low priority of gaming cases in the criminal justice system, none had served time for bookmaking. The bookmakers ran their business through a wire room, which was a space with telephones manned by clerks, also known as writers. The clerks, paid a flat salary, took bets, and a manager oversaw the clerks and maintained records. One wire room studied accepted about 150 bets in a typical day, which ran from 11 A.M. to 8 P.M. A collector, runner, or bagman collected payments from and dispersed winnings to bettors. In larger operations, sheetholders referred new customers to the bookmaker, monitored their betting, and served as collector.[32]

Bookmaking continued to cross state lines, though the degree to which it did so was subject to debate. Both the 1972 report and Strumpf's 2003 study (using data generated during the 1990s) revealed that bookmakers continued to rely on long-distance handicapping services. Strumpf's data show bookmakers paying between $100 and $250 per week for a "line subscription service."[33] This is consistent with Hirschfeld's original practice of running his service strictly as a news dissemination network and not as a lever to gain control of bookmakers.

The studies did not agree on the prevalence of the other interstate betting link, layoff betting. The 1972 study described it as a complicated procedure "working all the way through a national system before equilibrium is established," and held that layoff betting was an essential business practice of all bookmakers.[34] Strumpf, on the other hand, found that bookmakers were hardly risk-averse businessmen and that larger bookmakers either did not lay off bets at all or did so only rarely. Smaller bookmakers, with presumably more-finite capital reserves, made more-frequent use of layoff betting, but the layoff was not an integral part of bookmaking and was only a hedge against excessive risk.[35] If organized crime did not use the line subscription service to force itself into bookmaking businesses, and these businesses did not need layoff service, one might conclude that sports betting had evolved to an illegal business not necessarily tied to traditional organized crime.

But links between sports betting and organized crime continued. The 1972 New York City report declared that the typical office manager of a bookmaking operation was "either a low-level member of a diversified criminal organization or an independent entrepreneur." Organized-crime agents were paid a salary and a share of the profits, while independents paid tribute, based on their business volume, to organized crime.[36] Strumpf reported that four of the bookmakers in his sample had reputed connections to organized crime, but he provided no detailed information about these connections. The ties that bound gambling to crime syndicates, while they could be loosened, could not be cut completely.

RICO: The Transformation of the Fight Against Organized Crime

During the Progressive Era agitation for gaming prohibition, the opponents of gaming strove mightily to convince the public that gaming inherently harmed the delicate fiscal constitutions of citizens. Painting lurid tales of men driven to the madhouse or to suicide by a friendly wager on the horses, and of youth lured into the demimonde after lounging in poolrooms, moralists ultimately failed to really make anyone care. In the new order of industrial capitalism, fiscal paternalism was decidedly outmoded; if a man chose to gamble, so be it. Attempts to force Congress to act against interstate gambling rings on strictly moral grounds for the personal salvation of defenseless gambling addicts proved futile.

Robert Kennedy succeeded where these moralists had failed because, building on the work of Estes Kefauver, he changed the question. While he heaped scorn on gambling as an intrinsically crooked con game that only enriched the bosses, he did not wish to stop interstate gambling to help its "victims," most of whom eagerly bet small amounts in the name of entertainment. Rather, he sought to smash gambling networks to deprive organized crime, defined as a growing menace within, of its fiscal breadbasket. Marrying gambling to organized crime, he got a ban on interstate gambling transmission primarily as an anti-racketeering measure.

But in the years that followed the enactment of the Wire Act, the nature of the fight against organized crime changed. Just as school administrators beset with teenage pregnancy and the specter of guns in the classroom might look back nostalgically at days when gum chewing and cigarette smoking provided the chief disciplinary headaches, police found that a new generation of organized-crime perpetrators had emerged. These gangsters derived profits from narcotics smuggling and distribution that dwarfed those from bookmaking and roulette wheels.

Most assessments of Robert Kennedy's attorney generalship hold that Lyndon Johnson effectively halted, or even rolled back, forward progress made against organized crime during the Kennedy years. Yet Johnson considered crime a major national problem, and in June 1965 he appointed a committee to analyze every facet of lawlessness. This commission, known prosaically as the President's Commission on Law Enforcement and Administration of Justice, condensed its findings into a report titled *The Challenge of Crime in a Free Society*. Published in early 1967, as urban disorder and crime rates were rapidly escalating, *The Challenge of Crime* devoted a chapter to organized crime.

The commission estimated annual gross revenue from illegal gaming at anywhere between $6 billion and $50 billion. Organized crime dominated gaming because it could provide an economy of scale making cumulative small bets lucrative and through the layoff betting network. "Most large-city gambling," the report stated, "is established or controlled by organized crime members through elaborate hierarchies."[37] This conclusion belied future studies of sports bookmaking, but it may have accurately captured the scene in the mid-1960s.

But gaming, though it was still organized crime's biggest-volume "public service," was only one of the chief enterprises. Loan sharking ran second, and narcotics third (the report stated that heroin consumption confined itself to only a few cities), followed by an assortment of other offerings including prostitution and bootlegging. Labor racketeering and, more ominously, infiltration into "legitimate business" represented even more serious problems; Americans could choose not to gamble, but with these extensions of racketeering into every facet of the economy, a simple trip to the grocery store to buy a loaf of bread presumably enriched racketeers.[38]

The commission found that Kennedy's increased emphasis on organized crime had resulted in several high-profile convictions and the disruption of major interstate gambling operations. But since 1965, the Camelot quest to slay the racketeering dragon had turned into a quagmire. Treasury Department officials had begun to question Kennedy's mandate that the IRS be used as a punitive and investigative arm of the federal prosecutorial effort rather than as a revenue collection agency. The Justice Department, thanks in part to the botched investigation into Las Vegas casinos, was accused of extensive use of illegal electronic surveillance. The once-fawning press began attacking the "intensity and tactics" of federal investigations and prosecutions. The Organized Crime and Racketeering Section suffered an astronomical turnover rate as disaffected attorneys headed for greener pastures and federal prosecutors throughout the nation demanded independence from OCR mandates.[39]

Local and state efforts were similarly at an impasse. Of the seventy-one cities surveyed by the commission, only nineteen admitted to having an organized-crime problem. Chicago and New York City had strong police intelligence units that worked to investigate organized crime, but most other cities were either unaware of a threat or unwilling to devote significant resources to fighting it. Public and private crime commissions worked to provide information on organized-crime activities, but, the report concluded, efforts to curb racketeering had not been successful for several reasons, chief among them difficulties in obtaining proof, lack of resources, lack of coordination, and the lack of public and political commitment. The report singled out gaming as an exemplar, complaining that street workers did not fear criminal sanctions and therefore had little compunction about joining criminal organizations and that judges only reluctantly jailed gambling criminals and imposed light sentences on those who were convicted. Fines were "paid by the organization and considered a business expense."[40]

The commission made several recommendations to increase the effectiveness of anti–organized crime efforts. Some dealt with procedural matters such as expanding the power of grand juries and easing the evidence rules for perjury prosecutions. Others were organizational, such as the directives that all major police departments should assemble intelligence units, all state attorneys general should dedicate staff attorneys to organized crime, and the federal government should maintain central computer records to house all organized-crime intelligence. But the most far-reaching was a proposal that federal and state legislation be enacted to provide for extended prison terms for those who committed felonies as part of a continuing illegal business.[41]

In response to the commission's report, and after serious legislative consideration, Congress passed the Organized Crime Control Act in 1970. Longtime rackets foe John McClellan proposed the act as s. 30, and President Nixon added several suggestions to the final version. It breezed through the Senate in January 1970 with only one dissenting vote but ran into stiff opposition in the House. The American Bar Association, which had endorsed Robert Kennedy's program a decade earlier, warned that s. 30 contained "the seeds of official repression" and suggested complete revision. Critics charged that, as the bill did not define "organized crime," its provisions could be used against any lawbreakers that prosecutors chose to harass. Advocates replied that if the act did not violate the rights of those engaged in organized crime, it did not violate those of any other criminals and was therefore appropriate. After making a few amendments, the House, under intense political pressure as the November elections approached, approved s. 30 in September. The Senate agreed to the House amendments, and President Nixon signed the bill into law on October 15.[42]

Title IX of the 1970 Organized Crime Control Act is known better as the Racketeer Influenced and Corrupt Organizations Act or RICO. As the legislative fulfillment of the commission's proposal, RICO provided formidable criminal and civil sanctions for persons engaging in "a pattern of racketeering activity" or collection of unlawful debts connected to an enterprise affecting interstate commerce. "Racketeering" included thirty offenses, ranging from murder to mail fraud, while two or more of these offenses taking place within ten years constituted a "pattern." An enterprise, while it could include chartered corporations and even government entities, also embraced any group of people associated in fact, even if they did not constitute a legal entity. Subsections of RICO made criminal the investment of proceeds of crime in "legitimate" interstate enterprises, the maintenance of an interest in an interstate enterprise through a pattern of racketeering, running such an enterprise through a pattern of racketeering, and conspiring to commit any of these offenses. Criminal penalties included twenty years in prison and a fine of up to twice the gross profits of the corrupt enterprise and forfeiture of assets.[43]

RICO was not an extension of the Kefauver/Kennedy program. Rather, it was a repudiation of its failure. Beginning in 1950, Estes Kefauver had argued that if Congress made illegal specific elements of organized crime, such as sending illegal gambling information across state lines, vigorous prosecution would quickly smash illegal gambling operations. With kingpin racketeers in prison, denied command, control, and capital, gambling syndicates would wither. This "attrition" strategy sought to disable criminal organizations by "incapacitating individual offenders under discrete statutes."[44] Thus Robert Kennedy's optimism that, if carrying the proceeds of a gambling operation across state lines were made criminal, gangster kingpins would swiftly be brought to justice and illegal gambling would collapse.

By 1970 the police, government attorneys, and even legislators had realized that no matter how many federal prosecutors were devoted to racketeering probes, the Kennedy program could not succeed, simply because when members of criminal organization were incapacitated, others advanced to assume their authority. One might even argue that the attrition strategy helped breed a more cunning and resourceful criminal; like antibiotics that led to the mutation of drug-resistant super-bacteria, attrition weeded out the clumsy and irresolute racketeers and let the strong and devious survive. RICO, therefore, advanced an entirely new paradigm: the "enterprise" strategy, under which prosecutors focused their energies on the entrenched criminal organizations themselves.[45] Organized-crime members would be prosecuted for more than just breaking the law; being part of the criminal organization itself became a crime.

By the time RICO had been enacted, gambling was only one of the many offenses considered part of a pattern of racketeering. Out of a total sample of 80 RICO cases heard in the appellate courts, gambling and related offenses accounted for a total of 6 convictions; extortion and mail fraud combined for 29.[46] Part of the reason for the relative paucity of gambling cases stems from RICO's protean nature; the statute has been used to prosecute cases ranging from the sale of substandard shrimp to drug smuggling.[47] Criminal RICO prosecutions against not only organized crime but also corrupt politicians, white-collar criminals, and hate groups became common after 1970, averaging about 125 annually. Only 39 percent of criminal RICO prosecutions were undertaken against classic organized-crime operations, with 49 percent attacking white-collar crimes and 13 percent directed against hate and terrorist groups. Civil prosecutions under the RICO statute, through which the aggrieved party could receive injunctions, triple damages, and court costs, became increasingly common after 1980.[48] Gaming no longer held any special fascination for those seeking to root out racketeering and corruption.

The use of RICO against organized crime made reliance on laws like the Wire Act an anachronism. Juries were far more likely to convict criminals for predicate offenses such as murder or extortion than for a "public service" like gaming. As such, RICO represented a profound shift in federal anti–organized crime strategies from sprawling investigations into violations of discrete anti-gaming statutes. After 1970 RICO shifted the emphasis to prosecution of entire organizations. "Gambling intensification efforts" in 1971 and 1972 yielded approximately one thousand convictions in each year, but prosecutors found that judges often gave convicted defendants probation and that "the game was not worth the candle." They therefore shifted resources into other areas of investigation.[49]

In 1977, when the FBI began a program management approach to organized crime that set clear national priorities for investigations, it listed gambling as a relatively minor concern, ranking it fifth of six priorities, below labor racketeering, corruption, infiltration of legitimate business, and loan sharking.[50] Up to that point, gambling prosecutions had been fairly routine; from 1962 to 1978, FBI efforts led to the conviction of more than ten thousand "hoodlums, gambling and vice figures."[51] In the early 1970s, according to Organized Crime Section deputy chief DeFeo, more than half of all law enforcement resources were devoted to illegal gambling. By the 1980s, only 10 percent of the resources were earmarked to combat "strictly illegal gambling businesses," while another 15 percent went to cases that might involve gambling tangentially.[52] A combination of limited resources, more-immediate criminal problems, such as major crimes, narcotics trafficking, and, after 2001, terrorism, meant a general slackening of the federal antigambling effort.

But this did not mean that the Wire Act had entirely outlived its purpose. Freed by RICO to attack racketeers for the eponymous crime of operating a continuing criminal enterprise, investigators and prosecutors used the Wire Act not as a general weapon against organized crime but specifically to stifle illegal bookmaking. Having fallen by the wayside in the campaign against organized crime, the statute would now be directed against gaming businesses as gaming businesses rather than as parts of larger criminal organizations.

Targeting Illegal Bookmakers

The original antigambling reformers of the Progressive Era considered gaming an evil beyond negotiation. No wager, no matter how friendly, could be socially or morally justifiable, as gambling inevitably led to the madhouse or to a pauper's grave. Gaming was inherently incompatible with a healthy society, and governments should no more sanction betting than they should decriminalize robbery or tax adultery. Such attitudes persisted, but by the 1960s they were lost in a growing torrent of American gambling. Even as Robert Kennedy complained that roulette wheels were "not only illegal, but fixed," and therefore by nature illegitimate, Americans gave gambling an increasingly prominent place.[53] The attorneys in Kennedy's own organized-crime section regularly played poker to unwind after a hard day of manning the battlements of the war on organized crime and gaming. In a nation where even federal prosecutors gambled, one might assume that gaming prosecutions would soon become a quaint reminder of past puritanical excesses.

But it was no paradox that the popularity of gambling demanded that illegal operations be prosecuted even more vigorously. With the positive explosion of public-interest gaming that began in the 1960s, legal, state-regulated gaming became the norm rather than the exception; by the turn of the twenty-first century, only two states were completely free of legal gaming. States did not merely decriminalize social gaming and allow citizens to merrily bet against each other. Rather, they became active partners in gaming enterprises, either by sponsoring monopoly lotteries or by extracting percentages of casino and pari-mutuel revenue. So by the 1970s cynics could say that states sought to stifle illegal gaming not to protect citizens from the ravages of gambling but to knock off the competition.

As illegal bookmaking became increasingly entrenched and continued to threaten state gaming interests, gambling investigations became routine elements of large-city policing. The FBI produced a training video in the early 1970s that explored the organization of three types of betting operations (numbers, bookmaking, illegal casino) and described effective investigation and arrest techniques for each.[54] A score of articles in police procedure journals and other law enforcement resources further explained the mechanics of effective antigambling police work.[55] A book-length volume published in 1992, *Practical Gambling Investigation Techniques*, provided all police officers (and, presumably, all bookmakers) a handy guidebook for how to conduct (or avoid) successful gambling investigations.[56] From initial background checks to infiltrating and raiding the operation all the way through court appearances, detectives had ample instruction on how to conduct effective operations. Though no longer a federal priority, gambling investigations continued to enjoy substantial law enforcement resources.

Illegal gaming investigations incorporated painstaking surveillance, meticulous tracking of telephone calls, and an almost playful cat-and-mouse game during the ultimate raid. Promptly securing the only smoking gun in gambling cases, a bookmaker's store of records, was an essential part of a successful raid. To give themselves time to destroy records, bookkeepers built barricaded rooms in which they conducted their business. Swiftly gaining access to the "bomb shelter" was perhaps the most important aspect of a gambling raid, for bookmakers used flash paper that incinerated at the touch of a flame or paper that rapidly dissolved in water. Less technically advanced bookmakers tried to flush incriminating records down a toilet or simply heft them out a window. To mitigate the former possibility, some police had one site's sewerage line disconnected before the raid; one can only hope that no one really had to use the toilet in the interim. During one raid, an enterprising bookmaker jammed his records into a series of balloons, which he filled with helium and tossed out a window before the police could break into his garrison. But the law was not so easily trumped—"a high-jumping detective outside the window managed to snare the evidence before it wafted away."[57]

Investigation handbooks described several humorous instances of bookmaking ineptitude and ingenuity. For example, an illegal operation run from a shoeshine parlor was broken up when an alert police officer noticed that an unusually large number of customers were leaving with dirty footwear. In another case, good weather became a bookmaker's bane as he made a poor decision to take advantage of a sunny day by bringing his work outside. He was arrested when police became suspicious of the steady stream of motorists stopping to visit a certain clump of bushes in a local park.[58] In another raid, ten people escaped by dropping two stories through a window, but a hundred others fell into the clutches of the police after a three-hundred-pound man became stuck in the window and sealed their avenue of escape.[59]

These entertaining vignettes aside, gaming investigations were serious and usually thankless jobs. Citizens typically felt that police non-enforcement of gaming laws was the result of corruption, yet they clearly demanded that police devote more time to catching "dangerous" criminals. The large 1978 survey *Gambling Law Enforcement in Major American Cities* found that citizens consistently rated a range of crimes from selling heroin and drunk driving to simple public drunkenness and the sale of pornography as more important priorities than gaming enforcement. They righteously demanded enforcement of these higher-priority crimes before low-level gambling offenses. Yet most citizens felt that police knew of active gaming operations, and a majority in most sections of the country believed that gaming flourished not because of public indifference but because the police had been paid off.[60] The police were stuck in an untenable position.

The police did in fact investigate gambling, though at each stage a range of factors complicated the process and limited its effectiveness. With public apathy and more pressing demands for limited resources, detectives faced difficulty in even getting permission to launch an investigation; *Practical Gambling Investigation Techniques* author Kevin Kinnee suggested that they could increase their chances of receiving permission if they tied the gambling operation to narcotics, money laundering, or a larger criminal enterprise.[61] After infiltrating the operation, a feat often requiring lengthy surveillance of persons and premises and risky undercover work, detectives then had to build a case for probable cause and secure a search warrant. Once permission to raid had been secured, the police had to prevent bookmakers from destroying records and other evidence.

Even if the police managed to preserve all evidence flawlessly and detectives presented the facts of their investigation at trial, the prosecutor had to convince a jury to convict a defendant for running a betting business, and this was sometimes not an easy task. Few gaming criminals had good reason to fear the justice system. The 1978 *Gambling Law Enforcement* survey reported an enviable 70 percent average conviction rate for gambling offenses, higher than that for other crimes. Yet this did not mean that juries liked to convict gamblers. Rather, most of these cases involved plea bargains, reduced charges, and recommended sentences. The survey conservatively estimated that only 15 percent of all gambling cases went to a jury trial.[62] Prosecutors clearly entertained strong doubts about the will of juries to convict gambling operators.

Though the police could not be sure that prosecutors would press gambling cases to the end, they did have another, even more imposing, ally: the Internal Revenue Service. "Remember that the suspects are more afraid of the IRS than your criminal charges," Kinnee advised detectives in *Practical Gambling Investigation Techniques*. "Use this to your advantage."[63] In 1952 Congress placed a 10 percent excise tax on bookmaking in a muddled effort to raise revenue and provide law enforcement with another tool to hound gaming operators. In deference to Nevada's legal industry, Congress eventually rolled this tax back to 0.025 percent, but the Internal Revenue Code Section 4401 imposed a 2 percent tax on wagers "placed in states where wagers are not authorized." Anyone in the business of accepting wagers in such a state was subject to the tax.[64] IRS agents were empowered to determine if a person was in the business of accepting wagers and, if so, to identify the volume of wagers accepted. Because bookmakers generally held only the current week's records, IRS agents were permitted to assess the wagering tax "on the basis of projections and extrapolations" from the available data.[65] In *Lucia v. United States* (Fifth Circuit, 1973), the seizure of one day's betting slips totaling $28,780 allowed auditors to compute annual wagers of $5,612,100 for a four-and-a-half-year period.[66] Even if bookmakers did not fear criminal sanctions, they could not help but feel terror at the prospect of an IRS excise and income tax liability audit.

Throughout the nation, state and local police continued to work against gambling, though they appear to have joined the FBI in losing ardor for gambling prosecutions in the final years of the century. Estimated national arrests for gambling fluctuated greatly in the 1970s, ranging from 79,000 in 1976 to 54,800 in 1979. Though 1980 saw 87,000 arrests, law enforcement never approached even half that number in the next two decades. Arrests steadily declined, with occasional bumps, until, by 1999, only 10,400 people were arrested on gambling charges. Of these arrests, bookmaking offenses accounted for, on average, less than 10 percent each year (FBI reports subdivided gambling arrests only until 1984, but the trend is clear enough before then). Bookmaking arrests were certainly still a possibility as the century waned, but they were not nearly as common as they had once been.[67]

Though gambling remained a large illegal enterprise, the actual size of gaming networks seems to have shrunk after the 1970s. In November 1974 the Brooklyn district attorney indicted 157 people who were allegedly involved in a vast gambling network linked to loan sharking, homicide, larceny, robbery, narcotics smuggling, and cigarette bootlegging. This investigation yielded evidence of corruption within the New York Police Department and a pervasive presence of gaming throughout the city; two of the defendants continued running their independent businesses from their hospital beds.[68] In 1993 the same office shut down an operation of "Mafia super bookies" by indicting three operators who reportedly accepted $86 million in wagers a year over the telephone.[69]

Bookmakers may have been working smarter and downsizing their operations, but the old characterization of illegal gaming as an essential part of organized crime remained. Brooklyn district attorney Charles Hymes asserted that bookmaking "is the cash cow that runs organized crime" when he announced the indictments of the three super-bookies.[70] Bookmaking investigations may have been difficult and time-consuming for the police and poorly regarded by the public, but for many in law enforcement they remained an essential element of the war against organized crime.

From the beginning, prosecutors realized that they could use the Wire Act against a range of gaming-related offenders. In addition to initial sorties against bookmakers, the federal government used the Wire Act to launch a massive crackdown against tipsters in 1964. These singular gambling professionals neither placed nor accepted wagers. Rather, they grew a multi-million-dollar business by telling clients how to bet. Though many of the twenty-seven operators snagged in the sting protested their innocence, because tipsters often had their clients place bets for them, authorities held that the transactions involved the transmission of gambling information over the telephone and hence violated the Wire Act.[71]

It was this kind of outside-the-box use of the Wire Act that pointed the way toward the future. As prosecutors shifted to RICO to battle organized crime, those wishing to target simple illegal bookmakers were free to use the Wire Act—certainly a different use of it than Kennedy had intended but one he might have approved of—so long as those bookmakers used the telephone to coordinate interstate betting.

Table 4.1: Estimated Arrests for Gambling, United States, 1974–2002

YEAR	ARRESTS
1974	61,900 (5,100 bookmaking, 8,200 numbers, 48,600 other)
1975	62,600 (5,500 bookmaking, 10,400 numbers, 46,800 other)
1976	79,000 (17,900 bookmaking, 12,700 numbers, 48,400 other)
1977	58,700 (5,500 bookmaking, 8,300 numbers, 44,900 other)
1978	55,800 (5,400 bookmaking, 8,200 numbers, 42,200 other)
1979	54,800 (4,600 bookmaking, 7,500 numbers, 42,700 other)
1980	87,000 (6,300 bookmaking, 10,400 numbers, 70,300 other)
1981	40,700 (3,300 bookmaking, 5,600 numbers, 31,700 other)
1982	41,000 (3,500 bookmaking, 7,300 numbers, 30,200 other)
1983	41,200 (3,400 bookmaking, 7,100 numbers, 30,600 other)
1984	34,700 (3,200 bookmaking, 8,800 numbers, 22,700 other)
1985	32,100
1986	30,500
1987	25,400
1988	23,600
1989	20,600
1990	19,300
1991	16,600
1992	17,100
1993	17,300
1994	18,500
1995	19,500
1996	21,000
1997	15,900
1998	12,800
1999	10,400
2000	10,842
2001	11,112
2002	10,506

Source: Bureau of Justice, *Sourcebook of Criminal Justice Statistics* (Albany: Hindelang
Criminal Justice Research Center, 1974–2002).

When authorities began using the Wire Act in a more expansive sense to
prosecute Internet sportsbooks in other jurisdictions, they argued that the
law had originally been meant as a catch-all anti-gaming measure. In fact,
two things seem certain. Congress held the original Wire Act to a strict construction, as it separately considered amending it to account for technological advances, and it had also done so for the anti–slot machine statute.
More important, the role of gambling in American society shifted dramat-

ically. Within thirty years of the Wire Act's passage, states and the federal government were treating gaming not as a crime to be eradicated but as a valuable revenue source to be regulated. As a result of this significant historical change, the United States had become a nation in which gaming was the rule, not the exception. As a result, the Wire Act would be pushed into a new, digital realm in unintended ways.

5 A Money Jungle From Sea to Sea

In a generation, the United States becomes a nation dedicated to public gaming for the public interest, reversing decades of anti-gaming sentiment.

Forty years ago, approval of gaming was not so strong. This began to change, however, as state governments in the 1960s began to sponsor lotteries and corporations took over casinos, bringing these entities under the strictest of regulatory controls. . . . These factors combined to make legalized gaming both more familiar and more trustworthy to a broader cross-section of Americans.

But within that broad cross-section of Americans is a generation gap. . . . In the AGA's Annual poll conducted in 2003 . . . adults over 50 indicated generally favorable opinions about casinos, but the opinions of adults ages 21 to 39 were consistently more positive.

This much is clear: While older Americans have come to like us, younger adults love us.
— State of the States 2003: The AGA Survey of Casino Entertainment

SPEAKING AT HIS FEBRUARY 1950 Conference on Organized Crime, Attorney General Howard McGrath proclaimed plainly that opposition to gaming was the reigning cumulative law of the United States: "Throughout the United States there is, and has existed for many years, a public policy that condemns organized gambling and makes its activities criminal."[1] Given that half the states in the Union regulated and taxed pari-mutuel betting at the time, and a clutch of others were experimenting with various legalized machine gaming schemes, this may not have been the literal truth, but he said it and no newspapers printed editorial retractions; no representatives seized the rostrum in Congress and protested. To that extent, McGrath's assertion was true: The official policy of the United States, federal, state, and local, dictated that gaming, with a few exceptions, was illegal.

Half a century later, one could say with equal fairness that support of gaming, particularly for revenue enhancement and regional economic development, was the public policy of the United States. Forty-eight of the fifty states, plus the District of Columbia, had some kind of legal gaming. The federal government, through legislative acts, executive decrees, and judicial decisions, sanctioned and even encouraged the development of casinos on Indian lands.[2] As of 2001, the federal government itself, through the armed forces, operated eight thousand slot machines in ninety-four locations, garnering an annual profit of more than $127 million; small potatoes, when compared to the $72 billion Americans annually spend on gaming, but a sizable piece of change nevertheless, particularly for a government that is ostensibly gaming-neutral.[3] America is now a nation nearly united in the pursuit of gaming.

This did not happen as the result of a single referendum or white paper. Rather, the country's embrace of gaming at nearly all levels has been the product of a series of individual choices made by citizens, public officials, and businesses. The culmination of these choices was an unwritten and even unspoken reversal of the McGrath doctrine of American opposition to gaming. These choices collectively changed the landscape of American culture and law. The United States is now a nation that aggressively promotes gaming, whether we want to admit it or not.

States Buy In: The Origins of Public-Interest Gaming

The twentieth century of gaming expansion began humbly with the permission of pari-mutuel wagering in the 1920s and 1930s, endured setbacks during the 1940s and 1950s with the anti-gaming movement, and regained its vigor in the 1960s, with the legalization of state-run or state-endorsed lottery monopolies. There are many similarities between lotteries and pari-mutuel betting, particularly in their uses by states for revenue, that make a joint consideration of their evolution appropriate.

Although horse racing—and betting on it—has been part of American life and culture since at least the time of the first British settlements, the system of race wagering that is now popular originated in the 1920s. Partly an adaptation in the face of political and economic pressures, partly the result of new technologies, pari-mutuel wagering offered several plums to several groups. For those involved in the business of breeding and racing horses, legal wagering permitted larger purses and a subsidy for the agribusiness of horse breeding and training. Public officials found a painless, entirely voluntary source of revenue that could obviate the need for higher taxes. The betting public gained the satisfaction and security of being able to indulge its urge to gamble without breaking the law and, indeed, in a way that directly benefited society. Everyone, it seemed, was a winner.

As the Great Depression ground the hopes of millions of Americans into the dirt, horse racing and betting actually grew in popularity. The pari-mutuel industry continued to broaden after World War II; by 1949 twenty-four states had legal pari-mutuel betting.[4] In the next twenty years, race betting saw modest expansion and then stagnation. In the early 1970s a total of thirty states permitted pari-mutuel betting on horse racing, greyhound racing, and jai alai. But around that time horse racing and betting began a steady decline marked by decreasing attendance, lower purse sizes, and shrinking state revenues.

Like other gaming forms, race betting has undergone significant organizational and technical innovations in the past quarter century in a drive to remain profitable. As racing began to decline in popularity, legal remote wagering became an option for those who wanted to sustain the industry. The operators of horse rooms and race wires in the early twentieth century were offering illegal, unsanctioned remote wagering, but there was nothing intrinsically illegal or even immoral about the idea of remote wagering. Provided that a formula of revenue sharing could be devised that would appease all of the interested parties—breeders' associations, racetracks, and state authorities—remote wagering promised to offer expanded revenues for the industry and government and more convenience and variety for bettors.

The first significant application of remote wagering to legal pari-mutuel betting was the institution of legal off-track betting (OTB). New York developed OTB in response to two connected facts: The state's revenues from pari-mutuel betting conducted at the tracks were declining, and illegal bookmaking far from the tracks was apparently booming. City voters had overwhelmingly approved a referendum on OTB in 1963, and the first state law to permit OTB, crafted to meet an immediate fiscal need in New York City, passed in 1970.[5] The law authorized a state commission to oversee the New York City Off-Track Betting Corporation, which in turn offered action to bettors. By 1974 the New York City OTB was the city's largest retailer, with more than a hundred branch offices that served between 100,000 and 150,000 people a day, as well as a telephone service that permitted account wagering.[6]

New York's adoption of OTB represented a significant technological achievement. It was the first time that any such organization operated a system based entirely on computers. The system required the dozens of OTB locations to be connected with a central network and to be able to handle large numbers of bets and compute the correct odds.[7] Within a few years of its establishment, it was clear that OTB was generating additional revenue for the three most interested parties: the government, the racetracks, and the horse breeders. In 1975, after five years of off-track betting, New York's racing revenue had increased by $96 million from the 1970 total. In response to fears that it would bleed revenue from live racing, OTB distributed a portion of its profits to the racetracks, which advocates insisted more than compensated for lower attendance. Finally, OTB allowed a 52 percent increase in purse money from 1970 to 1975, something that redounded directly to the benefit of horse owners.[8] To square these increased revenues with charges that off-track betting would lead to rampant public gambling, OTB supporters argued that it did not represent an extension of gaming. Anyone who placed bets with OTB could place the same bets in person at a track, but OTB provided more convenience.

Simulcasting of races also opened up more opportunities for race betting without "expanding" gaming dramatically. Authorized under the 1978 Interstate Horseracing Act, in the 1990s simulcasting expanded throughout states that had racetracks. Simulcast races are broadcast to tracks, casino race books, and OTB locations throughout the world, which take bets on the races. Because of the success of remote wagering, the dollar amount wagered on horse races has actually increased, even though attendance at racetracks has declined. While on-track bets have fallen to little more than $2 billion a year, off-track wagers have risen to more than $13 billion, thus contributing to an increase in the total amount of pari-mutuel betting from approximately $9 billion in 1990 to more than $15 billion in 2002.[9] This speaks to a broader trend in American life, as the convenience of remote wagering is perfect for a nation with an increasingly short attention span. Why drive to a racetrack and sit in uncomfortable bleachers to see two minutes of racing action when you can see and wager on races from around the world in a comfortable race book or OTB facility, or from home, for that matter?

Remote wagering alone has not been enough to save the racetracks; slot machines have emerged as the latest savior for racing. Like those who championed remote wagering, advocates of installing slot machines at racetracks claimed that this is not a true expansion of gaming—rather, it only adds another flavor of wagering to a site already dedicated to it. Although many racetracks blamed casinos and lotteries for declining revenues, the combination of casino-style slots with racing has created a renaissance at several tracks. Many states have allowed tracks to install video lottery terminals (VLTs), video-based versions of the traditional slot machine, usually owned and always regulated by a state's lottery commission or board.[10] These slot doppelgängers created a ripple effect, as the revenues from VLTs allowed tracks to offer larger purses, which attracted a higher caliber of racing action and in turn drew more fans. In theory, according to VLT proponents, everyone wins: The tracks get increased revenues and attendance, the horse breeders get larger purses, the state gets more revenue, and live audiences get more "gaming entertainment."

The track record of tracks with slots, or racinos, speaks for itself; VLTs have brought a measure of prosperity to the racing industry in many states. In West Virginia, for example, VLT revenue soared from around $82 million in 1997 to nearly $642 million in 2002. Using VLTs as a base, track operators expanded their sites into full-destination resorts offering video gambling, racing, simulcasting, entertainment, sports, and shopping. By the summer of 2003, both Mountaineer Park and Wheeling Downs had added hotels, and the two other state tracks were planning them. The growth of VLTs boosted racing business as well; the state's racing handle climbed from under $181 million to more than $205 million from 1997 to 2002. Thanks to improved quality of racing, West Virginia tracks made more than $450 million from exporting their signals for simulcast in 2002; in 1997 they could not sell their signals at any price.[11]

The horse racing industry has used new technologies and new partnerships to survive during the past two decades, a time when consumer interest in its live product has flagged considerably. In this regard, horse racing is typical of gaming industries in general, which frequently use the latest technological advances. The transition from on-track wagering to off-track betting to account wagering over the telephone and eventually the Internet has been a natural, if not seamless, evolution and a function of the industry's desire to perpetuate itself by adjusting to new delivery systems. State governments have been an interested party as well, as each new variant of wagering opens up a new revenue stream.

Originally, proponents of legalized off-track betting in New York claimed that the practice would eliminate organized crime from gambling and drive out illegal bookmaking. Rather then extending the market for gaming, it would sanitize it and channel this inevitable activity toward the public good. But a New York Police Department white paper circulated in early 1974 concluded that, on the contrary, illegal betting had grown by 62 percent. The study, as well as a host of anecdotal reports, also suggested that OTB had created a new class of "losers," as bettors at off-track facilities, presumably less familiar with racing, lost more on average than track bettors. Grizzled bettors may still have pored over the *Daily Racing Form* before selecting bets at the tracks, but the off-track bettors, observers reported, tended to be housewives given to "hatpin picking" of horses. One detective claimed that several housewives had descended into prostitution to recoup money lost at betting and that others had progressed to betting with illegal bookmakers.[12] Though OTB may not have delivered on all of its promises, states that adopted it for revenue enhancement were loath to abandon it. No longer viewing OTB as a panacea that solved a number of law enforcement and budgetary problems, they accepted it as a revenue device with problems that could be mitigated, or at least managed.

In addition to pari-mutuel wagering, many states sought to tap the public desire for gaming by authorizing lotteries, usually with the proceeds dedicated to education or other budget areas. In 1963 New Hampshire voters approved the first American lottery of the twentieth century; forty years later thirty-seven states and the District of Columbia had legal lotteries.[13] This was an impressive reversal, given that lotteries had been universally condemned as regressive and predatory as late as the 1950s.

Business and policy expert Richard McGowan has argued that three waves of lottery (not legal gaming in general) activity coincided with the financing of a war or postwar reconstruction. The lotteries held in the South during Reconstruction, he argues, were the only way for unpopular "carpetbagger" governments to finance needed improvements.[14] This argument belies the facts that some states—Georgia for one—specifically outlawed lotteries in their Reconstruction constitutions and that the Louisiana lottery endured until it was throttled by the federal government in the 1890s, long after the end of Reconstruction and in a period when an essentially one-party Democratic state had all the power it needed to raise taxes.[15]

On far firmer ground, McGowan argues that the 1980s boom in lotteries was a direct consequence of the Cold War, which diverted limited tax resources to defense spending. With the "New Federalism" of the Reagan years, the federal government shifted the burden of many social welfare services to state governments, which found themselves suddenly strapped for resources. State legislators, understandably reluctant to take the politically suicidal dive of a tax hike, chose instead to authorize lotteries to raise money. Nationally, both the breadth of lotteries—the number of states that have authorized them—and the depth—the seemingly limitless opportunities to bet that they provide—serve as evidence of an unprecedented national embrace of lotteries that far outdistances earlier "waves."[16]

It is often said that all politics are local, and indeed, the real story of lotteries begins at the local level in New Hampshire. Voters approved the New Hampshire Sweepstakes to plug holes in local school budgets, which were chronically underfunded because the state's tax structure eschewed sales and income taxes and relied instead almost entirely on property and "sin" taxes. As initially approved, the Sweepstakes held two drawings a year, with tickets costing $3 each. Distribution was limited and required the registration of ticket buyers. Though this sweepstakes failed to earn the projected revenues, New York authorized a lottery in 1967, with $1 tickets and monthly drawings.[17] Like New Hampshire, New York organized its lottery around the principles of limited access and strict regulation to curb moral objections and organized-crime infiltration. In New York, as in the Granite State, only limited revenues were realized.[18]

As in so many other areas of American life and culture, New Jersey provided a major breakthrough in state experimentation with legal lotteries. In a desperate attempt to forestall a state income tax in 1970, New Jersey adopted a lottery scheme designed not to limit the opportunity to gamble but to maximize revenues. The state offered tickets as cheap as 50 cents and held weekly lottery drawings. This offered direct competition with illegal numbers operations and proved wildly successful; in its first year the New Jersey lottery grossed three times the amount of the New York lottery. Throughout the 1970s, this lottery would generate tens of millions of dollars for schools and state institutions annually and inspire New York and New Hampshire to switch to weekly 50-cent games.[19]

The New Jersey formula proved a popular one (though the state ultimately got an income tax in 1976 anyway), and in 1972 Connecticut, Pennsylvania, and Massachusetts followed suit. Suffering from budget crunches brought on by economic malaise, more states followed, including Maryland in 1973 and Illinois, Maine, and Ohio in 1974.[20] Suddenly the lottery was firmly established throughout the Northeast. By the mid-1970s, nearly half of all citizens in lottery states actually bought tickets, signaling the ultimate acceptance of this previously vilified gaming form.[21]

As morning was breaking across America in 1981, fourteen states had legal lotteries. The weekly 50-cent "draw games," the cutting edge of gambling a scant decade earlier, now appealed only to "hard-core" lottery devotees; daily and even instant games reigned as popular betting options. Daily numbers games, frankly borrowing their name and concept from the illegal numbers rackets, featured daily (except Sundays and holidays) drawings of three-number combinations. Tickets ranged from 50 cents to $10 and could usually be bought through linked computer terminals. With drawings televised nightly and printed in the following day's paper, the daily numbers became part of everyday life in many states.[22] Weekly lotto games, led again by New Jersey's Pick 6 Lotto, which offered escalating jackpots, were just establishing themselves as powerful games.[23]

Instant games offered the random, no-skill elements of the lottery along with the instant gratification of casino-type games. Indeed, opponents labeled them "paper slot machines." These games, offered by Massachusetts in 1974, allowed a player to rub off an opaque film and discover instantly if she was a winner.[24] Soon to become part of fast-food marketing campaigns throughout the nation, instant games took the United States by storm upon their introduction, and most states moved to offer a constantly shifting variety of these "scratchers."[25]

From its beachhead in the Northeast, the lottery movement expanded throughout the Midwest and West in the 1980s and 1990s to twenty-two additional states, including California, Arizona, New Mexico, and Washington (but not Nevada) in the West and such Bible Belt states as Texas, Georgia, and Kentucky. Feeding on the needs of states for revenue and the political toxicity of raising taxes, lotteries steamrolled across the political landscape in the last two decades of the twentieth century. Innovations like keno and sports pool betting failed to displace lotto as the leading lottery game, but the development of VLTs created a new wave of lottery mania in the 1990s.[26]

What were the mechanics of this newly legal gambling monopoly? States, which usually authorize the lottery as an administration within the state hierarchy, frequently have a lottery board or commission charged with ensuring an honest and fair lottery and an executive director who actually administers the lottery and answers to the commission. Lottery tickets are sold in virtually any retail establishment, and lottery retailers get a 5 to 7 percent commission on sales at their location. As of 2001, 184,396 lottery retailers sold tickets in the United States.[27] Primarily convenience stores, grocery stores, taverns, and other community retail outlets, these locations represent the backbone of the current national culture of gaming. Some states feed lottery revenues directly into the state's general funds, while about twenty earmark lottery dollars either wholly or partially for education. Kansas splits its proceeds between economic development and prisons, Iowa allots a portion for problem gambling treatment, and Wisconsin dedicates its lottery to property tax relief, no doubt a politically salable prospect.[28]

In response to national complaints about the abuses of the Louisiana lottery, in 1895 Congress deemed the interstate shipment of lottery tickets to be a federal offense. Other states felt powerless to stop "the Serpent" from peddling its materials in states with no legal lotteries and turned to the federal government for remedy. But less than a century later, states banded together to offer multi-state lottery games; by forming a consortium and pooling their revenues, the states could offer a higher jackpot, which would in turn attract more sales. The first and largest such group, the Multi-State Lottery Association, came together in 1988. It currently has twenty-four member states, which together own and operate the association. Its chief product, launched in 1992, is Powerball. In twice-weekly drawings, five numbers are selected out of 53, and a sixth is picked from 42 numbers.[29] Jackpots for hitting all six numbers have run as high as the $190 million won in October 2003 by a group of sixteen Holdingford, Minnesota, school district employees.[30] A rival multi-state lotto game began in 1996 as the Big Game and offered what was at the time the largest lottery jackpot in North American history, $363 million, in May 2000 (it was ultimately split by two winners). Following that jackpot, however, sales lagged, and the game's directors reorganized it in 2002 as Mega Millions, with a higher initial jackpot and projected jackpot totals as high as $500 million.[31] Multi-state lottery games illustrate the inventiveness with which lottery commissions and boards can attack the problem of increasing their sales and demonstrate that these arms of state governments have become very active purveyors of gaming entertainment.

Both lotteries and pari-mutuel gaming have offered state governments a chance to create revenue without directly raising taxes. Lottery opponents charge that gaming taxes are in effect regressive tax schemes because they invariably target less-affluent citizens who are least able to afford new burdens, while supporters point out that buying lottery tickets or playing VLTs is never compulsory. Lotteries and pari-mutuel betting expanded as the direct result of economic and political realities that have left states short of funds and taxpayers with little tolerance for higher taxes. They speak, however, to the growing acceptance of—and reliance on—gaming as an engine of economic redistribution in the United States. This is tremendously ironic, as one of the original thrusts of anti-gaming laws in England was to restrict redistribution of wealth through gaming and to prevent moneyed but dissolute estate owners from losing their holdings. Today, it seems, state governments use gaming precisely to reallocate wealth, though it is hardly the large estate owners they target; rather, it is anyone with "a dollar and a dream."

A Casino Boom Lights the Skies of America

As lotteries proliferated, the expansion of casino gaming dramatically transformed the American landscape, leaving in its wake multibillion-dollar edifices and regional economies beholden to casino-related tourism and development. The first stage of casino growth took place more or less vertically, as casinos became increasingly powerful economic drivers in the only state to permit them legally at midcentury, Nevada. In the second stage, beginning in the late 1970s but rapidly accelerating in the early 1990s, commercial casinos also expanded horizontally, spreading to eleven states throughout the nation. As has been the case in all gaming expansions in the United States, the proliferation of state-regulated commercial casinos happened as the result of a series of decisions made in the public and private interest.

In the early twentieth century, legal gaming in the United States was at its low ebb. "Wide-open" gaming, which had lingered in the state of Nevada and the territories of New Mexico and Arizona, was illegal everywhere. But when Nevada outlawed gaming in 1909, it never completely slammed the door on betting games. Gambling continued in back rooms and hotels, though counties now had no legal means of using it to raise revenue (corruption, as in other jurisdictions with flourishing illegal gaming, quietly subsidized law enforcement and judicial salaries). In 1915 legislators voted to permit games played for drinks, cigars, or sums under $2, as well as nickel slot machines. A lingering moral apprehension allowed the anti-gaming lobby, composed primarily of women's and reform groups, to thrash full legalization proposals in the 1920s, but with the slide of the state into the Depression in 1930, the time was ripe for pro-gaming forces to complete the *reconquista* of Nevada for gaming interests.[32]

Nevada decriminalized "wide-open" gaming in 1931 as part of a burst of legislative desperation that included a "quickie" six-week divorce bill. Lawmakers believed that these measures would spur tourism and business, primarily in the Reno area. They did not, however, intend gaming tourism to become the state's main source of economic strength. Gaming operators obliged the legislators' low expectations of their newly legal establishments by keeping them decidedly low-rent. Gaming remained restricted to taverns and gambling halls that catered primarily to locals and the divorce trade, particularly in the north. In the south, the small town of Las Vegas showed little more creativity. A few gaming halls that catered to dam workers appeared on Boulder Highway in the early 1930s, and Hollywood royalty sometimes gambled in downtown halls as California gambling dried up in the late 1930s, but gaming remained mostly a local curiosity.

In 1941 California motelier Thomas Hull opened a new kind of gaming establishment that would redefine Las Vegas gaming and ultimately change the ways Americans conceived of gaming. His El Rancho Vegas, built on fifty-seven acres of land on the Los Angeles Highway outside the city limits, was the first bona fide casino resort, a self-contained vacation destination with lodging, dining, entertainment, shopping, and a casino featuring both table games and slot machines. Subsequent casinos elaborated on this basic model, and by 1952 the Los Angeles Highway had become the Las Vegas Strip, a collection of isolated insular casino resorts that captured visitors from Southern California before they had a chance to visit downtown.[33]

By the mid-1950s, casino resorts had established the Strip as a national vacation destination and the economic engine of Nevada. The state of Nevada, which originally collected taxes from gaming halls but otherwise showed only a perfunctory interest in regulating them, faced a quandary. A series of scandals encouraged the belief that the industry was beset by corruption and possible infiltration by organized-crime figures. In response, Nevada instituted a rigorous regulatory regime that promised to keep the industry clean of allegations of mob influence and guarantee its integrity. At the same time, the resorts of the Strip actively sought to broaden their market by reinventing themselves as convention hotels. Beginning with the Stardust in 1958, casino resorts courted business travelers, a strategy underscored by the opening of the Las Vegas Convention Center in 1959.

Financing for these resorts had come from the same sources that had funded illegal gaming operations for generations: syndicates of investors, some with ties to other illicit enterprises. Three structural tensions within the casino industry forced changes in ownership beginning in the late 1960s. First, the tremendous profits that could be realized from a well-run casino resort attracted the interest of large hotel operators, who surmised that, with their hospitality management expertise and brand recognition, they could make the jump into the casino business. Second, as resorts got bigger, pushing the thousand-room mark, they simply became too expensive for the relatively small syndicates of investors to afford. Finally, the state of Nevada, in its continuing mission to seek out legitimacy for its fiscal foundation, believed that large, publicly held corporations would guarantee acceptance by the economic mainstream and facilitate new growth.

According to the existing gaming laws, each stockholder in a casino had to be investigated and licensed by Nevada authorities—something that precluded publicly traded corporations from owning casinos, as it was impossible, even theoretically, for gaming regulators to investigate every "owner" of a corporation with thousands of shares of stock. This didn't entirely shut the door on corporations in Nevada gaming—the Del Webb Corporation owned and operated the Sahara and Mint casinos through an ingenious feat of organizational trickery by which a wholly owned subsidiary of Del Webb actually owned the casinos, which were managed under contract by a management company consisting of three principals in Del Webb.[34] But other corporations found this juggling act unpalatable, because it presented both the appearance and the very real possibility of impropriety.

To mitigate these problems, Nevada amended its gaming laws in 1967 and 1969 to permit ownership by publicly traded corporations by requiring only the licensing of controlling stockholders, officers, and directors of a corporation seeking to operate a casino. Regulators were so wary of the possibilities for mob infiltration into the industry that they reserved the right to remove any stockholder from a corporation if his or her presence was deemed "contrary to the best interests of Nevada," a condition to which investors in most other industries would never assent.[35] But the lure of profits to be made, and the understood importance of maintaining the integrity of the industry by keeping it free from "undesirables," prompted prospective investors to make this concession willingly.

Following the passage of the Corporate Gaming Acts in 1967 and 1969, some casino companies, like Harrah's in Northern Nevada, took themselves public, raising money for improvements and expansions. Hotel companies, like Hilton, purchased Las Vegas properties like Kirk Kerkorian's Flamingo and International (rechristened the Las Vegas Hilton). Lum's, a Florida corporation that owned hot dog eateries, purchased Caesars Palace and eventually divested itself of its restaurants and took the name Caesars World. The resulting investments changed the fabric of the Nevada gaming industry, allowing the value of its physical assets to skyrocket. State gaming revenues soared from $358 million in 1967 to $2.5 billion from gaming and $1.3 billion more in non-gaming revenue in 1981.[36]

During the 1970s the United States faced national economic problems, felt most acutely across the industrial Northeast and Midwest. The seem-ingly painless bonanza provided by Nevada casinos for the state's coffers and Southern Nevada's booming tourist economy intrigued open-minded citi-zens in Atlantic City, New Jersey, a seaside resort and convention center that had decayed and essentially imploded. Conditions in Atlantic City were cer-tainly dire. A 1980 report spoke of "a sustained decline of catastrophic pro-portions" beginning in the 1960s as room occupancies dropped and eighteen hotels closed their doors.[37] As a result of this sustained depression, Atlan-tic City's population fell as those who could left, and prospects for further tourist development dimmed. The once-proud resort was caught in a cycle of economic misery.

Proponents argued that by building Strip-style casino resorts in Atlantic City, the area's tourist infrastructure would quickly revive, leading to new in-vestment and jobs for all, as well as additional monies for state programs. In the years when the state was trying to avoid levying its first income tax, this was no small part of the bargain. Although the first referendum to legal-ize casinos throughout the state failed in 1974, a second go-round in 1976 proved fruitful. After gaming began in 1978, forecasters predicted an even-tual casino win of up to $1.5 billion and the creation of at least 41,000 jobs, speculating optimistically that casinos would spark a wave of ancillary devel-opments.[38]

As it happened, the actual gaming revenue dwarfed predicted revenue; by the late 1990s, Atlantic City casinos won more than $4 billion annually and paid more than $300 million in taxes.[39] But the ancillary development did not take place. A prescient review by the New Jersey Department of Communi-ty Affairs warned that the Atlantic City economy would become "more one-dimensional and casino-dependent . . . because casino-related tourist invest-ment will outbid other sectors of the economy for labor and land."[40]

The reasons for the mixed results of casino gaming in Atlantic City—soaring revenues but not a great spillover into ancillary tourist develop-ment—were rooted in the framework created for the industry. The 1976 referendum restricted gaming to prescribed areas of Atlantic City, and the enabling legislation, enacted the next year, specified that all gaming take place within casino resort complexes (with casino, hotel, dining, and enter-tainment all mandatory) and under extremely strict regulatory guidelines. Public officials held that this regulation, though sometimes absurdly strict (particularly to Nevada operators used to that state's less intrusive approach) was necessary to guarantee the integrity of the new gaming industry.

From the opening of Resorts International in a converted boardwalk hotel on Memorial Day weekend in 1978, Atlantic City casino gaming proved to be incredibly profitable and a dynamic engine of regional, though not local, growth. While the regulations specifying that all casinos be insular resorts that totally provided for all their guests' needs left in question the efficacy of casino gaming as a "unique tool for urban redevelopment," there was no denying what casinos did in Atlantic City; after twenty-five years, casinos had created 45,000 permanent jobs, paid more than $5 billion into a state fund that gave assistance to senior citizens and those with disabilities, and brought more than $7 billion in investments to Atlantic City.[41]

Atlantic City casinos thus pleased three constituencies: casino owners, who in calendar year 2002 could boast total gaming revenues of more than $4.3 billion; state legislators and officials, who received nearly $350 million in taxes on those revenues (and were thus spared the specter of raising funds through taxation); and residents of New Jersey, about 45,000 of whom worked directly for casinos, in addition to thousands more who gained from industries supplying the casinos. In addition, all residents of the state shared in the tax bonanza and redevelopment projects made possible by casino funds.[42] The interplay of these three groups—owners, state officials, and the electorate—would ultimately result in the expansion of casino gaming across the United States.

As the Atlantic City roll of the dice proved increasingly lucrative for casino operators, budget-minded public officials, and the general public, arguments against the spread of casino-style gaming seemed progressively less persuasive. Southern Nevada had prospered for a generation with an economy largely based on gaming-derived tourism, and New Jersey had proven that an economically diversified state could successfully regulate a gaming industry harnessed for regional redevelopment. As Americans woke up in the early 1980s to discover a nation that could no longer guarantee funding for government programs or full industrial employment, the use of casinos—stringently monitored and optimally taxed—to spur economic growth began to make sense to former foes of gaming.

Iowa won the race to be the next state to legalize casino gaming by a nose when it approved a new form of gambling in 1989. Iowans adapted the successful casino resort idea to a mélange of historic myth and political logrolling to create the casino riverboat. Such vessels putatively harked back to the riverboat gamblers of lore, with several convenient elisions: The colorful blacklegs of Mark Twain's childhood were known cheats and, for that matter, paid no taxes to the state.

The riverboat casinos of Iowa, however, were pitched to do no less than revitalize flagging regional economies and pour millions of dollars into state coffers—something completely at odds with the traditional social construction of the riverboat gambler as an avaricious, deceptive parasite at worst and a rakish, bombastic scoundrel at best. But the Iowa model provided for the development of an industry that could, theoretically, be strictly controlled by the state and provide maximum good with minimal harm. Gaming legalization in Iowa followed a classic pattern. Since statehood in 1846, gaming had been expressly illegal. In 1973 charitable gaming—bingo and raffles—was deemed acceptable. In 1983 Iowans legalized pari-mutuel betting at horse and dog tracks, and two years later, they adopted a state lottery.[43]

So the 1989 decision to permit riverboat gaming by county option entirely conformed to the trend toward liberalization of Iowa's anti-gaming laws. In that year, eight counties approved riverboats; within three years, two more would join them. The state's first boat launched in April 1991, under stringent rules that would supposedly shield Iowa from the excesses of gaming but permit the flourishing of a healthy industry that could be optimally taxed. Among the restrictions were the requirements that all gambling take place while the boat was actually cruising, that no more than 30 percent of the boat's square footage be taken up by gambling, that bets be limited to $5, and that losses be limited to $200 per trip.[44]

These limitations were all passed with the best of intentions, but they produced an industry that was only reasonably profitable when it had a monopoly and quite disappointing after boats began cruising in Illinois in September 1991. Illinois, though it restricted the number of licenses to ten and maintained the cruising requirement, eschewed any loss limits, with the result that players gambled and lost more, making more money for the operators and, by extension, the state. Even though the initial 20 percent tax rate of Illinois was higher than that of Iowa, the Illinois boats, with their players losing more, could afford it. Predictably, as other jurisdictions (like liberal Mississippi) opened, boats began leaving Iowa, until Iowa waived cruising requirements. Loss limits, too, crumbled before industry protestations and the desire of legislators for "enhanced" revenue sources.

States without famously navigable waterways also wished to cash in on the casino gaming express, but balked at creating a full-blown casino industry along the lines of Nevada's or, for that matter, Atlantic City's. They therefore turned to "limited gaming," a compromise between gaming proponents and the anti-gaming lobby that has been surprisingly durable. Colorado and South Dakota both experimented with land-based limited gaming in the 1990s, with somewhat different results.

Colorado had a rich tradition of gaming. During the state's first mining booms, in the 1860s and 1870s, gamblers proved to be as ubiquitous a presence there as they were elsewhere on the mining frontier, and continued mineral strikes meant that gaming remained widely present into the twentieth century. The state's constitution did not specifically prohibit forms of gambling besides the lottery. As in many parts of the nation, illegal public gaming survived Progressive Era attempts to root it out, only to finally succumb to the midcentury anti-gaming movement.[45] Though the state continued to sanction horse and dog race betting and charitable gambling, casino-style gambling was curtailed. During the 1980s, attempts to introduce casino legalization failed. But with the success of casinos in Atlantic City, arguments to allow decaying mining towns to host casinos began making more sense to more people.

In early 1990 the Colorado legislature rejected an initial proposal to allow limited gaming in "historical communities," but supporters took the fight to the people, who ultimately approved an amendment to permit "limited gaming" in the historic mining towns of Blackhawk, Central City, and Cripple Creek. The amendment as passed limited gambling to slot machines, poker, and blackjack, with maximum bets of $5 per play, and specified that gaming must take place in structures conforming to "pre–World War I architectural designs." Funds collected as gaming taxes were to benefit the state general fund, the state historical fund, the counties and cities with gaming, and a fund for the promotion of tourism.[46] In their eight months of operation (October 1991 to June 1992), Colorado casinos, laboring under significant restrictions (in addition to their betting limits, the casino towns were difficult to reach and had too few hotel rooms) brought in nearly $100 million.[47] By 2002, a mature Colorado limited gaming industry brought in more than $700 million in revenue each year, from which it paid nearly $100 million in state taxes.[48] As of 2003, Colorado soldiered on with a $5-per-bet limit, the only state still clinging to the letter and spirit of its original "limited gaming" promise.

Low-stakes gaming met a different fate in South Dakota. Legalized gambling began in Deadwood on November 1, 1989, with several provisos, among them that gambling operations be owned by "bona fide" South Dakota citizens and that they accept no wagers higher than $5. For those looking to revive the mining and lumbering center, gambling offered another tourist attraction. In a year when gaming had not yet proliferated throughout the nation, the $5 bet limit was not viewed as a large impediment. But as other states rolled out their own gaming regimes throughout the 1990s, the low stakes of South Dakota proved less salable to tourists and less profitable to operators and the state.

In 2000 state voters lifted the bet limit to $100—certainly nothing to raise eyebrows in the Bellagio's baccarat pit but clearly enough to allow gambling halls to pursue "high-end play." The higher bet limit has been held responsible for casino and hotel expansions and a rise in convention bookings. Although slot machines still generate more than 90 percent of Deadwood's gaming revenue, the higher bet limits have allowed a resurgence of blackjack, which permits more interaction and presumably a more authentic "Western" gambling experience. This may be true, as many visitors to Deadwood say that the town's "colorful history" resonates with them.[49] In any event, South Dakota's willingness to abandon low-stakes gaming in favor of increased revenues reflects the realpolitik that shapes most gaming expansion—satisfying the hopefully complementary desires of gaming operators, state officials, and the voting and working public.[50]

Tantalized by the seemingly painless benefits of riverboat gaming and low-stakes gaming, other states speedily jumped aboard. The state of Mississippi had been home to a thriving illegal gambling scene in Biloxi on the Gulf Coast. Indeed, Biloxi frequently emerged in discussions of national gaming syndicates as a major center for layoff betting. But by the 1980s state and local authorities had effectively eliminated public illegal gaming. Still, Mississippians wanted to gamble, and in 1987 "cruises to nowhere" began. Ships sailed from Biloxi ports into international waters, where otherwise illegal gambling took place, rendering state police powerless to enforce anti-gaming ordinances, since the activity took place outside of their jurisdiction. With poverty a tremendous problem (the state was frequently depicted as the poorest in the nation), the Mississippi legislature approved a liberal, market-driven model of riverboat gaming in 1992. Though facilities had to float, they did not have to cruise, and most were barges connected to larger hotel and entertainment complexes. The state placed no wagering limits on its casinos and no restrictions on the number of licenses, preferring to let the market, rather than the government, determine the optimum number of operators.

As a result, applications for licenses flooded the state, and three Iowa riverboats relocated to Mississippi.[51] Soon gaming thrived in three areas: Tunica County, near Memphis, Tennessee; the central Natchez/Vicksburg region; and the Gulf Coast area (Biloxi and Gulfport).[52] Mississippi has been so successful at creating jobs and revenue that promoters utter the phrase "Mississippi miracle" without any pretense of irony. In 2001 casinos generated more than $1 billion in direct and indirect wages, paid nearly $330 million in gaming taxes, and spent about $2.23 billion more on operating expenses and other spending. Tunica County, once one of the nation's most impoverished rural counties, has become the nation's third–largest casino destination.[53] That casinos provided such a bounty seemed a vindication of Mississippi's permissive regulatory regime, particularly when contrasted with Louisiana's restrictive approach. Confronted by low oil prices and a generally stagnant economy, the legislature in 1991 authorized fifteen riverboats.

Louisiana's cap on riverboat licenses made them scarce, valuable commodities and opened the door to tremendous corruption. In 1998 prosecutors indicted former Louisiana governor Edwin Edwards and six others for racketeering and extortion. Edwards and his codefendants stood accused of having blackmailed prospective licensees out of more than $3 million in payoffs; former San Francisco 49ers chairman Eddie DeBartolo testified that he had given Edwards $400,000 after Edwards had threatened to use his influence to block DeBartolo's license application.[54] The allegations were so damning and the evidence of wrongdoing so blatant that the jury had no option but to convict Edwards, who had emerged unscathed from two trials and no less than twenty-two grand jury investigations.[55]

Illinois, which capped its riverboat licenses at ten, had a less spectacular scandal erupt when the Illinois Gaming Board declared Emerald Casino, the recipient of the tenth license, unfit to operate the casino because of investors with reputed connections to organized crime. In states with an unlimited number of licenses, this would be no great difficulty—the operator would simply be denied and the next application accepted—but because of the limit on licenses, the state was unable to simply allow another casino to open. This gave holders of the license some leverage in negotiating a settlement with the state, which was desperate for the additional revenue a tenth riverboat casino would bring in.[56]

Thus, those favoring limited regimes of riverboats gaming had little to show but frustrated operators, scandals, and lower-than-projected revenues, while Mississippi, following its own permissive path, developed the nation's third-largest gaming industry. Of course, the entire point of dampening the acceleration of gaming in riverboat states has been to avoid becoming the third-largest casino state in the nation, but that is little consolation to state legislators mulling a tax increase while gazing across the river at their more liberal neighbors rolling in the casino taxes.

By the mid-1990s, it was apparent that gaming in Atlantic City had succeeded in creating both jobs and revenue and that riverboats had brought similar gains to the heartland, though legislators sought to balance revenues against the potential social ills of "runaway" gaming by limiting gaming. Around this time, some major cities, facing budget crunches and unemployment problems of their own, saw few cogent arguments against joining in the casino bonanza. This did not mean that all legalization campaigns succeeded, however. Ambitious city officials and curious gaming industry executives floated opportune trial balloons in several cities, only to see them burst by a well-financed casino lobby from a neighboring state or a genuine anti-gaming campaign. In two notable instances, though, land-based casinos have opened to somewhat mixed results.

Given New Orleans's rich tradition of gaming, much of it legal, it seemed only natural for that city to give casino gaming a try. After all, many of the visitors to Biloxi casinos who had made the "Mississippi miracle" possible came from Louisiana, and, with the already existing tourist attractions of New Orleans, the addition of casino gaming would supplement the carousing of the French Quarter and give tourists a place to visit after downing the obligatory Hurricane on Bourbon Street. In 1992 the legislature authorized a single land-based casino in New Orleans (continuing the policy of limiting licenses). This lone casino, proponents forecast, could earn as much as $1 billion in revenue and provide 50,000 jobs.[57]

After fierce rounds of bidding, Harrah's Entertainment won the casino franchise. Located in a converted building on Canal Street, in the heart of the tourist district, the casino began operations with several limitations, including an onerous $100 million annual minimum tax burden and restrictions against offering dining and lodging—provisions that local merchants, seeing the impact of insular casino resorts on Atlantic City, had demanded. A temporary casino, Harrah's Jazz, filed for bankruptcy in 1995, and the permanent facility, Harrah's New Orleans, was also forced into bankruptcy, unable to meet the state's $100 million tax. In early 2001 Harrah's negotiated with the city and state for tax relief and fiscal concessions. Still, without an attached hotel and entertainment complex, the casino did not approach the original sanguine estimates for its performance.

Even as Harrah's difficulties in New Orleans indicated that casinos in major cities, even ones with thriving tourism economies, were no cakewalk for generating jobs and revenue, the city of Detroit spun the wheel on its own variant of controlled urban gaming. The city's hand was forced by the opening of the Casino Windsor across the Detroit River in 1994. This casino, owned by the province of Ontario, attracted many Michigan gamblers. Michigan legislators, facing the usual postindustrial suspects—low employment, high taxes, shrinking revenues—decided that three casinos in Detroit could absorb those already gambling in Windsor and provide a stimulus to the state's and city's economies and revenues.

Once bid upon and licensed, the three Detroit casinos began operating at temporary sites under the original master plan for four years while the city acquired waterfront land to serve as a permanent location. MGM Grand opened the first of these casinos in 1997, and by 2000 all three were in operation; in 2001 they generated revenues of more than $1 billion. Rising land prices and ongoing court challenges precluded the city from realizing the original waterfront plan, however, though an agreement reached in 2002 permitted the casinos to open permanent locations away from the waterfront.[58] In addition, a legal challenge by the Lac Vieux Desert Band of Lake Superior Chippewa Indians, which charged that the bidding process was marred by preferential treatment extended to two of the ultimately successful candidates, delayed the building of "permanent" casinos. In late 2003 the Lac Vieux band finally settled with the Greektown and Motor City casinos, agreeing to drop all legal challenges in exchange for a total payment of $79 million.[59] Still, doubts remained about Detroit's casinos. One of the selling points of permitting casinos was that they would provide upscale accommodations for guests to the planned 2006 Super Bowl, but 2003 ended with no construction planned and doubts as to whether it would proceed.[60]

In any consideration of the history of gaming in the United States, few years recommend themselves as such stark turning points as 1989. In that year, after all, Iowans approved riverboats, opening the floodgates of slot machines along the rivers of the Midwest and the South. But that year is also significant because of an event that marked the beginning of the transformation of the Las Vegas Strip from a schmaltzy collection of rather bland casinos into a glitzy, cosmopolitan stage that can seriously promote itself as the world's gaming and entertainment capital.

That punctuation event was the opening of the Mirage Resort, Hotel, and Casino by Steve Wynn on November 22, 1989. Wynn had parlayed a controlling stake in the downtown Golden Nugget into an extremely successful Atlantic City casino, which, hamstrung by regulatory barriers, he sold in 1986. He used the proceeds of the sale to begin the Mirage. The Mirage was not the largest casino or hotel on the Strip, but it was the most expensive. Steve Wynn's then-revolutionary dictum that the casino with the highest overhead would also be the casino with the highest profits was borne out by the Mirage.[61] Yet the success of the Mirage was predicated on more than simply the concept "if you build it, they will come." It involved a thorough reconceptualization of the very nature of a casino resort. Wynn himself emphatically told his stockholders in 1992, "Simply put, *gaming is not enough.*"[62] According to Wynn, the casino had to be more than a casino—it had to provide the customer "with an entertaining experience . . . that will inspire the customer to return again and again, regardless of whether he or she wins in the casino." Certainly his Mirage, with fourteen restaurants and lounges and more than three thousand rooms, two thousand slot machines, and one hundred table games had all the elements of a basic casino. But the $20 million erupting volcano outside signaled that this was to be something different, an entertainment destination with a dolphin habitat, a tropical rain forest, Siegfried and Roy performing nightly, and, for wealthier guests, posh villas and an invitation-only golf course.[63] Wynn set the bar for spectacle and luxury higher than ever.

Other operators soon scrambled to overtake the Mirage. Up and down the Strip, the blasts of hotel implosions were followed by the boom of new construction. The Excalibur, already well under way when the Mirage opened, debuted in 1990, and it provides a point of departure for how a Las Vegas Strip without Steve Wynn would have looked: its more than four thousand rooms eschewed any pretense at anything more than comfort, and the casino was geared toward budget-minded gamblers and vacationers. Though the Excalibur was successful, its owners, Circus Circus Enterprises, began building first the Luxor and then Mandalay Bay (now the flagship of the renamed Mandalay Resort Group) as upscale casinos in an attempt to out-Wynn Mirage Resorts. With its "Masterplan Mile" south of Tropicana Avenue, Circus sought to create a "Strip within the Strip." The company saw Mandalay Bay as its chance to step up to the plate as a "designer of dramatic space" rather than just a casino company.[64] Indeed, the theme, the color scheme, and even the smell of Mandalay Bay, replete with a South Seas setting and an "isle of escape" identity, trod dangerously close to outright imitation of the Mirage. But only Steve Wynn himself improved on the Mirage; when he opened the Bellagio in 1998 as an even more expensive casino built from the Mirage template, that casino became the undisputed leader of the market.

By 2004 the Las Vegas Strip had completely reinvented itself. While older casinos, like the Flamingo, the Riviera, the Sahara, and the Stardust endured, the center of gravity had shifted, quite naturally, to the newer and more elaborate offerings. Though the industry saw a decline in 2001 owing as much to the general economic downtown as to the travel shakeup in the wake of the tragedy of September 11, it rebounded over the next year, and soon expansion projects were under way and completed. With many on the Strip anticipating Steve Wynn's next project, the Wynn Las Vegas (slated to open in April 2005 on the site of the former Desert Inn), operators looked to the future with a fair sense of optimism.

People obviously cherish success, but it seldom leads to serious introspection or self-analysis. This is unfortunate, because many Strip casino operators seem blissfully unaware of the tremendous historical shift that they have authored. In 1940 legal gaming was a sawdust-and-spittoon affair, and it remained so until the casinos of the Strip made it palatable to middle-class vacationers in the 1950s. Until the 1990s, though, a casino was an uncommon place in American life, seen only on special trips to Nevada or Atlantic City. Within the past decade or so, casinos have become a routine part of most Americans' worlds. Given that in 2002 approximately 51 million Americans—about one-quarter of all Americans twenty-one and over—visited a casino and more than half of the Americans polled would favor a casino in their area because of its economic benefits, it stands to reason that Americans' comfort level with legal, state-sanctioned gaming knows few limits.[65]

Tribal Government Gaming as Public Policy

In the 1980s and 1990s, Indian tribes began opening casinos that paid no direct state taxes and were not subject to state regulation. Though this development has been decried as unfair and even un-American, it makes sense when considered within the context of historic white-Indian encounters and relationships. From the initial colonization of the North American mainland by European settlers in the seventeenth century, the new arrivals systematically pushed Native Americans off their lands. Throughout the nineteenth century, Indians found themselves relocated to progressively more-marginal lands. When Americans found things they wanted from even these lands, such as gold in the Black Hills of South Dakota, they often violated treaties to get them.

With the passage of the Dawes Severalty Act in 1877, the U.S. government committed itself to the deconstruction of tribal governments and traditional identities. Laboring under the assumption that "Indianness" held Native Americans back from advancing to a middle-class Protestant lifestyle, reformers actively attempted to suppress all traces of traditional culture and language. The act also dissolved tribal governments as legal, landowning entities, allotting lands to be held in trust for Indians as individual landowners and selling the remainder on the open market. This did little to help Indians "become white," but it did disrupt the continuity of tribal government and culture. At the turn of the century, Indian landholdings had shrunk to a fraction of their former size.

By the 1930s it was clear that such policies had not helped Indians assimilate into white American life or achieve material success. Under John Collier, who became commissioner of the Bureau of Indian Affairs in 1933, the "Indian New Deal" attempted to strengthen tribal identities and reinforce collective ownership of tribal lands and businesses. The Indian Reorganization Act of 1934 scrapped the allotment system, renewed collective land ownership, provided for acquisition of tribal lands for reservations, established procedures for self-government, and generally sought to renew communal life.

But these efforts did little to improve the lives of Indians. In the early 1970s, when state deficits across the Northeast dictated a turn to lotteries and the sustained depression of Atlantic City began to drive that city toward considering casino legalization, the national plight of American Indians was even more serious. Native Americans had an average income 75 percent less than the national average, with a 40 percent unemployment rate, and they suffered infant mortality rates far in excess of the national average. Nor was there much hope for the future. Half of all Native American students did not finish high school, and Indian teenagers had a suicide rate about one hundred times greater than that of white youths.[66] Around this time, the federal government renewed its commitment to encouraging self-determination and self-sufficiency—political, cultural, and economic—among Indian tribes.

Half a century of well-meaning reforms had left Native Americans with little more than sovereignty and reservation lands. But in the late 1970s tribes began using these two assets, virtually the only ones left them, to their advantage by offering bingo jackpots that exceeded those mandated by state law. As sovereign political entities, tribes argued, they had no responsibility to adhere to the civil laws of the state where they were. Thus, if gambling was permitted in a state, an Indian tribe could offer that form of gambling without any regulation or restriction being imposed by the state.

The Indian tribes believed they had the right to offer gambling, but their non-Indian competitors tended to disagree. Questions over the legitimacy of Indian gaming ended up in the courts, though Congress later set the legislative foundation for today's Indian gaming industry, and the Bureau of Indian Affairs and other arms of the executive branch have made decisions to facilitate the development of Indian gaming. Thus, Indian gaming has the imprimatur of each of the three branches of the federal government.[67] As a solution to endemic underdevelopment on tribal lands, gaming can reasonably be said to be the public policy of the federal government.

Executive toleration and encouragement of Indian gaming began in 1924 when the Bureau of Indian Affairs adopted tribal gaming laws as federal laws. Since no federal statute gave states jurisdiction over gaming on Indian lands, and no federal statute comprehensively addressed the subject, the uneasy authority over Indian gaming remained in the hands of the executive branch.[68] By the 1980s the development of high-stakes bingo on Indian reservations provided a ready tool for the realization of President Reagan's stated Indian policy to reduce the dependence of tribes on federal funds and to encourage private development.[69] As a result, the Department of the Interior approved tribal ordinances that established and regulated gaming activities and financed the development of bingo operations through both grants and insured loans under the Indian Finance Act. In addition, the Departments of Housing and Urban Development and Health and Human Services provided financial assistance to tribal gaming enterprises. At least three executive bodies, then, put the federal government in the business of financing gaming operations on Native American lands. Lest anyone protest the propriety of the U.S. government's bankrolling of start-up bingo operations, Congress noted as it considered legislation on the topic that the tribes were only "doing what many state governments are doing, using gaming as a means of generating revenues to provide governmental services."[70]

Those already in the gaming business expressed strong misgivings about their new competitors. The first legal challenge to Indian gaming came from

Florida, where in 1978 Seminole bingo operators in South Florida waived the state jackpot limits on their bingo. They thus undercut the trade of other charity bingo halls, which predictably turned to the authorities for relief. Though the jackpots offered clearly violated the laws of Florida, in *Seminole Tribe of Florida v. Butterworth*, a federal court of appeals ruled that games permitted elsewhere by states could be allowed without limits on reservations. Thus, unless states banned gaming entirely, they had no power to close gaming halls on Indian reservations.[71]

The *Seminole* decision provided an important legal precedent but did not go to the Supreme Court, thus leaving open the possibility that another challenge to Indian gaming, taken to the nation's highest court, could quash the legality of Indian gaming. Soon, *State of California v. The Cabazon Band of Mission Indians* provided such a test case. The Supreme Court would ultimately rule on this case, thus settling any doubts about the status of Indian gaming. In the late 1970s the Cabazon band had twenty-five enrolled members on its reservation near Indio, California, in the San Joaquin Valley, near Palm Springs. In October 1980 the band opened the Desert Oasis Casino, a poker parlor, on its reservation, under the theory that since card rooms were legal in California the tribe was free to open its own card room. Since the city of Indio had rejected a referendum on card rooms, though, municipal authorities believed that they had the right to shut down the Cabazon operation, and their attempts to do so triggered a legal battle that ultimately went before the Supreme Court.[72]

The Ninth U.S. Circuit Court of Appeals ruled that the reservation was not in Indio, so it could have a poker room even if Indio didn't permit it, but this did not end the legal challenges. Riverside County then sued the tribe, and the case once again went before the Ninth Circuit, which ruled in early 1986 that the county had no right to interfere with the tribe's business, which included the card room. Attorneys argued the case to the Supreme Court, whose decision was not subject to appeal, thus giving both sides in *California v. Cabazon*—and those with much to gain or lose in the debate over Indian gaming throughout the nation—the test case they wanted.

On February 25, 1987, the Supreme Court ruled on the *Cabazon* case, deciding that since both poker rooms and bingo were legal in California, neither cities, nor counties, nor the state could interfere with tribal gaming.[73] Tellingly, the Supreme Court ruled that in light of the numerous state-sanctioned gambling operations in the state, California regulated, rather than prohibited, gambling. This decision was stronger than the *Seminole* decision and made it clear that the Supreme Court favored the right of Indians to conduct gambling operations on reservation land. With the *Cabazon* decision, the Court affirmed the legality of tribal gaming operations, going so far as to say that as a major source of employment and revenue, tribal gaming was consonant with the goals of the federal government to inculcate sovereignty and self-determination on tribal lands. Justice Byron White's majority decision boldly stated, "The Tribes' interests obviously parallel the federal interests," in offering high-stakes bingo.[74] Throughout his decision, Justice White cited efforts by the Bureau of Indian Affairs and the Department of Housing and Urban Development to assist tribes in developing gaming operations. Clearly gaming was no longer a social menace but a force for social progress.

With the question of tribal casinos now out of state hands, state governors urged Congress to create a framework that might constrain untrammeled casino development, and Congress moved to regulate Indian gaming with 1988's Indian Gaming Regulatory Act. This legislation established the three-member National Indian Gaming Commission and declared that casino gaming was to be regulated under rules established by compacts between state governments and individual tribes. The act delineated three classes of gaming. Class I gaming included low-stakes games played among tribal members and was to be regulated only by tribes. Class II gaming included bingo and similar games as well as non-bank card games such as poker, where players bet against each other rather than the house. Class II gaming was initially to be regulated by the commission, but successful operations could eventually apply for self-regulation.[75]

Casino gaming, the most profitable form of gambling, was subsumed under Class II gaming. For tribes to conduct Class III gaming, according to the IGRA, they must enter a compact with their states. Such a compact would specify the exact nature of the games to be allowed on the reservation and provide for the regulation of the gaming. Tribes were free to contract non-Indian companies to manage reservation facilities, though limits were placed on the share of revenue that this outside company could receive. States were given no power to tax Indian gaming and thus no effective power to regulate it. Thus, many Indian tribes were free to use their marginal lands and self-government for economic development in a way that few could have foreseen before the 1980s.

Congress passed the IGRA to balance the interests of tribes and those of the "gaming public," principally to guard against infiltration by organized crime into Indian gaming operations.[76] In its preamble to the IGRA, Congress found that federal Indian policy had as a principal goal the promotion of "tribal economic development, tribal self-sufficiency, and strong tribal government." With an "exclusive right" to regulate gaming on Indian lands when not prohibited by federal law or state criminal law, tribes were free to use gaming to pursue these ends. Indeed, the avowed purpose of the act was to "provide a statutory basis for the operation of gaming by Indian tribes as a means of promoting tribal economic development, self-sufficiency, and strong tribal government."[77] With the IGRA, Congress gave its blessing to the use of gaming for economic development as a public policy of the U.S. government.

Just as some states turned toward the commercial casino industry for casino development and revenues, others negotiated with the tribes. Connecticut, in fact, flirted with casino mogul Steve Wynn's proposal to build a Las Vegas–style casino resort in that state before approving compacts with the Mashantucket Pequots and later the Mohegans to allow slot machines in their casinos. In the final agreement, tribes guaranteed the state $80 million or 25 percent of their slot revenue annually, whichever was greater.[78] Connecticut was happy to share the bounty of Class III gaming; in the ten years since it began receiving one-quarter of the Pequots' Foxwoods casino's slot revenues, the state received more than $1.7 billion from Foxwoods alone.[79] The state's two Indian casinos produced about $100 million more for the Division of Special Revenue than the state lottery did.[80] Such revenue-sharing deals necessarily took the form of compacts between sovereign political entities, but they emerged from the same political and economic realities that pushed other states into the casino industry.

In the decade after the Seminoles opened the door to high-stakes bingo, Indian bingo became a cottage industry; by 1988 Congress estimated that more than a hundred bingo games generated more than $100 million in annual revenue.[81] But with the signing of IGRA, Indian gaming exploded across the United States as states, eager to reap revenue from tribal gaming, raced to ink compacts. By 2002, 221 tribes were operating 348 facilities in thirty states.[82] In that year Indian gaming operations in the United States produced revenue of nearly $15 billion, more than three times that of the Las Vegas Strip. This growth was not evenly distributed: the 41 largest operations produced about 65 percent of all revenue, while the 200 smallest accounted for 10 percent of revenue.[83] Connecticut's Mohegan Sun and Pequot Foxwoods casinos accounted for more than $2 billion of Indian casino revenue in 2003.

Indian gaming had a positive impact on Native Americans, who a scant twenty years earlier were possibly the most economically disadvantaged group in America, and even on the U.S. economy. Indian casinos directly paid $7 billion in wages to nearly 230,000 employees in 2002. The combined direct, indirect, and induced economic impact of Indian gaming on the economy was stunning: It created nearly $39 billion in sales, about $15.5 billion in wages, and nearly half a million jobs.[84] Although the economy as a whole struggled in that year, Indian gaming emerged as a vibrant growth industry, vindicating those who had embraced it as an engine of economic development and self-sufficiency for tribal governments.[85]

Fifteen years after becoming the espoused public policy of the federal government vis-à-vis tribal development, Indian casinos can be found throughout the United States, from Connecticut and New York to Florida, from Michigan and Wisconsin to New Mexico and California. As a fruit of its success, tribal gaming has generated envy and denunciation of "casino Indians." An unbelievably biased 2002 cover story in *Time* magazine summarized the major points of casino opponents by stressing the uneven distribution of casino revenue and the "fraud, corruption and intimidation" that has reportedly accompanied the development of the industry.[86] A measure of the enduring gains made by the tribes, though, is the fact that the California Nations Indian Gaming Association used its Web site to issue a retaliatory press release that contained as fine a summary of the progress of the previous years as can be written:

> Gaming has enabled tribes to become an economic force, contributing to the prosperity of those on Indian lands and surrounding communities. It has allowed tribal governments to be a partner in U.S. commerce and industry. It has given Native Americans a voice in national and state politics. It has restored to American Indians a sense of pride and self-respect. It is helping Indians recapture their past, preserve their culture and insure their future.[87]

Indian gaming has become an important part of tribal identity and an inextricable part of the American legal, political, and cultural landscape. It is yet another manifestation of the larger political/economic/cultural web of gaming that Americans have woven around themselves in the past thirty years.

Why Not Sports Betting?

During the midcentury crest of anti-gaming sentiment, legal sportsbooks existed in only one state, Nevada, and even there they barely survived the anxious 1950s. The 1951 federal law that forced all bookmakers to pay an annual $50 excise tax and a ruinous 10 percent tax on the gross handle, or total amount bet, drove many illegal bookmakers out of the public eye and underground, where they continued to thrive, but it throttled the legal Nevada betting parlors that graced most of the major casinos.[88] Since these betting rooms operated on a profit margin of about 5 percent of the gross handle, they would in effect be paying the federal government for the privilege of running an inherently unprofitable business. The law didn't do much to slow the proliferation of illegal bookmakers (one source estimated that by 1960 there were 300,000 of them at work nationwide), but it drove Nevada casinos out of the sports betting business.[89]

A handful of "turf clubs," small, poorly capitalized, sawdust-and-peanuts establishments, popped up in Las Vegas to take bets, but they often skirted the law to survive the 10 percent tax burden. Recording a $500 bet as a $5 one, for example, allowed these clubs to avoid most of the tax, and taking bets from known customers completely "off the books" removed any evidence that such bets had taken place.[90] When, in 1974, Nevada senator Howard Cannon succeeded in passing legislation that lowered the gross tax on betting to a manageable 2 percent, however, casinos stepped back into the sports betting world. The race and sports books of first the Union Plaza and then the Stardust pioneered, giving sports bettors comfortable, even airy places to bet, with large-screen televisions broadcasting sports events. By the late 1980s the turf clubs had been driven out of business, and every casino resort worth its salt had its own sportsbook.[91] Las Vegas–based oddsmakers set the "line" or point spread for college and professional games, and although Nevada sportsbooks could not accept bets from outside the state, they emerged as the most visible symbol of the national sports betting mania.

The success of legal casino gaming in Nevada inspired New Jersey to roll the dice on Atlantic City, and New Hampshire's lottery experiment began a wave in legal gaming that swept through most of the United States. Sports betting increased in popularity throughout America in the 1970s, so intelligent observers might have assumed that it would soon become legal throughout the nation. But because of structural differences between sports gambling and other forms of gambling, this did not happen.

Proponents of legal sports betting did not fail for lack of effort. The New York legislature approved off-track betting (OTB) for horse racing in 1970. Even before setting up betting offices, the chairman of the New York City Off-Track Betting Corporation suggested that legislators pass additional laws to allow OTB to handle sports betting as well. Howard Samuels contended that wagers on sports made up 80 percent of New York's $1.5 billion a year illegal bookmaking market. Though the legislation he advocated would have required a constitutional amendment, Samuels argued that since France and England had successfully adopted legal sports betting, there was no compelling reason why New York could not do so.[92]

But seven years later, the legislature had still not acted, and the window of opportunity for legalizing sports betting was closing, for although sports betting seemed a sensible enough proposition to OTB chairman Samuels, political and structural exigencies combined to collapse hopes for legal sports betting. Speaking before the Commission on the Review of the National Policy Toward Gambling, Major League Baseball commissioner Bowie Kuhn and National Football League commissioner Pete Rozelle insisted that legalizing sports betting would jeopardize the integrity of professional sports. Both professional and collegiate sports leagues offered unstinting opposition to legal betting, despite the fact that they directly profited from sports betting.[93] This opposition gave the anti-legalization side potent political allies, but it does not completely explain the fundamental failure of legal sports betting.

The best explanation is rooted in the very nature of the business and the steep competitive disadvantages any legal system would face. Though bookmakers strive to keep a balanced book by evenly dividing bets on any given contest, in practice this was easier said than done. Hometown favorites usually attracted such high levels of play that a bookmaker often ended up having an unbalanced book, which meant that he stood to lose if the favored team won. Illegal bookmakers, of course, mitigated this problem by placing layoff bets with larger bookmakers. But New York's legal OTB could hardly buy this kind of insurance.

One proposal for legalizing sports betting went so far as to suggest that the government could successfully get revenue from sports bets and avoid the risk of layoff betting by giving organized crime a major role in the system. Donald R. Cressey, a law professor and expert on organized crime, proposed during the Nixon administration that Cosa Nostra (as he styled organized crime) be allowed to keep some profit from bookmaking in exchange for its withdrawal from political corruption and the infiltration of legitimate business. "This state of affairs," he wrote, "could be achieved by legalizing free enterprise bet taking shops while giving Cosa Nostra, not the government, a monopoly on the lay-off system needed by the owners of these shops."[94] On its face, this proposal seems flatly ridiculous, but at a time when the United States was attempting to negotiate a peace settlement in Vietnam and was facing civil unrest at home, it may not have seemed so outlandish. State governments, however, did not begin negotiations along these lines. They ruled out this possibility for legal sports betting and searched for other solutions.

Horse racing used a pari-mutuel odds system that guaranteed a profit to the bookmaker no matter the outcome of the contest, but point-spread betting, the most popular form of sports betting, could not be forced into this system. Its inherent unpredictability obviated a state-run sports betting operation. Illegal bookmakers granted extensive lines of credit to players; that the state could not do so further diminished its attractiveness as a bookmaker, as did the fact that, unlike patrons of illegal bookies, winners at a state-run betting facility would have to pay income tax on their jackpots. Any state-regulated betting system, even if it assigned the risk of operations to private operators, would assume liabilities, as it still could not place layoff bets and it would still require winners to pay income taxes. Even the most sanguine supporters of legal betting admitted that illegal operations had insurmountable advantages over contemplated legal ones. Though legalizing sports betting would not end illegal gambling, "at least the state would get some of the fun out of the fun of betting on people," as a New York Times writer editorialized in 1977.[95]

Yet even the modest ambition that the state capture a fragment of the sports betting market proved too much for other regimes of legal gaming. Nevada's casino sportsbooks, after the 1970s, had the luxury of serving as side dishes in the buffet of gambling offerings; they had only to break even and at worst could be operated at a loss, as the fiscal vitality of the casino itself was rarely tied to the performance of the sportsbook.

Illegal sports betting, though popular, operated on a narrow profit margin. In 1972, the Fund for New York City estimated that whereas illegal numbers games kept nearly 50 percent of their proceeds to pay costs, protection, and profits, sports betting retained only 4.5 percent. The fund's report therefore recommended against the state operating or licensing legal bookmaking, as there was "little prospect" that it could be operated on such a low profit margin.[96] Compared to lucrative lotteries, legal sports betting would be small potatoes. Any attempt to license and tax stand-alone sports betting operations, therefore, would have to somehow allow the government to eke out a meaningful share of revenue on this already paltry revenue and was seemingly doomed to failure.

Because of the single glaring fact that illegal gaming could run profitably on a lower margin than legal gaming, and the risk inherent in a state-licensed sports betting scheme, the few attempts to offer state-sanctioned sports betting ending unhappily for all involved. Montana adopted a minimalist strategy in the 1970s, permitting anyone who wished to do so to operate legal betting pools; all money bet had to be paid out to the bettors, and the state collected no license fees or taxation.[97] In 1989 Montanans voted to allow limited sports pools, as well as fantasy sports leagues, in bars already licensed to have video gambling machines. Legal sports betting was therefore an adjunct to existing gambling at best. The state still prohibited full-blown sports betting, and its authorities continued to vigorously prosecute illegal sports betting operations.[98]

In the fall of 1976 Delaware's attempt to launch a football lottery ended as such a spectacular failure that it discouraged any further experiments for more than a decade. The lottery initially offered players the choice of two games, Football Bonus or Touchdown. Touchdown required players to mark point spreads as well as winning teams, though neither game featured straight-up betting on single games—players had to correctly pick at least four winning teams to win. Winners were not paid guaranteed prizes, but out of a pari-mutuel pool. With three weeks left in the season, Touchdown II, which offered fixed point spreads and payoffs, replaced Touchdown, but though it might have competed with illegal betting, it still required players to successfully pick at least three winners.

Because of the arcane bet structure, less than favorable odds, and the fact that players who won more than $600 had to pay income taxes, the game failed to attract a substantial player base. The state had estimated that the football lottery would yield $6 million; it actually produced only $725,000 in revenue. This was not nearly enough to cover operating costs, and the lottery finished the season $371,000 in the red.[99] Although the state won a legal victory against the National Football League in August 1977 that would have allowed it to continue the football lottery, it hardly had a sterling operational record. With complicated rules and few advantages, the lottery could not offer a product to legitimately compete with illegal sports betting.[100] Though

Delaware had begun the effort with high hopes, the state abandoned the football lottery.

Despite this failure, it was clear that many otherwise law-abiding Americans enjoyed betting on sports, even when it was illegal. The possibility of legal sports betting continued to entrance states like Oregon, which in 1989 began an ultimately unsuccessful experiment with football and basketball lotteries. "Sports Action" tickets allowed Oregonians to bet up to $20 for or against the spread for between three and fourteen events. While smaller bets paid guaranteed odds, the longer-shot, higher-paying bets paid out of a pari-mutuel pool, thus guaranteeing that the state lottery could not lose.[101] But this system still required players to correctly pick a number of games for a single payoff, and it eventually folded, but not before gaming industry pundits predicted that the Oregon sports lottery would pave the way for a new expansion of legal sports betting. These predictions became moot when, in 1991, the U.S. Congress moved to prevent the spread of legal sports betting. In that year it passed a blanket ban on legalizing sports betting, carving out exceptions for Nevada, Oregon, and Delaware but otherwise slamming the door on even the possibility of new attempts to find a workable solution.

Before Congress, the most fervent opponents of legal gaming continued to be the representatives of professional and amateur sports. Sports leagues gave what seemed to be straightforward reasons why they opposed sports betting. Red Auerbach, president of the storied Boston Celtics, represented the National Basketball Association before the House Judiciary Subcommittee on Economic and Commercial Law and stated quite plainly, "Gambling and sports do not mix."[102] Auerbach conjured up the specter of sports fans who were more interested in the point spread than the outcome of the game and implied that the spread of legal sports betting would contaminate the very integrity of the game.

One can imagine the political problems of the Massachusetts legislator who presumed to know more about sports than the great Red Auerbach at the height of the 1980s Celtics dynasty and voted against the leagues' proposal to halt the spread of legal sports betting. Herein was the dilemma many members of Congress faced: The sports leagues were politically potent and, as advertisers had learned, sports figures commanded respect and even reverence among Americans of all backgrounds. Both the House and the Senate moved quickly to pass legislation that barred gambling on sporting events. Oregon, Nevada, and Delaware, which already had or were considering sports betting, either through the lottery or in casinos, were exempted from the ban by a grandfather clause.[103] Now sure that no more "cash-starved states" would profit from the public's desire to wager on sports, the leagues claimed victory for integrity and honest sports everywhere.

 Perhaps the leagues were merely obtuse. They may have been positively disingenuous. College and professional sports profit from betting, illegal and legal. Though Auerbach bemoaned the possibility of fans with more interest in their team beating the spread than winning the game, betting on the outcome of a game gives millions of Americans an added incentive to watch televised games. When the ultimate outcome of the game is secure but the point spread is still in doubt, these bettors continue watching avidly. As sports leagues get a major portion of their revenues from television contracts, this is no small point. The higher the ratings, the more a league can garner for its television rights. Televised sports are big business. The NCAA received $6 billion for the rights to their games in 2000.[104] If anything, it would seem that, as a purely business decision, sports leagues would overtly encourage the proliferation of sports betting. Some allege that in fact they already do this, by mandating that teams disclose all injuries to the media, making it easier for handicappers to gauge team performance.

 Despite the fact that legal sports betting is only a pittance compared to the illegal market—estimates range from 1 to 5 percent—league representatives insisted in 1991, and continue to insist, that legal sports betting is bad for sports. In 2000 Arizona senator John McCain introduced legislation that would have banned betting on college sports in Nevada casinos. Seemingly a violation of that state's right to regulate gaming, the bill was proposed as a way of stemming gambling on college campuses. While some in the Senate believed that Nevada's sportsbooks' taking bets on college games fed a culture of betting that threatened to corrupt a generation of students and athletes, Nevada senator Harry Reid threw the problem back in the face of the NCAA, charging that the bill was merely an attempt to divert attention from its incompetence in stopping campus betting.[105] Despite the protests of Nevada's senators, the bill passed the Senate Commerce Committee in April 2000.[106] Nevada's congressional delegation was able to scuttle the legislation during the 2003 legislative session, though it continued to rear its head in new bills.[107]

 Throughout the NCAA's drive to make the world safe for college athletics untainted by legal wagering, it continued to tacitly encourage illegal betting. The sanctioned hype for the annual NCAA championship tournament, better known as "March Madness," actively abetted wagering activity by providing printable "brackets" on the NCAA tournament Web site. Though the site cautioned that the brackets were "for entertainment only," a Reno Gazette-Journal editorial took the organization to task, noting that the NCAA did little to even discourage the millions of office pool bets made on the tournament, each of them illegal, while it attacked Nevada's legal sportsbooks.[108] The paradox of the NCAA's decrying legal wagering while winking at an avalanche of illegal betting captures the position it shares with the professional sports leagues—while they refuse to condone legal sports betting, they profit immensely from illegal wagering.

The flourishing of illegal sports betting gives the lie to one argument in favor of legal gaming: that it will trump competing illegal forms. While it may be true that state-run lotteries have reduced the scale of illegal numbers games, one form of gaming simply doesn't substitute for another. Bettors looking to get action down on football are not likely to buy lottery tickets or take up blackjack at the local Indian casino instead. The spread of legal gaming in America is impressive, but it represents only the tip of the larger iceberg of Americans' apparently unquenchable desire to bet.

6 Point, Click, and Bet

The birth of an industry in the new world of e-commerce. Congressional efforts to rein in Net wagering ignore international experiences in legalization, regulation, and taxation of Internet gaming.

The advent of the internet has brought gaming into every household that possesses a computer and a modem. Yet despite the web's growing popularity, many questions remain regarding the legality of internet gaming. In the absence of a comprehensive legislative solution, courts have been forced to provide answers on a case-by-case basis using pre-internet precedents.
— Jarvis et al., *Gaming Law*

IN THE MID-1990S, the sudden popularity of the Internet appeared to be an overnight phenomenon, but it had in fact been quietly evolving for decades. The technology to link computer systems has existed since 1965, when computer scientist Larry Roberts demonstrated the feasibility of long-distance connections between computers. In 1969, as Americans walked on the moon, computer scientists took a small step into cyberspace when they created the ARPAnet under the auspices of the Advanced Research Projects Agency, a Department of Defense division that sponsored open-ended research.[1] By the early 1990s, the development of the World Wide Web hypertext data system, which allows users to access tremendous amounts of information in a flexible and convenient way, made it clear that the Internet could make knowledge more accessible and facilitate communication.

Beginning in 1993 and intensifying through 1995, governments, businesses, and media outlets raced to get themselves online, acquiring domain names and setting up Web sites. Many entrepreneurs and investors believed that this new technology was both a promise and a threat. A 1996 report on the prospects of online commerce described the Internet as an unstoppable new force similar to "the railroads of days gone by" and cautioned that those who failed to embrace the challenges of this new environment "may not get out alive."[2]

Into this bold new frontier stepped several technical geniuses and determined visionaries, each with a desire to harness the inexorable new force and, like railroad barons of the late nineteenth century, grow rich. Some developed business plans and pitched ideas for selling computers, books, and hardware online. Others jumped in with both feet. The two most immediately proliferating online industries, pornography and gaming, share a reputation as "vices," and their wild popularity probably says something about the United States in the late twentieth century. Unsurprisingly, the ambivalent prohibitions against gaming that provided only perfunctory control over sports betting operations were completely ineffective at dissuading entrepreneurs from opening online gaming sites or discouraging Americans from gambling at them.

"If You Can Use a Mouse, You Can Place a Wager"

From the earliest days of the Internet, its users likened it to a frontier. Indeed, one of the first Internet advocacy groups, the Electronic Frontier Foundation, embraced the ideology of cyberspace as a new Wild West; its mission statement claimed that the group was established to "help civilize" this new frontier.[3] Others likened the possibilities of Internet commerce to the gold rush. There are several parallels between the prospecting argonauts of the mid-nineteenth century and the dot-com pioneers of the late twentieth century: In both cases, relatively open access (placer mining and open-source exchange of ideas) quickly lost out to control by large business enterprises (banks and railroads and the Microsoft Corporation). It may be a quirk of history, but it happened that gaming was a driving force on both frontiers.

American businesses moved online haltingly, using the Internet as a place to post promotional material and other information rather than as a new way to sell their products and services. Concerns over encryption and security kept many companies from making the jump to cyberspace, but by 1997 true online commerce, in which buyers purchased from sellers with a single mouse click, was clearly the wave of the future. Within a few years, customers felt at home shopping over the Internet. Amazon.com, for example, started allowing customers to buy books online in 1995. Founded by Jeff Bezos, a former New York hedge-fund manager, the site became a paragon for online commerce by taking a traditional activity—buying books—to its logical online extension.[4] Amazon.com did more than let customers place purchase orders over the Internet; it allowed them to read and post reviews of books and other merchandise, create their own lists of recommended products and media, and generate personal "wish lists" from which others could buy products for them. Other online shopping sites soon followed its lead, offering everything from jewelry to automobiles to pets, and traditional retailers like bookseller Barnes and Noble and category-killer chain Wal-Mart brought themselves online as well.[5]

As in the nineteenth-century American West, gamblers proliferated on the lightly policed online frontier. The first Web sites permitting online play for visitors appeared in 1995. Initial "beta" sites offered only "free" games on which visitors played with imaginary money, but observers were already predicting that the nascent online gaming industry could surpass annual revenues of $10 billion, about the take of the Las Vegas Strip and Atlantic City combined.[6] Soon, sites began allowing bettors to play for prizes, and some began taking actual bets, using credit cards and wire transfers to move money.

At almost exactly the same time that betting over the World Wide Web became feasible, the tiny island nation of Antigua created a free-trade zone in which cross-border betting operators could take bets without paying corporate taxes, though they did pay licensing fees and were subject to regulation.[7] Antiguan policy had long been to lure offshore businesses, including ship registry and financial institutions. To further shore up its economy, Antigua wooed betting operations like any other business.[8] Some bookmakers took advantage of Antigua's betting haven and began taking bets by telephone there. These bookmakers insisted that they were licensed by Antigua and therefore completely legitimate. Sports publications and radio stations accepted their advertisements.[9] Many began to also advertise on the Internet, and by 1995 some had made the leap and gone "virtual."

At first, existing offshore gambling operations just posted static odds and directed potential bettors to a 1-800 number where they placed their actual wagers.[10] As simple outgrowths of existing offshore sportsbooks, they were not primarily Internet businesses. Gaming suppliers in the United States took similar steps. Capital OTB, a New York off-track betting corporation, announced its plans to go online in late 1996. By that time it was already providing a "virtual tote board" on its Web site, possibly a violation of the Wire Act's prohibition on transmitting information assisting in the placement of bets.[11] By 1999 New York OTB's system of remote access and account wagering was well established; bettors could open an account with the New York Racing Association and make bets against that account using a home telephone. To help them place bets, they could use the betting information on the NYRA Web site and listen to (and eventually watch) races live via streaming audio (later video).[12] Technically not online gambling because players actually placed their bets over the phone, this system nevertheless used the World Wide Web to transmit wagering information.

Other domestic American gambling operations went online as well. In 1997 the Coeur d'Alene Indian tribe began offering digital lottery games as an electronic adjunct to its existing bingo hall. Since the Indian Gaming Regulatory Act had given tribes significant latitude in offering Class II games such as lotteries, the tribe argued that its online lottery was completely legal.[13] The attorney general of Wisconsin disagreed and promptly filed suit against the tribe, spurring a court battle.[14]

The first online sportsbooks used the Web like New York's OTB did—primarily as a way to transmit odds information. But with the proliferation of online commerce, it was only a matter of time before an enterprising entrepreneur took the next logical step: the creation of a true Web betting site. Such pioneers soon appeared. Jay Cohen and Steve Schillinger, a pair of traders on San Francisco's Pacific Stock Exchange, brought the World Sports Exchange (http://www.wsex.com) online in early 1997 as a full-service Internet sportsbook, updating odds and game information in real time and allowing bettors to use the Internet to actually place wagers. The venture grew out of Schillinger's office pools, which allowed fellow traders at the Pacific Exchange to trade sports futures and bet on other events, like the O. J. Simpson trial. Cohen convinced Schillinger that he should stake a claim in the wide-open Internet gaming market by taking his office pool online.[15]

The WSE partners, of whom only Schillinger had any experience with sports betting, consulted the financial filings of Sports International, a publicly traded offshore telephone wagering company that was in the process of supplementing its phone wagering with a Web site. Cohen, intrigued by the possibilities of an online sports futures trading business, persuaded other employees of Group One, the trading firm for which he worked, to help him fund a start-up. In a year when Internet start-ups made their share of millionaires, this was hardly unusual. Cohen and Schillinger retained accounting and consulting firm KPMG Peat Marwick to help set up the company, steer it through licensure, and give tax advice. As setting up an online sports betting operation was clearly illegal in the United States, Cohen researched nations that had licensed Internet sports betting and settled on Antigua because it had the "most stringent regulations" of any of the jurisdictions then permitting wagering businesses.[16]

Cohen chose to model the new company on an existing wagering busi-

ness, New York's Capital OTB, which accepted telephone wagers from established customers with accounts. The World Sports Exchange offered few
bells and whistles, but as was soon revealed by its booming business, customers without broadband or cable Internet connections appreciated that
its low bandwidth requirements meant quick load times.[17] In addition to offering fully interactive, completely online straight sports betting (with one
caveat—winners were mailed hand-cut checks when they chose to cash out
their winnings), the WSE allowed bettors to purchase futures contracts for
sports events, down to specific golf shots and baseball pitches, and individual players.[18] Garnering laudatory write-ups in the *Wall Street Journal*, the *New
York Times*, and other mainstream news outlets, Cohen and Schillinger found
themselves with an exploding client base.[19] They were no longer stock traders taking side action on the Academy Awards—they were the leaders of an
online revolution that promised to do for sports betting what Amazon.com
had done for retail.

Other operators were far from shy about accepting bets online. By the
time Denver upset Green Bay in the 1998 Super Bowl, about twenty-five legal, licensed sportsbooks were flourishing in Antigua, providing license
fees to the government as well as more than two hundred jobs to local
residents.[20] Gaming thus provided a boon to a sunny, remote, and under-
developed place—neatly paralleling the history of Las Vegas, which in less
than a generation transformed itself from a minor desert railroad town to an
international gaming and tourism destination, thanks to its casino resorts.

Las Vegas was not the only historical precedent for Antigua. Since at least
the eighteenth century, jurisdictions with few other natural resources or economic development have used both gaming and tourism to attract invest-
ment, jobs, and revenue in Europe.[21] In the United States, the Constitution
allowed gaming legalization to devolve to the states, and many states used
various forms of gaming to create jobs and revenue. In the 1990s states raced
to create commercial casino industries in hopes of spurring the development of gaming-related tourism that could siphon income from surrounding states. Antiguans embraced what they have termed "cross-border" gaming for exactly the same reasons—jobs and revenue. In doing so, they have
imported not only the entrepreneurial verve of the United States; Antiguans
have acted in concert with a generation of American lawmakers and voters
who have consistently chosen to legalize gaming as an antidote to higher
taxes and unemployment.

Several other nations joined Antigua in seeking to capitalize on the Internet gaming gold rush. The government of Liechtenstein began offering a public lottery online in 1995.[22] Other Caribbean nations offered havens to online sportsbooks, as did Costa Rica. Regulatory regimes varied wildly: Antigua insisted that all operators pay license fees and submit to background investigations, whereas Costa Rica vaguely told prospective operators that they would have to "reach a settlement" with local officials.[23] To the government of Antigua, and to the men and women who paid their license fees and began operating there, online bookmakers were not at all virtual cowboys, moving their faro layouts one step ahead of the cyber sheriffs. They were, instead, following in the footsteps of previous generations of gaming entrepreneurs who had exploited new technologies and set up shop in newly available jurisdictions.

The gush of favorable write-ups in the business and technology pages, though, was often eclipsed by pessimistic reporting of the bad potential that easy online gambling betokened for some. During the decade of the 1990s, legal gaming proliferated through the United States at an unprecedented rate; perhaps not coincidentally, awareness of problem gambling increased. Experts could not conclusively argue that the expansion of gaming had triggered higher rates of pathological gambling, but they suggested that during the decade pathological gambling rates either stayed constant or increased.[24] News reports seldom provided actual statistics on the relative rates of addiction for traditional and online gaming or supplied the actual numbers of online gamblers who had developed gambling problems. Instead, using anecdotal horror stories, they painted a lurid picture of corrupted Web surfers.

A 2000 Pew Internet and American Life study estimated that in that year about one million Americans gambled online every day.[25] Drawn in by the convenience and anonymity of the online gaming experience, an undetermined number of this one million found themselves unable to control their wagering, betting and losing far more than they could afford. When describing this aspect of the industry, writers replaced the fresh-faced wunderkinds and bookies on the make of the Internet gaming success stories with victims of online gaming, like a forty-one-year-old architect who, intrigued by a magazine advertisement, began playing blackjack online. After maxing out seven credit cards, he joined a gambling addiction program. To those who would minimize the seriousness of pathological gambling, he offered chilling words, stating that he was more troubled by his gambling addiction than by his Parkinson's disease.[26] For those who could not avoid the temptation to gamble, the reality of a "casino on the desktop" would be an inescapable snare. In the words of economist John Kindt, "People will be trapped. . . . They won't be able to get away."[27]

To those not swayed by compassion for people who could not control their gambling, opponents of Internet wagering played another card—credibility. Even those who played online recognized that not every Web site was trustworthy. "There are a lot of shady operations. . . . They are so deceitful," complained an avid online bettor in a 2001 news story, yet she continued to play.[28] Kindt, an outspoken critic of gaming, summed up the sentiments of those suspicious of the new industry when he decried it as a lose-lose proposition that threatened to "destroy the credibility of the Internet system." At online casinos, Kindt argued, "if you lose, you'll lose, and if you win, you could lose because there's no way to collect from these offshore operations."[29]

When faced with the reality that fly-by-night Net casinos have cheated customers, such an assertion seems sensible. But it confuses the issue by tarring every operator with the brush of deceit. Postal delivery opens up the possibility of mail fraud, and telephone service makes possible fraudulent telemarketing. Yet these activities are not viewed as threatening the credibility of the post office or the telephone or legitimate businesses that use them. Certainly the potential for criminal deception existed on the Internet, but so too did the possibility for regulation and reputability. But since U.S. state governments actively competed with Internet gaming sites for gaming revenue, they instead took the position that the entire system of wagering over the Internet was inherently fraudulent.

National policymakers noted with alarm the illicit possibilities of Internet gaming. The Republican Policy Committee's position paper on online gaming noted that it facilitated the theft of deposited money from accounts and credit card numbers from customers. Disreputable operators could use Internet casinos to bait identity theft schemes. Even if they did not baldly steal customers' money, operators could tamper with casino software to deprive customers of an honest chance (this would not, presumably, be possible in sports wagering). Finally, the remote access and "anonymity" of online wagering, the paper argued, allowed money launderers to deposit money, wager a small amount, then withdraw the remaining funds.[30] Such reasoning ignored the possibilities of documenting every betting transaction (which is not feasible in a terrestrial casino), yet it showed an ingrained distrust of online gaming. As early as 1997, New York attorney general Dennis Vacco warned that fraudulent virtual casinos might "leave a wake of victims" and asked for laws that would let him "smash crooked computer gambling rings."[31]

Just how the attorney general of New York would "smash" a business licensed in Antigua, Australia, or Great Britain was unclear at the time, but most law enforcement authorities agreed that online wagering was bad. When operators found havens in other jurisdictions, locating their entire business offshore, there was little that the police could do. But some online wagering companies were caught flat-footed, with assets and employees in the United States. The World Interactive Gaming Corporation, based in Bohemia, New York, was one such operation. In 1997 Attorney General Vacco, the Federal Trade Commission, and the Securities and Exchange Commission began an investigation that targeted nearly sixty gaming companies, resulting in an FTC complaint and a prosecution against World Interactive Gaming. A judge subsequently upheld the seizure of World Interactive's assets, ruling that the bet took place in New York, where an undercover investigator opened an account, and not Antigua, where the company's computer server resided.[32] American companies could not shield themselves from prosecution by locating only their computers in a country where Internet gaming was legal.

A consensus of legal experts held that while those who profited from online gaming might be subject to prosecution under the Wire Act, those who placed bets with online casinos were not.[33] Most of the states that criminalized Internet gaming ostensibly desired to protect consumers by shutting down unregulated online casinos, asserting that they would never target bettors. But as early as 1996, the National Association of Attorneys General urged the federal government to amend the law to permit the arrest of "gamblers from in front of their computers."[34] Though Congress and the Justice Department balked at this measure, in 2003 the North Dakota attorney general's office investigated the betting of Jeffrey Trauman, a former car salesman and self-described professional gambler. Trauman, who began betting on sports full-time in 2000, reported his income to the Internal Revenue Service and paid taxes on it, blissfully unaware that North Dakota law prohibited placing bets of more than $500. Trauman ultimately pled guilty to a misdemeanor gambling charge, paid a $500 fine, and relocated his family to Kentucky, where he continued his betting career.[35] His conviction, though, established the precedent that states could indeed prosecute Internet bettors.

Still, despite the warnings of law enforcement, many Americans chose to wager online. In 2000 the *New York Times* cited a Pew report that placed the number of Americans who had ever gambled over the Internet at approximately 4.5 million.[36] This hardly means that there are that many serious Internet bettors, though; according to a survey commissioned by the River City Group in 2001, only 28 percent of those who played online did so for real money—most simply played at wagering "for free" at sites that let them simulate casino games without risking money.[37] Whatever the actual number, Americans were clearly gambling via the Internet increasingly in the late 1990s, often winning and losing real money.

A growing number of gaming sites stood ready to compete for the Internet gaming dollar. In 1996 industry observers estimated that there were 40 online gaming sites, of which only 15 accepted wagers. Most were free-play sites waiting to develop software and payment systems that would allow them to handle money.[38] A year later, more than 200 gambling sites could be found, many of which accepted real money, like Antigua-based World Interactive Gaming, which reported accepting bets from as many as 5,000 visitors in a week.[39] In 1999 online gamblers could play for real money at about 650 sites. The number more than doubled, to 1,400, in 2000. By 2002 approximately 1,800 online casinos, lotteries, bingo games, and sportsbooks operated.[40] That number remained fairly static into 2005.

Most online casinos and sportsbooks had similar features, differing only in thematic depth and the probity of the operator. Some had a fancy, graphics-rich splash page introducing visitors to the site, while others preferred a more utilitarian approach, but once inside the site, a visitor would find virtually the same elements. Sports betting sites displayed the most recent odds information and betting lines on upcoming games, while casinos had listings of their games. Other pages listed site rules and regulations, information about the operation, and answers to frequently asked questions; most also had links to information about problem gambling. Many online casinos and betting sites offered visitors the chance to play for free or for money, and nearly all listed promotional offers, such as bonus cash for deposits and referrals, similar to land-based casinos' player loyalty and comp programs. Most important, all online gaming sites gave players directions for depositing money into their accounts, with several options, including credit card, calling card, electronic funds transfer, bank wire, and bank check.

Perhaps the surest sign of the online gaming industry's maturity was the interest shown by land-based casino companies in creating online adjuncts to their existing operations. The British firm Aspinalls, which had been operating casinos since 1962, launched an online casino that was still active as of late 2004. The casino firm outsourced the operation of its Web site to Golden Palace, an established online casino, thus benefiting from its own name recognition and Golden Palace's knowledge of the market.[41] But not all casinos made a seamless transition to cyberspace. Many found that restricting their activities to jurisdictions where online gaming was permitted made the venture unprofitable. Kerzner International, operators of Atlantis, Paradise Island in the Bahamas, launched an online casino, only to close it in 2003. Las Vegas–based Station Casinos had already pulled out of its half-ownership stake in the Kerzner online operation.[42]

MGM Mirage, which ventured online in 2001 with a casino based on the Isle of Man, a British dependency, began with great expectations. To preserve its Nevada gaming license, the company allowed free play for all visitors but restricted money bets to visitors from six countries; the United States was among those excluded. The company was not interested in quick profits; rather, as spokesman Alan Feldman explained, it was interested in "establishing an operational model" that would show the world that online regulation was workable.[43] In June 2003 the company shut down its online casino, citing the unsure legal and political climate in the United States. Still, MGM Mirage chief executive officer Terry Lanni deemed the online experiment a success, as the site demonstrated a successful working model that had checks for jurisdictional control, age verification, and transaction security. In other words, MGM showed that Internet gaming could be run with the same level of scrutiny as land-based gaming. It was now up to the legislators and regulators to draft laws that would permit the industry to flourish. Once the industry was legalized in the United States, MGM Mirage would "participate fully."[44]

Traditional casinos' forays into the online realm might have faltered in the uncertain climate that kept them out of the world's most lucrative online gaming market, the United States, but that they even tried to gain a foothold among virtual casinos is important. Rather than perceiving the online gaming industry as a high-tech short con, major casino operators began viewing it as simply another way of offering their product, casino entertainment. Casino floors had evolved from table games and mechanical slot machines to include linked networks of video slot machines, their payouts determined by random-number generators. Although casino patrons interviewed in 2000 saw worlds of difference between Las Vegas Strip casinos and online ones, others were not so sure. *New York Times* reporter Matt Richtel wrote that the

Strip casino offered "an unparalleled opportunity to sit in the dark in front of a monitor . . . compulsively hitting buttons and pulling levers," much like online gambling.[45] There was less difference than was readily apparent between traditional casinos and virtual ones. That consumers might choose one over the other seemed more a matter of personal preference than public policy.

Congress Ponders Prohibition

But not everyone was enamored of the possibility that Americans could now place sports bets with the simple click of a mouse. Members of the U.S. Congress almost immediately resolved to have that body criminalize Internet betting. Senator Jon Kyl quickly took offense to online gaming, citing its accessibility to children and its "highly addictive" nature.[46] In a Republican Policy Committee position paper, Kyl asserted that Internet gambling was linked to organized crime and "rife with fraud," that it threatened the integrity of amateur and professional sports, and that it was "more dangerous and addictive than regulated gambling," particularly for young people, who could clandestinely "build up thousands of dollars in debt on their parents' credit cards."[47]

Kyl hit the trifecta of anti–Internet gaming sentiment: fraud and crime, pathology, and unrestricted access. Those in charge of issuing licenses for Internet gaming operations in places like Antigua and the Isle of Man may have chafed at Kyl's blanket statement that online wagering was by definition unregulated, corrupt, and riddled with fraud, and some may have chuckled at the notion that cheating at gaming is strictly an online phenomenon—a flood of historical artifacts and documentary evidence provides testimony that gaming, whether conducted by hand, machine, or software, is almost universally subject to cheating.

This position paper offered myriad reasons why the activity was the scourge of the digital age. But, tellingly, it did not mention one of the chief objections to online gaming: that it circumvents the monopoly on gaming granted by states or tribes to licensees and therefore short-circuits the entire system of legalized gaming in the United States, whereby states permit gaming in order to get a slice of the $72 billion or so in annual gross revenue that gambling generates.[48] To mention that point might force opponents of Internet gaming to ask some troubling questions about the differences between traditional and online gaming.

Truth be told, the same charges made against Internet gaming could be made against state-regulated and tribal government gaming operations. There have been corruption scandals associated with casino licenses in Louisiana and Illinois. The New York Racing Association, which oversees the largest racing market in the United States, has been charged by New York attorney general Eliot Spitzer with "a lack of appropriate financial and operational controls and rampant criminal activity."[49] Thousands of compulsive gamblers have brought themselves to ruin at state-regulated gaming facilities. Underage gamblers can just as easily obtain a fake identification and visit a land-based casino as they can swipe a parent's credit card, and controls over access can be lax or stringent in both the real world and cyberspace, depending on the operator.

Opposition to online gaming might just be about preserving state monopolies on gambling. American citizens, in addition to enjoying the thrill of gambling, relied on gaming revenues to keep taxes low, or at least to circumvent new tax increases. Rhode Island, not known to be the home of particularly ardent gamblers or a destination gaming industry of any size, was typical of many states in its creeping dependence on gaming. In 1992 money garnered from gaming revenues made up 1.4 percent of the state's budget, but by 2003 the proportion had increased to 11 percent, and gaming stood as the state's third-largest revenue stream.[50] So it appeared that, in opposing online gaming, states and the federal government were not as concerned with the public health impact of increased gaming as with maintaining their lucrative sources of revenue.

Opponents of Internet gaming outside of the government fell into three discrete categories, which had competing agendas. Casinos, racetracks, and other gaming industries sought to stifle the competition. Religious and social conservatives were appalled at the moral decay that would doubtless follow if every PC could be used as a slot machine. Professional sports leagues saw Internet gaming as a serious threat, since it encouraged betting on games, which the leagues ostensibly opposed. Most commercial gaming interests and those who simply hated all gambling thus opposed online wagering.

Existing gaming industries might have had the most to lose, economically, from the growth of Internet gaming, but many casino operators have evolved from early hostility toward online gaming into cautious proponents. In 1996 Hilton Hotels CEO Stephen Bollenbach spoke for the industry when he proclaimed that online wagering was "not very interesting" and that it was an entirely "different business" from the hospitality offered by casino resorts.[51] American Gaming Association CEO Frank Fahrenkopf stated in 2001 that Internet gaming was not a competitive threat to the American commercial casino industry. Still, as late as that year the industry's lobbying group continued to oppose "unregulated Internet gambling."[52] Subject to strict regulations and sizable tax burdens, commercial casinos instinctively looked askance at new arrivals that potentially could operate without regulation or taxes. Even if they did not fear competition from online casinos, traditional casinos felt that underregulated online casinos might tarnish the solid reputation of casino gaming as a fair recreation. Initially, the commercial casino industry was virtually unanimous in its condemnation of online gambling. Racetracks and lottery interests also opposed online competitors, but they usually did not support bans on Internet gaming unless the measures specifically legalized simulcasting and off-track betting networks.

Gaming businesses may have had self-interest in mind, but they had allies in the fight against Internet casinos in those who opposed Internet gaming because it was a new and insidious form of gambling. There are still elements in American society that remain opposed to any form of gaming, legal or illegal. Faith-based groups like the Christian Coalition and Focus on the Family hold as a matter of principle that "addiction, child abuse, domestic violence, marital dissolution, destruction of families, suicide, crime, exploitation of the poor, government corruption, the demise of local businesses, economic instability and gambling-induced bankruptcies are well-documented injuries that gambling inflicts on people, communities and states."[53] Such groups generally expressed hostility toward the Internet, since it permitted virtually uncontrollable access to a diversity of unfiltered content, including gambling and pornography. The American Family Association went so far as to begin a campaign to end the American Library Association's "chokehold on the library system" because the ALA pledged to oppose blocking any kind of material from library computers, including pornography.[54] For those with certain religious or moral principles, Internet gaming represented a devilish cocktail of temptation.

Even those not known for evincing publicly religious sentiments opposed Internet gaming as a new form of gambling. Consumer advocate Ralph Nader decried the move by Las Vegas casinos toward "family entertainment," complaining that casinos were "more brazen" than tobacco companies in trying to addict children to their product.[55] His disapproval of gaming did not stop at the door of Circus Circus's Adventuredome. Though Nader frequently championed the use of the Internet for consumer protection and civic awareness—he proposed making congressional voting records and government

contracts more easily accessible online—he was among those who supported Jon Kyl's Internet Gambling Prohibition Act.[56] The protection of America's consumers apparently outweighed any jurisdictional or personal liberty
issues that might have argued against a ban on Internet gaming.

Internet gaming also ran afoul of another well-established lobby, the
professional sports leagues. The major American sports leagues, particularly Major League Baseball and the National Football League, had for years
registered official opposition to all forms of sports betting. MLB commissioner Bowie Kuhn testified before the Commission on the Review of the National Policy Toward Gambling in 1975 that professional baseball had long
labored to bring "scrupulously honest and wholesome entertainment for
American families." Though betting on games took place, Kuhn and other
sports commissioners held that to legalize betting would create the suspicion of dishonesty and therefore threaten the integrity of the game itself.[57]
Although they recognized that a significant share of the general public—and
their own athletes—gambled, American professional sports steadfastly opposed any expansion of legal sports betting. Though they did not enunciate
any true position on virtual blackjack or poker, the sports leagues easily extended this animus against betting to online sports wagering. In testifying in
favor of a bill to restrict Internet gaming, a National Football League official
sounded the party line—"we don't want our games or our players used as
gambling bait"—officially extending the league's gambling opposition to
cyberspace.[58] Thus, whether in the name of religious principles or consumer
protection, online wagering attracted a diverse coalition of opponents.

Advocates of the practice were fewer. Internet casino operators themselves obviously supported it, but as quasi-foreign businesses they were in no
position to effectively lobby Congress for regulation instead of prohibition.
Internet service providers voiced the loudest objections to the first round of
anti–Internet gaming legislation, primarily because it would have placed
the burden of enforcement squarely on their shoulders, requiring them to
block gaming sites.[59] Indian tribes with casinos also objected to prohibition
of online gaming, taking the position that tribal governments could effectively regulate Internet casinos.[60] Internet advocacy and privacy rights groups
pointedly remained mum on the issue.

Though the commercial casino industry originally opposed Internet gaming, in 2001 some of the largest casino companies in the nation abruptly
changed course and instead embraced online wagering. By that year, Harrah's
Entertainment, MGM Mirage, and Park Place Entertainment had each es-

tablished online casinos that took no cash, and Terry Lanni, CEO of MGM Mirage, openly stated that his company was looking to "move ahead" onto the Internet with full-scale gaming operations. Nevada's congressional delegation, which had been among the strongest opponents of Internet gaming through 2000, followed suit, expressing reservations toward prohibition and even a willingness to study the possibilities of regulation.[61] With the support of some of the largest casino companies in the world, online gaming had finally found an influential champion.

Gaming was not alone in expanding onto the Internet; most other areas of American life and business also found an online outlet. Many observers drew analogies between the popularity of online gambling and that of online pornography. Both are borderline vices that were once criminalized but have, in the past generation, become thriving industries. Religious and moral groups frequently target pornography as a sign of moral lassitude and societal decay. Family-oriented groups, successful at pressuring some retailers into discontinuing the sale of pornography, were aghast at the sudden availability of indecent material over the Internet to anyone, including children. Many such groups began beating the drums for Congress to take action against Internet indecency, showing a vehemence that far outstripped their opposition to gambling.

Congress obliged the morality police with the Communications Decency Act, signed into law by President Bill Clinton in early 1996. The law criminalized indecent content and the knowing transmission of offensive content to minors. Free speech and individual liberty groups like the American Civil Liberties Union and the Electronic Frontier Foundation, founded to protect the civil liberties of Internet users, immediately began a legal challenge to the law.[62] The Supreme Court declared it unconstitutional in 1997, but in the next year Congress passed the Child Online Protection Act, viewed as the "sequel" to the CDA. Though President Clinton signed it into law, an appeals court quickly struck it down. The Supreme Court upheld the ban but did not rule on the core issues of the case, sending it back to the Third Circuit Court of Appeals, which again ruled the law unconstitutional in 2003.[63]

Bans against online indecency, despite the vehemence with which traditional values coalitions and religious groups supported them, were consistently challenged. Any mention of censorship, even of the most depraved materials, attracted the attention of the well-intentioned and well-funded privacy lobby. But few individual rights organizations offered any support for the rights of online gaming operators to accept bets, or of bettors to place them. When faced with the morally noisome task of protecting the cyber-rights of child pornographers, rights groups countered that existing criminal penalties were sufficient to deal with those who criminally exploited others without infringing on their online rights. Yet they made no similar arguments against proposed bans on Internet gaming. While the fight against online gambling made strange bedfellows, the struggle to preserve it found few friends.

It is somewhat surprising, then, that congressional efforts to proscribe gambling over the Internet fared worse than anti-indecency measures. While Congress delivered two acts that would have cleaned up the Internet if not stopped by the courts, it did not pass even one measure to stop online wagering. With so many forces arrayed against online gaming and so few champions, a bill to ban betting online seemed imminent several times, but efforts to pass one fell short time and time again.

This was not for lack of trying. Jon Kyl opposed online gaming as early as 1996, arguing that since there was "no effective way" of regulating gaming online, the only solution was to ban it entirely.[64] His Internet Gambling Prohibition Act, originally proposed in that year, would have criminalized both the operation of a betting business (which the Wire Act already did) and the placing of bets. The Justice Department expressed its doubts over the Kyl bill, making no secret of the fact that it was unlikely to arrest "blue-haired grannies for playing virtual bingo."[65] Despite the support of the commercial casino industry, the original bill did not make it out of committee, but even as it perished, Kyl vowed to offer it again.[66]

Kyl was nothing if not persistent. In 1998 he reintroduced the bill and saw it pass the Senate by a vote of 90 to 9. Representative Robert Goodlatte, a Virginia Republican who prided himself on his leadership in the area of the Internet and technology, attempted to shepherd the bill through the House of Representatives, but that body adjourned before taking any action on the bill, thus killing it.[67]

In 1999 Kyl revived his bill, dropping the provision calling for the prosecution of bettors and during the fight to get the bill approved adding amendments that would have permitted horse race and lottery betting over the Internet. This attempt to placate the commercial gaming lobby served only to attract the opposition of anti-gaming groups, who felt the act mandated the legalization and spread of online betting. The measure again went down in defeat.

Having no luck with their attempts to foist enforcement onto Internet service providers, opponents of online wagering took a new tack in 2000. Reasoning that if online casinos could not collect money they would quickly disappear, legislators now sought to make illegal the most common ways that such establishments received their funds: by credit card, check, and electronic funds transfer. Representative Jim Leach, a Republican from Iowa, joined with the ranking Democrat on the House Committee on Banking, Housing, and Urban Affairs, John LaFalce of New York, to introduce H.R. 556, better known as the Unlawful Internet Gambling Funding Prohibition Act. Although Leach designed the bill to complement the Kyl-Goodlatte prohibition bill, he felt that it could also stand alone as an effective enforcement mechanism.[68] Ultimately, however, the bill did not pass the House. The funding prohibition bill and the criminalization bill failed to pass in Congress in both 2001 and 2002.

Banning Internet gaming, it seemed, would never be a high priority for Congress. Still, Kyl came achingly close to having restrictions on online wagering passed in 2003, when the Unlawful Internet Gambling Funding Prohibition cleared the House, only to fail in the Senate. The Leach-LaFalce bill passed the House on June 10 by a large margin, leaving hope that Kyl could get a companion bill through the Senate. But the chair of the Banking Committee, Richard Shelby, deleted a provision that would have allowed states to regulate online gaming within their own borders. Given that Station Casinos was already offering its sportsbook customers intranet gaming in the Las Vegas Valley, this amendment made the once-tolerable bill offensive to the commercial casino industry, which had traditionally opposed any erosion of a state's right to regulate its own gaming. AGA president Frank Fahrenkopf objected to the bill on the grounds that it would permit the pari-mutuel industry to offer Internet betting and leave the casino industry at a competitive disadvantage. Because tribal governments were not permitted to regulate their own Internet gaming, Indian tribes also opposed the measure.[69]

Facing stiff resistance from the most interested parties, as well as a logjam of other, arguably more critical legislation dealing with Medicare reform and homeland security, Kyl still put a brave face on the bill's chances, proclaiming in September that Congress was "as close as it's ever been" to passing the payment ban. Credit card companies, including Visa and MasterCard, began blocking payments to online gaming sites in anticipation of the ban, forcing operators and bettors to find alternate payment solutions.[70] But as the year drew to a close, the Senate failed to vote on the bill, and the attempt to stymie Internet gaming ended in futility for the fourth consecutive Congress.

In trying to get anti–Internet gaming legislation through Congress, Senator Kyl and his cosponsors ran into problems nearly identical to those encountered by the original proponents of anti–interstate betting laws in 1950. Though Congress had no problem passing a bill to ban the interstate transport of gaming machines, a ban on the use of interstate wire facilities failed to pass, chiefly because the Justice Department argued that it was a regulatory matter and therefore under the purview of the FCC, while the FCC took the view that local police were best suited to handle criminal uses of telephones and telegraphs. In addition, the telecommunications lobby expressed reservations about any laws that would give it responsibility for policing the wires. It would take eleven years and the strident support of the most powerful attorney general in U.S. history to get a version of the Wire Act passed. The proponents of Internet gaming prohibition, facing even thornier questions of jurisdiction and equally resolute opposition to their proposals, had company in a generation of earlier anti-gaming legislators.

Legalizing Internet Gaming

Although the U.S. Congress successfully avoided taking action on the challenges posed by domestic and cross-border Internet gaming, other nations eagerly jumped into the breach. The first jurisdictions to embrace online gaming were primarily Caribbean island nations seeking to use it as a source of revenue and jobs.

Caribbean basin nations enacted control schemes, termed "self-regulation," that are a libertarian's dream. Industry analyst Mark Balestra has identified several characteristics of such regimes. On the positive side, they offer low or no business taxes, impose low start-up costs on licensees, and place few restrictions on how operators run their businesses. On the negative side, this laissez-faire attitude can be viewed as lax, with few mandated controls on problem and underage gambling, few provisions on money laundering, inadequate auditing, and, in general, virtually no accountability for either regulators or operators.[71]

Antigua and Barbuda, for example, began regulating online gaming to boost economic development. Declaring a free-trade zone that left telephone and Internet gaming operations exempt from local taxes, licenses, and import duties, Antigua actively courted gaming entrepreneurs. The national government's licensing power, in the eyes of operators like Jay Cohen, added an extra measure of legitimacy.[72] Essentially, Antigua required online sportsbooks to get a license, but collected no business taxes and offered no real auditing or enforcement of its regulations. This kind of laissez-faire regulation is politically impossible in the United States.

As competing jurisdictions began offering a maturing industry more-stringent regulation and presumably more legitimacy, Antigua tightened its control, creating the Directorate of Offshore Gaming in 1999 to oversee the industry. In 2001 Parliament amended the gaming regulations to include stricter controls against money laundering and a greater emphasis on player protection.[73] Consequently, some operators, chafing at the higher costs of Antiguan regulation, have decided to relocate to less strict jurisdictions, like Curaçao and Costa Rica. Antigua's evolving Internet gaming regulations mirror the development of Nevada's gaming law, which has grown from a six-page statute passed in 1931 to a comprehensive system of financial oversight and procedural requirements.

Costa Rica provides an instructive contrast with Antigua. In its initial experiment with offshore gaming, Costa Rica became an even more lax model of regulatory control than the island offshore banking haven. In a byzantine series of decisions, the Costa Rican Supreme Court and attorney general concluded that although gaming is illegal in Costa Rica, Internet gaming is not considered gaming if operators do not accept bets from Costa Ricans who are physically in the country. Though a company can locate its server and process transactions in Costa Rica, it must find another country to host its merchant account. Costa Rica required its offshore gaming operators to get a business license but imposed no real regulation on them.[74] By 2003 Costa Rica had framed a system for taxing, licensing, and regulating Internet gaming businesses, though, signaling the evolution toward the kind of increased control found in Antigua.

Still, compared to the regulations imposed on commercial casinos in the United States, the "stricter" requirements of latter-day Caribbean regulation seemed ridiculously lenient. In New Jersey, for example, the license application includes a fifty-two-page business entity disclosure form and multijurisdictional personal history disclosure forms (sixty-eight pages each) for all directors and officers, plus a thirteen-page supplement to that form. Atlantic City casinos bear the costs of their regulation by funding the Casino Control Commission and Division of Gaming Enforcement (to the tune of $62 million in 2002).[75] Simply to submit a license application will cost a company $200,000, and that does not include the expenses of the investigation, billed to the applicant and likely to exceed $1 million. In addition, applicants pay an effective tax rate of 9.25 percent (8 percent for the Casino Revenue Fund and 1.25 percent of revenue mandated to be reinvested in approved redevelopment projects) on casino revenue and must adhere to more than six hundred pages of regulations.[76]

Certainly, casinos are more highly regulated in the United States than are other hospitality industries, but every industry in America, from diaper manufacturing to funeral home operation, is regulated rather heavily. The American regulation of industry and commerce developed only after extensive industrialization with few controls made it necessary. Modern regulation dates to the Progressive Era, when reformers, seeking to blunt the excesses of large-scale enterprises, attempted to limit concentrations of economic power and provide a measure of consumer protection. As a result, American businesses contend with a sometimes arcane system of regulations that blankets virtually every area in American life, from agriculture to aerospace. Other industrialized nations went through similar experiences, developing equally strong—and often stronger—models for state regulation and intervention into industrial policy and operations.[77]

Caribbean basin nations, by contrast, have not had this historical experience with industrialization and regulation. Most regulation is therefore reactive. Once Americans began raising questions about possible money laundering in Caribbean financial institutions and online gaming sites, Antigua and other nations sought to increase their oversight of financial transactions. In general, though, Caribbean leaders perceived their lack of regulation as a boon to economic development and aggressively pursued any possible finance or industry that could bring wealth. The Caribbean was therefore an ideal location for the development of an industry that was, in its earliest years, chiefly self-regulating.

To provide self-regulation, several online gaming companies formed the Interactive Gaming Council in 1996. The IGC drafted a code of conduct covering a variety of key issues, from regulatory compliance to dispute resolution to financial transaction processing. The IGC bestows a seal of approval on member companies that meet its criteria. Even its own members, however, recognize that self-regulation is a "short-term solution," and most view it as a prologue to stricter governmental regulation.[78] To this end, the Interactive Gaming Council proselytizes the cause of U.S. regulation.[79]

Self-regulation has been accompanied by a welcome innovation of the Internet—consumer regulation. On most e-commerce Web sites, of which Amazon.com is the supreme exemplar, customers can post comments on their purchases, praising a psychologically taut thriller or warning would-be buyers away from buggy software. Online bettors are no different, using sites like "the Prescription" (www.therx.com), created by former physician Ken Weitzner, to serve as a consumer advocate Web site for offshore gaming. On message forums, bettors share their thoughts on honest and fraudulent online sportsbooks.[80] MajorWager.com is a similar site, offering sportsbook reviews and news resources.[81] In a rational world, a betting site that cheated its customers would be driven out of business by the decisions of informed consumers.

Operators cherished this libertarian nirvana of self-regulation and low taxes as a digital re-creation of the Wild West's gaming frontier. It was, however, paradoxically unpalatable to Nevada operators, who were ostensibly the lineal descendants of real Western frontier gamblers. In reality they benefited from stringent protectionist regulations that maintained high barriers to entry in the market and guaranteed a solid reputation for casino gaming. While start-up offshore sports betting, with no legal operations in the United States, had little to lose by incorporating in the Caribbean (should they heed the warning of Jay Cohen and remain abroad if indicted for violating Section 1084), established casino companies had the world to lose and relatively little to gain. MGM Mirage, with approximate assets of $10 billion tied up in land-based casino resorts, could hardly be expected to jeopardize its American casino licenses to poke a foot into the brave new world of online gaming, no matter how lucrative it might be.

Therefore, when established casino companies did venture into cyberspace, they looked for more heavily regulated environments. The Isle of Man, a dependency of the British Crown, offered such a niche. In September 2001 the Isle awarded three online gaming licenses. It promised strict regulation, including background investigations, data-protection checks, "know your customer" money-laundering controls, and statistical analysis of payouts. Licensees would be prohibited from accepting bets from minors and from nations where online wagering was illegal.[82] The Isle awarded two additional licenses in 2002, and established companies like MGM Mirage and Sun International opened online casinos, but by late 2003 each of the Isle's five online casinos had closed. Though established companies enjoyed the security and reputability provided by the Isle of Man's stringent regulations, with the legal status of online gaming undecided in the United States and other major markets, Internet casinos based there were at a supreme competitive disadvantage. Though the Isle of Man may have been too exacting in its regulation, most casino companies joined MGM Mirage in deciding to wait until the United States enunciated a clear public policy on gaming before relaunching online casinos.

Australia, which also gained renown for its strict regulation, once appeared to be a sure bet for reputable online casinos. Initially, regulation of such casinos and betting sites devolved to Australia's states and territories. Many Australian jurisdictions permitted existing casinos and betting operations to offer online services as an extension of their traditional gambling. State regulators simply extended existing regulatory guidelines for betting and casino games to the online arena, thus giving Australia a strict regulatory regime.

Lassetter's of Alice Springs, Northern Territory, took its operations online in 1999 to much success, but a subsequent political tug-of-war effectively halted the growth of the Australian online casino industry. Because of fears over problem gambling, Australians began almost immediately to roll back their experiment in legal Internet gaming. In 2000 the commonwealth government imposed a moratorium on new Internet gaming, and in 2001 the Interactive Gaming Act made it illegal to provide interactive gambling services to anyone in Australia. Though online wagering and sports betting were still permitted, online card games and slot machines were banned. Wagering sites proliferated, with no fewer than twelve active by 2002.[83] Australians continued to play casino games online too, but they now lacked the Australian regulatory protections enjoyed by American citizens, whose bets Australian sites accepted.

With the growing interest of the commercial casino industry in online gaming, the state of Nevada began to seriously consider the question of regulating cyber casinos. Though the question seemed academic given the federal government's continuing ban on Internet gaming in the Wire Act, legislators felt the need to create a framework for this potential industry. In April 2001 the Nevada legislature passed Assembly Bill 578, which opened the door for the eventual licensing and regulation of online gaming operations within the state. Under the statute, existing casinos could apply for an online gaming license, which would cost $500,000 for two years. This would take place, though, only after the federal government had decriminalized Internet gaming and the Gaming Control Board had established the requirements for a license.[84] Although the state had not, by late 2004, drafted any regulations for online wagering, its foresight in at least developing a procedure for doing so indicated that should the federal policy change, Nevada casinos would quickly move into the online realm.

Nevada was not the only state to explore Internet gaming. In March 2002 New Jersey, the state with the nation's second-largest casino market, began looking into online wagering. A joint resolution proposed the formation of an Internet Gaming Study Commission, which would consist of legislators, executive branch officials, and members of the public (including representatives of the gaming industry). This commission would conduct "a comprehensive study of the social and economic impact of legalizing Internet gambling in New Jersey."[85] New Jersey legislators could not match Nevada's biennial body for speed, having produced no study of Internet gaming two years later, but the consideration of a study commission pointed the way toward eventual regulation, pending a resolution of the federal policy.

Although prohibition bills garnered attention with their consistent near misses in Congress, some farsighted lawmakers conceded that perhaps prohibition was not the best answer. Representative John Conyers, a Michigan Democrat, introduced a bill in late 2002 that would create a federal commission to investigate online gaming and explore its alternatives, including regulation. Though the bill failed, Conyers reintroduced it in March 2003 to coincide with the reintroduction of the Leach bill, which would ban most payment methods to Internet gaming sites.[86] The proposal to study Internet gaming, cosponsored by Nevada representative Shelley Berkeley, accepted that Americans were already choosing to gamble on the Internet. Prohibition would not end this, but regulation, the bill's sponsors understood, might provide a measure of consumer protection and guard against money laundering. Of course, it might also create a new source of state revenue—no small consideration, as the history of legal gaming in the United States has shown.

7   March Madness

**How the most famous application of the Wire Act sent an Internet gaming
operator to jail and sparked an international trade dispute.**

But the fact is, Judge, that if ever there was a case that is outside the heartland of cases that are
normally prosecuted as 1084 violations, this is the case. That statute has been used repeatedly
to prosecute bookie operations, a back wire room with no law firms, no accounting firms, no
advertising firms, nothing off-shore, everything happening inside the United States where
everybody in place recognized full well that they were involved in an illegal gambling operation.
—Benjamin Brafman, Sentencing Hearing, *United States* v. *Jay Cohen* (2000)

THERE WILL PROBABLY ALWAYS BE SOME TENSION in the United States
between the policing imperative to curtail some citizens' actions in the name
of law and order and those citizens' wishes to pursue their pleasures unmolested. The growth of the Internet, a communications medium that slash-
es through national borders, has only complicated the collision between law
enforcement and personal privacy. Because of the supranational nature of
the Internet, simple issues of gaming law enforcement have become international legal disputes. To date, the U.S. government has chosen to criminalize online gaming, attempting to use the Wire Act to bind the digital beast.

But the inherent slipperiness of the Internet has rendered meaningless
the fight to subdue online gaming operators and "protect" American citizens from gambling online. As soon as prosecutors succeed in tying down
one tentacle of the Internet octopus, it seems, another is free to deal digital
blackjack to paying customers. From an enforcement perspective, it is an opponent even more elusive than Robert Kennedy's hated boss gamblers and
their syndicates. As national boundaries become progressively more porous,
attempts to effect a national prohibition on online gaming by enforcing the
Wire Act against foreign operators may prove futile.

United States v. Jay Cohen

Although Congress could not pass a bill to ban Internet gaming, law enforcement officials found they did have a few tools to use against Web casinos and
betting sites. Although the most striking prosecutions of Internet gambling

operators came with a spate of federal prosecutions in March 1998 involving violations of the Wire Act, state attorneys general used other laws to strike at Internet gaming as well.

Missouri attorney general Jeremiah W. "Jay" Nixon took one of the first legal stabs at Internet gaming providers. He was already inclined to challenge gaming outside of the jurisdiction of state authority, since in 1996 he had sued the federal government to guarantee that Missouri could fight any attempt by Indian tribes to acquire state land for gambling purposes.[1] When the Coeur d'Alene tribe of Idaho began offering an online lottery, as Class II gaming, under the assumption that it was permitted to do so, Nixon sued the tribe. The Missouri attorney general argued that since the tribe was offering gambling to Missouri citizens, the laws of that state applied. Although a U.S. district court judge ruled that tribal sovereignty prevented Nixon from prosecuting the Indian tribe, the Eighth Circuit Court of Appeals ruled in Nixon's favor, granting a temporary restraining order to stop the Coeur d'Alene tribe from offering online gaming.[2] The ruling that bets placed in Missouri took place in Missouri, not on tribal lands, effectively derailed the tribe's online lottery.

Nixon also sought to protect the citizens of Missouri from Sports International, a Pennsylvania-based online sportsbook with a server in Grenada. Nixon filed a civil suit to prevent the site from accepting wagers from Missouri residents. After the site's operator, Interactive Gaming and Communications Corporation, agreed to forgo bets from Missourians, a state investigator accessed the site and placed bets.[3] Nixon then brought criminal proceedings against the head of Interactive, Michael Simone, charging Simone with promoting gambling in the first degree.[4] Despite his attorney's argument that Missouri lacked the jurisdiction to try him, Simone eventually pled guilty to the criminal charges and paid a fine of $25,000.[5] Online gaming operators, it seemed, needed to keep themselves far from the wrath—and jurisdictional authority—of zealous attorneys general.

Attorney General Nixon was not alone in prosecuting online gamblers. Other states, including Wisconsin, joined him in the fight against the Coeur d'Alene lottery site. Dennis Vacco, attorney general of New York, successfully fought to freeze the assets of World Interactive Gaming, which maintained a server in Antigua but was essentially a New York company.[6] The attorney general of New Jersey brought suit against three Internet casinos in 2001.[7] The companies behind these virtual betting dens accepted bets from residents of the Garden State, advertised in the state, and even had the temerity to splash their pitches across billboards in sight of Atlantic City casinos, a leading state revenue source and employer. In 2002 the state settled two other civil suits brought against online casinos when the companies agreed to refuse bets placed by New Jersey residents.[8]

State attorneys general could, then, successfully win cases against Internet gaming operators that exposed themselves to prosecution by remaining partially based in the United States. With the determination that the betting activity took place at the site of the bettor, not at the gaming site, attorneys general gained free rein to prosecute out-of-state operators that permitted state residents to bet. Within their own borders, even states that condoned legal gaming held that the right of other states to prohibit it was inviolable. If a blackjack dealer from Nevada, for example, walked across the state line and began taking bets in Utah, Nevada agreed that though the casino gaming was legal, licensed, and taxed in the Silver State, once the dealer entered Utah the activity became criminal. Nevada would as a matter of routine jurisdictional courtesy surrender the dealer to Utah authorities for trial in that state. Prosecutors in Wisconsin and Minnesota followed Jay Nixon's lead in Missouri and successfully sued domestically based operators who presumably promoted gambling to their residents, forcing some operations to shut down.

Prosecutions along these lines, though, could snare only those who, because they kept part of their operations in the United States, were vulnerable to civil and criminal proceedings. By 1997 the savviest operators avoided this pitfall. The founders of the World Sports Exchange meticulously adhered to what they believed to be the law, locating all of their equipment and employees in Antigua.[9] They thus believed themselves to be operating legally and therefore to be immune from prosecution under Section 1084 of Title 18, or the Wire Act.

But online sportsbooks had aroused a powerful foe—professional sports. The major American sports leagues—the National Hockey League, the National Basketball Association, the National Football League, and Major League Baseball—had expressed official opposition to any sports betting. The leagues, though, seemed to accept the presence of a flourishing illegal sports betting market, and league policies such as the mandatory publication of player injuries actually helped sports bettors by giving them a better feel for the next game's matchups. NFL commissioner Pete Rozelle, seemingly unaware of his own inconsistency, stated in 1975 that the league maintained this practice to allay suspicion when the odds suddenly shifted.[10] He thus acknowledged that betting was an important part of the national sports complex.

The leagues vociferously opposed any discussion of legalizing sports betting and favored congressional attempts to enact a national ban on college sports betting that would prevent Nevada sportsbooks from legally accepting wagers on college sports. One gets the feeling that, if they could have, they gladly would have prevented the state of Nevada from sanctioning betting on professional sports as well. Though the leagues were wealthy and politically potent, they were no match for the commercial casino industry, which had equally deep pockets and, as the employer of several hundred thousand Americans, had no small political leverage. Internet sportsbooks, however, had nowhere near the political and financial clout of state-sanctioned casinos, so they undoubtedly made a far better target.

To protect their interests, the sports leagues retained Debevoise and Plimpton, an international law firm based in New York that specialized in corporate, litigation, tax, and trusts and estates law, and Internet, new media, and intellectual property practice groups.[11] Debevoise hired Joseph Daglione, a private investigator experienced in intellectual property cases, to probe the World Sports Exchange's possible use of National Football League trademarks.[12] Attorneys at Debevoise instructed Daglione to discover whether the WSE had "customers in New York or connections to New York."[13] Daglione placed a call to the WSE telephone number in May 1997, spoke with Steve Schillinger, and learned that the sportsbook did indeed accept bets from New Yorkers. The WSE even sent Daglione an unsolicited letter (postmarked in California, as it was mailed by the WSE's American advertising firm, Ingalls Moranville Advertising Agency) in August inviting him to fund his inactive account and receive a $50 credit.

Debevoise did not ask Daglione to investigate the Web site's use of NFL trademarks—his specialty.[14] Still, the National Football League threatened litigation against the World Sports Exchange for the unauthorized use of NFL logos and trademarks, since the company used team names and insignias on its Web site, which the league rightfully claimed were its intellectual property. Bruce Keller, a partner at Debevoise, sent a letter in May 1997 serving notice that the company's activities violated the rights of the NFL under the civil Racketeer Influenced and Corrupt Organizations Act (RICO) and an assortment of federal and state copyright, trademark, and unfair competition laws. Keller also did the WSE the favor of informing it that in his considered legal opinion the company was violating Section 1084.[15]

Keller insisted that the World Sports Exchange take immediate action to prevent Debevoise's clients—including the National Football League, the National Basketball Association, and the National Hockey League, from taking "any steps they may deem necessary" to protect their rights. Specifically, Keller requested that the WSE stop transmitting gambling information concerning Debevoise's clients into the United States, stop accepting bets on its clients' games, stop using its clients' trademarks, and sever links between the WSE Web site and NFL, NBA, and NHL sites.[16]

Once notified of the legal implications of using the official trademarks of the National Football League and other sports leagues, the WSE dropped the practice. Instead of accepting wagers on the "Philadelphia Eagles" football team, it merely accepted them on "Philadelphia." Since the site no longer used league insignias, the National Football League dropped its litigation. Cohen and his partners at the World Sports Exchange believed that they were now in the clear.

But the sports leagues and their law firm were not so easily satisfied. At the urging of Debevoise and Plimpton, the U.S. Attorney's Office for the Southern District of New York began investigating Antigua-licensed wagering sites for violations of U.S. law. A litigation partner from Debevoise met with representatives of that office to discuss the proliferation of offshore betting operations, forwarding news articles about the WSE and other companies to the office beforehand. A former Debevoise associate, Thomas Rubin, spearheaded the office's investigation of online betting sites and continued to receive correspondence from Debevoise lawyers, including audiotapes of remarks made by Jay Cohen at the First International Symposium on Internet Gambling Law in Washington, D.C. Debevoise attorneys specifically identified as potential targets for the U.S. attorney five sports betting companies out of the nine that the office investigated.[17]

Next the computer crime section of the New York FBI office launched an inquiry into online sportsbooks, including the World Sports Exchange. In an undercover capacity, special agents set up accounts with online wagering sites and funded the accounts via Western Union wire transfer. They then placed wagers on various sports events and had telephone conversations with representatives of the World Sports Exchange and other gaming operations.[18]

After several months of gathering evidence, the Justice Department felt confident in charging the operators of six Internet sportsbooks with using telephone and telegraph wires to illegally transmit bets. A generation after its passage as an anti–organized crime measure, the Wire Act had emerged into the digital age. The six companies were Island Casino and Galaxy Sports of Curaçao, SDB Global and Real Casino of Costa Rica, and Winner's Way and World Sports Exchange of Antigua.[19] Three employees, in the United States at the time of the charges, surrendered themselves and were arrested. The other individuals, however, were not in the United States at the time, and since they were operating legal, licensed businesses in foreign countries, they had little pressing reason to return to the United States to face prosecution.

Of those charged, ten subsequently pled guilty in Manhattan federal court to conspiring to violate the Wire Act, three pled guilty to related misdemeanor counts, and seven, including Steve Schillinger, Spencer Hanson, and Haden Ware, of the World Sports Exchange, chose to remain outside the United States, free from prosecution but unable to return to the country under penalty of arrest.

But Jay Cohen, the outspoken president of the World Sports Exchange, chose to fly to New York, surrender himself to the FBI at its 26 Federal Plaza office, and face trial for violating the Wire Act. Cohen wished to clear his name and have his day in court.[20] The World Sports Exchange, which had offered a betting pool "for entertainment purposes only" on whether the Kyl Bill would advance, now found itself in the midst of the debate over online gaming.[21] If the U.S. Justice Department and the offshore Internet gaming industry wanted a test case for the applicability of the Wire Act to the digital medium of the Web, they now had it. The stage was set for a legal showdown between an "online outlaw" of the virtual gaming frontier and the law.

The trial of Jay Cohen for violating Section 1084 of Title 18, the Wire Act, began on February 14, 2000, in the New York Southern District courtroom of Judge Thomas P. Griesa. In an ironic twist, it was fifty years earlier, nearly to the day, that U.S. attorney general Howard McGrath had convened a conference to address the problem of gaming crime that crossed state lines, which produced an early draft of the Wire Act. Mary Jo White, the U.S. attorney for New York's Southern District, delegated Joseph DeMarco, assisted by Teresa Pesce, to present the government's case. DeMarco and Pesce intended to prove that Cohen, assisted by three indicted, fugitive coconspirators (Steve Schillinger, Haden Ware, and Spencer Hanson, founding partners of the WSE), had engaged in a conspiracy to violate Section 1084 by accepting bets on American sporting events from residents of the United States.[22]

DeMarco and Pesce alleged that Cohen had masterminded a thriving sports betting enterprise in defiance of U.S. law, arguing that the free-trade zone enacted by the government of Antigua did not give him safe harbor to run a betting operation targeting American citizens. They maintained that the World Sports Exchange was a bookmaking business that, using telephones and the Internet, accepted bets from the United States. The prosecutors noted that the WSE retained American advertising and public relations firms to increase its business in the United States. Through audiotapes of conversations between undercover agents and WSE representatives, videotapes of gaming transactions being enacted via the WSE's Web site by undercover agents, bank records showing money transfers between undercover bettors and the WSE, and advertisements placed by the WSE in American print media, DeMarco and Pesce bolstered the contention that the World Sports Exchange was, in fact, a bookmaking operation that posted odds and took wagers on sports events.[23]

In his opening statement, DeMarco alleged that the case was that of "a bookie and his sports book." Jay Cohen abandoned his job on the Pacific Stock Exchange and went to Antigua to set up the World Sports Exchange "because he knew that bookies make money, lots of money." Cohen was no ordinary bookie, using a spiral notebook and pen to record wagers, but one who used high technology—the Internet and phone lines—"to collect as much money as he could from Americans and their sports bets." Cohen had been praised in the *Wall Street Journal* as an innovative Internet entrepreneur, but DeMarco chalked up the World Sports Exchange to little more than old-fashioned greed and unwonted "dreams of riches."[24] Cohen was nothing more than a bookie who had taken advantage of technology to accept bets from Americans while basking in the offshore safety of Antigua.

The prosecution's case rested on the fact that although Cohen and his co-conspirators were licensed to run a sports betting operation in Antigua, they used the phone system to accept bets from Americans—a violation of Section 1084(a), which made illegal the use of "a wire communication facility" in transmitting bets or information assisting in the placing of bets. "We are here in court today because this bookie took phone bets from Americans over phone lines. That is what this case is about," DeMarco told the jury. That the World Sports Exchange was a lawful business in another country and that Cohen and his partners had labored to follow the laws of the United States in incorporating their company had no bearing on the direct issue—Cohen had violated the Wire Act.[25]

Cohen retained as counsel Benjamin Brafman, a high-powered litigator whose clients included Sean "P. Diddy" Combs and reputed mafia chieftain Vincent Gigante and who specialized in complex white-collar criminal cases. Brafman countered the seemingly airtight prosecution case by claiming that if jurors simply exercised their "common sense," they would conclude that Cohen was not a bookie. Bookies, Brafman claimed, did not retain major accounting firms, advertise in the Wall Street Journal or Sports Illustrated, use American financial institutions like the Chase Manhattan Bank or Western Union, or testify before Congress urging the regulation of their business.[26]

On some of these points Brafman was either misinformed or disingenuous: One of the original purposes of the Wire Act was to stifle the use of telegraph and telephone wires—owned by Western Union, AT&T, and other telecommunications giants—to transmit gaming information to bookmakers. There really was nothing antithetical in the idea of an illegal gambling business's use of legitimate business channels. Nor were those involved with illegal gambling shy about public advocacy. "Betting commissioners" James Carroll of St. Louis and Frank Erickson of New York had testified before the McFarland Committee fifty years earlier. Erickson's experience was instructive; three days after he testified, New York detectives raided his office. Once a prosperous bookmaker, he ultimately served three prison sentences for bookmaking and tax evasion and for the remainder of his life was intermittently a target of police investigations.[27]

Some bookies had suggested legalization and regulation, and, truth be told, most successful bookies have cultivated reputations for integrity. But, Brafman insisted, Cohen was not a bookie (a "sinister word," in Brafman's estimation) but a "an honest citizen, a responsible entrepreneur, a brilliant young man who left a position at the stock exchange in California, where he was very successful and already very rich, to open a business in Antigua where that business is legal, licensed and regulated."[28]

Brafman emphasized that as market makers on the Pacific Stock Exchange, Cohen and others had in effect been gambling, and that although the World Sports Exchange did happen to take straight-up bets on sporting events, it was primarily a futures market in which customers bought and sold contracts for teams on the basis of their individual judgments on the teams' future performances, something that stock traders did quite legally in the realm of business. Cohen and his partners moved to Antigua not to evade the law but rather to legally establish a business through which Americans, using "the magic of the Internet," could enjoy the entertainment of trading in sports futures.[29]

Cohen was not motivated by avarice, Brafman claimed, because as a stock trader he had already accrued significant personal wealth. Nor was he a criminal, because he had complied with the law of Antigua and taken pains to pay foreign taxes as a U.S. citizen—hardly the actions of a scofflaw. Brafman argued that the criminal investigation of Cohen began at the urging of Debevoise and Plimpton, who sought to drive online betting sites out of business and protect their powerful clients, the sports leagues; the case was not a story of a greedy bookie but one of big business trying to crush a young upstart.[30]

Far from being a bookie blinded by acquisitiveness, Brafman proffered, Cohen was a visionary, and even a statesman of the Internet frontier, who was targeted precisely because of his rectitude and public profile as a paragon of the digital age:

> You will learn from Mr. Cohen that he became an outspoken advocate of this new business, and I submit to you that's why he is here: He became a public person. He spoke out for the right of a new business idea, to be run in a country where it was legal, and he went out front, up close and personal, the cover of *Newsday*, a several page article in *Sports Illustrated*, debating issues with former attorney generals on the radio, publicly speaking on internet gambling symposiums, questioning, probing, learning, taking the good with the bad, and trying to make this a business that could work honestly, and even publicly inviting regulation by the United States so that the United States could earn from this operation.[31]

Cohen did not seek to profit from the weaknesses of Americans, or to scam them. Brafman asserted that Cohen had signed up the World Sports Exchange site with four "Internet protection servers" to prevent underage visitors from accessing the site and that he placed a link to Gamblers Anonymous on the site—measures that any "legitimate" gambling operation would take. Cohen, who within days of hearing that he had been charged with violating Section 1084, chose to return to the United States to face trial, was a completely "responsible, legitimate business person," the polar opposite of "bookie in a smoke filled room with flash paper that burns on touch when the police arrive."[32] As the WSE was a legitimate, licensed, multimillion-dollar industry, founded and run by respectable, intelligent young men, the jury would have no choice but to find Cohen not guilty.

Brafman did not attempt to dispute any of the facts that the prosecutors offered as evidence. On the contrary, he asserted that he and his client embraced "95 percent" of the government's case. "This is not a whodunit," Brafman declared. "There is Mr. Cohen, president of the World Sports Exchange." Faced with a mountain of evidence that the WSE had accepted bets from the United States, Brafman did not seek to challenge any of these matters of fact, but rejected the "import and spin" that the government placed on the recorded betting transactions. As the president of a legal business, Cohen broke no laws, and, furthermore, he did not personally accept any bets placed by undercover agents, so he could not be convicted of any crime.[33]

Before the trial, the prosecution attempted to prevent Brafman from arguing that because Cohen had not believed he was breaking the law, he was not a criminal; he could not claim that because in his interpretation he was not violating Section 1084, he was innocent. Although Judge Griesa agreed that the government would not have to prove whether Cohen knew his actions were in violation of U.S. law, he did not prevent Cohen from testifying as to his state of mind. Rather, Griesa cautioned Cohen that although he could "testify about what he wants to testify about," the judge would instruct the jury that ignorance of the law did not constitute a valid defense.[34]

In the ten days of trial, the prosecution produced testimony from FBI special agents and entered into evidence recorded conversations and other documentary evidence that proved conclusively what Brafman had granted in his opening statement: that Cohen was the president of the World Sports Exchange, a company that accepted bets on sporting events via the Internet and telephone from the United States. Having proven the mechanics of the World Sports Exchange, the prosecution considered its case closed.

Brafman presented a multi-tiered defense, arguing simultaneously that Cohen was innocent because no bets took place in New York, that placing a bet was not illegal in New York anyway, and that Cohen had attempted to comply with the law, so he had no criminal intent. Cohen testified that he had modeled the WSE on New York's Capital OTB, which accepted telephone wagers using account wagering. In account wagering, the bet took place at the location where the account was set up—whether it was New York or Antigua. Capital OTB had not been charged with violating the Wire Act, Brafman argued, so neither should Cohen be so charged. To counter this claim, prosecutor Teresa Pesce used the World Sports Exchange's own words, noting that the advertisements invited customers to "bet with the click of a mouse." In questioning Cohen, Pesce tried to explode the idea that customers themselves did not bet but only instructed employees to place bets:

Q. And your web site actually invites customers to place wagers too. In fact it asks to click on the word "wager," correct?

A. Directing a wager be placed in Antigua.

Q. It doesn't say on the web site "click here now and direct us to place the wager for you," does it?[35]

Cohen cited the Web site's "rules and regulation" page, which stated clearly that all wagers took place at the server in Antigua, but the prosecution was able to produce taped conversations in which undercover agents appeared to place bets on various sports teams; Cohen merely countered that they only directed Antiguans to place bets on their behalf, which was not betting and therefore was not illegal.

Another thrust of Brafman's defense hinged on Cohen's mens rea, or criminal intent: As there was no criminal intent, and as the Wire Act could not cover the WSE because the Internet had not yet been invented when the Wire Act was written, Cohen must be innocent. The prosecution brushed aside this assertion. Under cross-examination by Pesce, Cohen stated that he sincerely believed that "the way my company was set up, with account wagering, with the money being down there first, that we would fall squarely under the exception of 1084, which is in Section 1084(b)."[36] In his closing, Brafman dramatically stated that the "heart and soul of the case" was "Did Mr. Cohen knowingly violate the law? Not did he pick up a phone" to accept a bet.[37]

Yet after both sides had presented their cases, and Brafman had conceded that the material facts of the prosecution were beyond dispute, Judge Griesa instructed the jury that it did not have to conclude that Cohen had intended to break the law but only that he was in a betting business that knowingly used a wire communication facility to accept wagers or information about wagers. The judge defined the meaning of "transmission of a bet" as a person calling from the United States to a foreign country, placing a bet, and specifying the amount of the bet, and that bet's acceptance on the other end—which was precisely what defense counsel conceded that the prosecution had proven. In no uncertain terms Griesa explained: "It is not necessary for the government to prove that [Cohen] knew that he was acting illegally" but only that he had done the deeds that constituted a violation of the Wire Act and that he was involved in a business that was effectively a conspiracy to violate the Wire Act.[38]

With these instructions, the jury had little choice but to find Cohen guilty of eight counts, including one of conspiracy to violate Section 1084 and seven substantive violations of that statute.[39] Cohen faced a maximum term of five years in prison on the conspiracy count and two years in prison on each of the seven substantive violations. In addition, on each count Cohen faced a maximum fine of $250,000, or twice the amount of profits derived from his operation of the World Sports Exchange.

Before he was sentenced, Cohen resigned as president of the World Sports Exchange, possibly in hope of receiving leniency—his continued tenure as president of the WSE was a thorny issue at trial. At sentencing, Brafman pleaded with Judge Griesa for a downward departure from sentencing guidelines and leniency on the grounds that no one had been defrauded by Cohen—a theme he had repeatedly emphasized during the trial. "I think the government concedes and the evidence demonstrates that every person who became a customer of World Sports Exchange got an honest count, got their money back when they asked for their money to come back and were not in any way defrauded or induced into participating in this activity," Brafman declared, though the government had not alleged any fraud, and Cohen was convicted not of questionable business practices but of violating the Wire Act.[40]

The government, for its part, argued for an upward adjustment of the criminal penalties, citing among other reasons that Cohen had perjured himself by claiming during the trial that the World Sports Exchange didn't take telephone bets and by stating that he had set up his business along the lines of Capital OTB, which accepted telephone bets from New Yorkers. Judge Griesa, believing that Cohen's opinions on the legality of his business did not represent distortions of fact, did not consider these statements to be perjury. In sentencing Cohen, Griesa denied both a downward departure and an upward adjustment, settling instead on the low range of the statutory guidelines, twenty-one months on each count, to be served concurrently. Following the end of his prison sentence, Cohen would have an additional two years of supervised release. Although he felt compelled under the law to sentence Cohen to a "very substantial" term in prison, Griesa imposed a fine of only $5,000.[41] Considering that he could have shackled Cohen with a total fine of $2 million, this outcome was quite lenient, though of little consolation to a man who believed that he had done nothing illegal.

Cohen was allowed to remain a free man while his attorneys appealed his conviction. Filing their initial appellate brief in November 2000, Cohen's legal team successfully received the chance to argue for a reversal of their client's eight convictions before the U.S. Court of Appeals, Second Circuit.

After trading appellate briefs with the U.S. attorney's office, Cohen's attorneys argued their case before two circuit court judges—Pierre Leval and Fred Parker—and a district judge, John Keenan of New York's Southern District. Ultimately, Cohen's attorneys appealed the convictions on six grounds, each of which attempted to point out faulty instructions to the jury by district court judge Thomas Griesa, which the defense argued irreversibly slanted the jury toward guilty verdicts.

First, they argued, the district court judge had instructed the jury to disregard Cohen's belief that his conduct was legal, arguing that in order to convict him of conspiracy, the jury would have to accept that he had a corrupt motive. They then faulted the judge's instruction to the jury to disregard the safe harbor provision in Section 1084(b); Griesa had denied this defense, as he asserted that placing a bet was not legal in New York, as the defense had maintained, and that the transmission of betting information was tantamount to placing the bet. The Cohen team further challenged Griesa's instruction that the jury, in order to convict, need only find that Cohen knew that the deeds prohibited by the statute (i.e., accepting bets from Americans) were being done, not that they were illegal.[42]

The defense team continued to argue that the rule of lenity required a reversal of Cohen's conviction. They charged that Congress, in drafting Section 1084, had left a "grievous ambiguity" in the statute, failing to provide clear guidelines as to whether the prohibition covered account wagering, whether transmission included the receipt of information as well as the sending of it, and whether a bet must be legal or simply not a criminal offense to be considered legal. Cohen's attorneys argued that even if none of the previous issues resonated with the appeals court, Cohen's conviction should be overturned because the district court judge constructively amended Cohen's indictment by failing to inform the jury that in order to convict Cohen of aiding and abetting his subordinates at World Sports Exchange (whom FBI agents had on tape actually accepting bets), they must first convict those subordinates of the crime. Finally, the defense protested the conviction on the grounds that Judge Griesa refused to adjourn the trial so that Cohen's counsel could depose a witness in Antigua.[43]

The appeals court, ruling on July 31, 2001, affirmed Cohen's conviction and refused to consider any of the six objections raised by his lawyers. Still, this was not the end of the legal battle. Cohen's legal team took the case to the next level, filing a petition in early 2002 for a writ of certiorari with the Supreme Court, asking that body to overturn the appeals court affirmation of the district court's judgment against Cohen. During this appeal process, Cohen remained free on bond.

Ian Gershengorn, of the Washington, D.C. law firm Jenner and Block, led Cohen's Supreme Court appeal effort. Melinda Sarafa, an attorney on the *Cohen* case since the beginning, stated that she believed that since the case presented compelling issues that would have a great impact on both the gaming industry and the nature of conspiracy law, the Supreme Court might grant certiorari and hear the case.[44] With Congress still unable to pass legislation clarifying the legal status of Internet gaming, it appeared that a Supreme Court decision might force the issue, much as the *Cabazon* decision had triggered the 1988 Indian Gaming Regulatory Act.

Gershengorn, a member of Jenner and Block's appellate and Supreme Court practice with substantive concentrations in telecommunications, media, and constitutional law, argued that the Supreme Court should hear the case for four reasons. First, the district court "rewrote" the Wire Act to cover Internet gaming, which Congress had not foreseen in 1961; second, the Second Circuit's interpretation of that statute criminalized sending betting information between jurisdictions where betting was legal; third, the Second Circuit ruled it irrelevant that Cohen used legal betting operations as his model and took pains to operate the business in a jurisdiction that permitted it; and fourth, Cohen's conviction would have troubling implications for both the offshore and the domestic off-track betting industries, both of which used account wagering.[45]

But after several delays in the filings of petitions by both Cohen's attorneys and the government, the Supreme Court denied the petition for a writ of certiorari on June 17, 2002. Cohen surrendered himself and began serving his prison term in October 2002. In a strange, and some might say cruel, twist, the Federal Bureau of Prisons assigned Cohen to serve out his sentence at Federal Prison Camp Nellis, a minimum-security prison camp located at Nellis Air Force Base, approximately twenty miles north of the Las Vegas Strip. The United States jailed Cohen for masterminding an offshore betting operation that had, by the government's calculations, accepted roughly $5 million in account wagering funds from Americans over the course of eighteen months and retained at the least 5 percent and at most 10 percent of it. From the confines of his desert prison, Cohen could see the glow in the night sky caused by the lights of the Las Vegas Strip, which grossed annual revenues of roughly $5 billion a year, powering Nevada's economy.

Though a 2003 ABC news article ranked Federal Prison Camp Nellis among the five "best places to go to prison" in the United States, it was far from a country club. True, the facility, the only freestanding prison camp on the West Coast, did have air-conditioning, but that was hardly a creature comfort in an unforgiving desert where the heat can exceed 100 degrees for weeks at a time. Prisoners at FPC Nellis did not have to languish in the shadow of a gloomy penitentiary, though, and access to Las Vegas's McCarran International Airport doubtless made visits from friends and family easier. Still, few would willingly trade the sands of Antigua for a cubicle shared with three other inmates, and the austere Mojave surrounding Nellis was certainly less conducive to personal tranquillity than the Caribbean.[46]

In his whirlwind of media celebrity, even before his indictment, Cohen took pains to insist that he was no gambler. Ironically, though, he gambled twice, for incredibly high stakes. First, he abandoned a lucrative job with Group One to start the World Sports Exchange in Antigua. When indicted, he wagered with his liberty—perhaps a person's most valuable possession—that his return to face charges in New York would result in his vindication. This was playing for astronomically higher stakes than a bettor buying a futures contract for Philadelphia to win the World Series. Even at trial, despite the mountain of documentary proof that the prosecution entered into evidence affirming that he had run a sports betting operation, Cohen remained confident that he would win, at least until the judge's jury instructions, which Cohen regarded as a virtual pep talk in favor of a guilty verdict. One might argue that Cohen, forced out of his remunerative position as president of the World Sports Exchange, expected to serve eighteen months of his sentence at Nellis, subject to structured release afterward, with the stigma of a felony conviction forever attached to his name, had lost. When asked if, in retrospect, he would make the decision to return to face trial if he could rewrite his life story, Cohen was almost apologetically ambivalent, sincerely believing on the one hand that he was in the right and had only been denied justice by a biased court and knowing on the other the reality of the jury verdict, his failed appeals, and his imprisonment.[47]

Convicted of accepting bets—in his belief fairly and legitimately—from Americans and confined to a prison camp in a city built on Americans' desires to gamble, Cohen could be forgiven for allowing himself to find his trial an exercise in hypocrisy. To salve his obvious disappointment in the impartiality of American justice, though, he had the comfort of believing that he was, at the very least, a footnote in history. "One day, people will look at my conviction and say, 'Did we really put someone in jail for that?'" Cohen mused, seeing in his case a reflection of someone convicted for violating the Volstead Act during Prohibition.[48]

Though the online gaming industry is still in its infancy and has yet to benefit from serious historical scrutiny, one can sense that Cohen will be more than just a footnote. Truth be told, Cohen saw himself as an innovator; at a time when other Internet start-ups were counting page hits, he and his partners were counting dollars, clearing a path for other online commerce to follow.[49] The future of betting, Cohen believed, lay online, and later pronouncements from industry leaders like MGM Mirage's Terri Lanni that his company was ready to move into cyberspace only confirmed what Cohen had known as far back as 1996.[50] If Cohen, Lanni, and a host of others were right, then it makes sense to see Jay Cohen as a true visionary and an important figure in the history of gaming.

A Berkeley graduate in nuclear engineering, Cohen made an unlikely candidate for the role of sports betting pioneer. Personally, he does not gamble or evince even a perfunctory interest in sports, failing to see the attraction in fantasy sports leagues, a burgeoning phenomenon with shades of similarity to the World Sports Exchange's sports futures markets. Obviously a driven worker (he once told reporters that though he had been in Antigua for months, he had not yet been to the beach), his only admitted hobby is a fondness for antique cars, a passion shared with casino pioneer Bill Harrah, who was visibly at ease only when conversing about classic automobiles and who, incidentally, studied engineering at UCLA before taking over his father's Venice (California) bingo game, the start of his career in gaming.[51] But if Americans do embrace online gaming, Cohen will certainly stand as one of the major figures in gaming history, being both advocate and cause célèbre of the new order. Small payment, perhaps, for his incarceration but also, perhaps, evidence that in the long run his gamble on the World Sports Exchange was worth it.

Regardless of the personal significance of Cohen as a gaming pioneer, his case is unquestionably the most consequential application of the Wire Act in decades. Originally drafted to assist in the Kennedy war on organized crime, the statute had never been exactly high profile. Though it never smashed organized-crime families or put their leaders in prison the way that the RICO statutes did, it still performed yeoman's service for prosecutors and police seeking to press the fight against bookmakers. Prosecutions of lowly bookmakers, though, rarely garnered the press that controversial organized-crime trials did.

But on March 4, 1998, the Justice Department brought Section 1084 into the forefront of an evolving debate over the Internet. Though prosecutor Joseph DeMarco told the jury that the *Cohen* case was no more than the story of "a bookie and his sports book," it was, in reality, far more.[52] At issue was not only the application of the Wire Act to a new technology but questions of jurisdiction that reverberate throughout what is, thanks in part to advancing technology, an increasingly linked world. Globalization has emerged in the early twenty-first century as an often divisive issue, but those demonstrating against the International Monetary Fund seemed to have little interest in a case that appears to be a reaction to globalization: Does the United States have the right to prosecute the owner of an Antiguan business for accepting American customers?

The United States v. the World (Trade Organization)

The "March Madness" prosecutions and congressional rumblings about prohibition, both of which influenced the decisions of credit card companies to cease processing online gaming transactions, chilled the balmy environment that Antigua had created for online sportsbooks. From a 1999 high of 119 licensed operators, who employed approximately 3,000 Antiguans and brought in about 10 percent of that country's gross domestic product, the number of operators declined precipitously, to 28 by 2003, when online gaming accounted for fewer than 500 jobs. Antigua's stiffening of its regulations might have been responsible for some of the decline, but it laid most of the blame at the feet of the United States, saying that the "increasingly aggressive strategy" of the United States led directly to the downturn.[53]

The government of Antigua, distressed at the sudden diminution of a leading industry, reviewed its options. Its best strategy seemed to be to pursue a settlement under the General Agreement on Trade in Services, a treaty of the World Trade Organization that is binding upon all members of that body (including both the United States and Antigua). Resulting from the Uruguay Round of negotiations on international trade, GATS took effect in 1995 and essentially extended the multilateral trading system to cover services as well as goods.[54] Antigua considered gaming and betting a service that it provided in a "cross-border" fashion to citizens of the United States. The United States was therefore bound, under GATS, to permit Antiguan businesses access to its markets.

In April, the United States and Antigua began consultations in an attempt to broker a solution. Since the United States maintained that gambling was a matter of criminal enforcement, not international trade, talks quickly broke down. By June, Antigua had asked the WTO's Dispute Settlement Body to establish a panel to adjudicate the dispute. In August, the WTO created a three-member panel to hear arguments from both sides. In addition to the United States and Antigua, the European Community, Mexico, Japan, Canada, and Taiwan joined the action as third parties.[55]

The WTO panel heard testimony in December 2003 and January 2003 and issued its first panel report in February. The Antiguans presented their case before the panel—that cross-border trade in betting services was in fact covered under GATS. Since the companies and states in the United States itself offered a broad array of gambling services, Antigua claimed, gambling was regulated, but not banned as a matter of policy. Antigua stressed that it hardly wanted to open the United States to unsanctioned gambling, but merely wanted to give its domestic gaming services industry fair access to the American market, "in an agreed regulatory context" amenable to both nations.[56] The U.S. Trade Representative countered that the prohibition of Internet gambling under Section 1084 was a necessary tool in the American war on organized crime and hence a domestic law enforcement matter. The USTR specifically cited Robert Kennedy as saying that "the restrictions on remote supply of gambling" of Section 1084 were necessary because "the use of wire communications technologies for the dissemination of gambling information frustrated local law enforcement efforts."[57]

When it released its interim report in March, the panel ruled that the treaty obligations of the United States under that organization required it to permit cross-border gaming, a repudiation of Section 1084 as strictly a law enforcement tool.[58] After briefly agreeing to negotiate a settlement with Antigua in the summer of 2004, the United States renewed its intransigence and ceased negotiations. The WTO panel then issued its final report to the public, which detailed its conclusion that "contrary to its specific market access commitments for gambling and betting services . . . the United States fails to accord services and service suppliers of Antigua treatment no less favorable than that provided for" in GATS.[59] The United States appealed the decision, and even if it lost that appeal, the penalties for violating Antigua's rights remained vague.

The WTO decision hardly meant the dismantling of American gaming prohibitions. The panel specifically said: "We have not decided that WTO Members do not have a right to regulate, including a right to prohibit, gambling and betting activities." Rather, in this specific case, it found that the ways that the United States chose to prohibit cross-border trade in gambling were inconsistent with its treaty obligations.[60] But the case raised some interesting questions. Negotiations raised the possibility that the United States might recognize Antigua's "remote gambling services" as legitimate businesses and let them flourish, unmolested by enforcement of federal anti-gambling laws.

Allowing Antiguan Web operators access to American cross-border trade in gaming services would likely be the first domino to fall in a series whose logical end would be domestic decriminalization and regulation of Internet gaming. If Americans are allowed to gamble at foreign Internet casinos, there is no compelling reason why they should not be allowed to do so at domestic ones that are already subject to stringent regulations and, more important, will pay taxes on their revenue. With many states facing a seemingly insatiable cash hunger and gaming expanding at an unprecedented rate, it would seem that a happy marriage could be consummated between consumers yearning to play online, gaming companies wishing to diversify into the online field, and states in need of more money. It seems probable that within two years of any negotiated settlement with Antigua, Las Vegas–based casino operators will be offering online wagering.

Certainly MGM Mirage, which briefly operated an online casino out of the Isle of Man, believes that it can run a successful online casino. The state of Nevada has already enacted a legal framework for Internet gaming; once the federal ban is lifted, it will be off to the races. Congress has been unable to pass an Internet gaming prohibition law, despite sporadic efforts since 1997. In an increasingly litigious country where a presidential election can end in the courts, it is only fitting that the next gambling frontier will be opened not by legislative initiative but by a ruling of an international court.

The Internet has enabled people to access information in entirely new ways, promising a revolution in the production and storage of human knowledge. Yet the most successful industries of the early Internet, gambling and pornography, seemed to appeal to people's baser desires. Whatever one's moral stance on gaming, though, the importance of gaming to the development of Internet commerce, often overlooked, is beyond question.

Since before the turn of the twentieth century, elements of law enforcement quailed at the use of telegraph wires to transmit gaming information. Yet it was not until 1961 that any restriction on the use of interstate wire communications facilities for this purpose became law. Even then, it happened only because of the energetic advocacy of Robert Kennedy. But once the Wire Act was in place, police and prosecutors found it useful, putting bookmakers in jail and disrupting betting operations.

The development of Internet gaming raised a host of questions for Americans. An international medium, the Internet did not respect state restrictions on gaming. As betting and gaming sites proliferated, some state attorneys general took action, but the federal government for the most part ignored the problem, at least until the U.S. attorney's office in Southern New York began investigating offshore sportsbooks. The twenty-two indictments of March 1998 did not stop online gaming, but the trial of Jay Cohen did not vindicate it, either. Even as Cohen appealed his convictions, Congress debated—and ultimately failed to make law on—the legal status of online gaming. The application of the Wire Act, though significant, did not clarify federal policy toward Internet gaming, and the continuing legal limbo of online wagering suggests that there is still no coherent public policy on it. But to those familiar with American's habitually uneasy embrace of gaming over the past two centuries, this is a sign that while new technologies can expand our capabilities, they do not always provide us with the wisdom to use them rationally.

Epilogue   Prohibition in a Borderless America

Is gaming a legitimate business and revenue source or is it "economic mor-phine"? What does the Wire Act say about Americans' embrace of gaming? How might the Internet transform the United States, and what does the popularity of Internet gaming mean for American democracy in the twenty-first century?

You'd think they'd have learned from Prohibition, but the more the government tries to stop Internet betting, the hotter it gets.
—Mr. Lotto, 2004

OVER THE PAST FIFTY YEARS, gaming advocates have triumphed in a pitched battle against anti-gaming forces, one that compelled Americans to choose between vestigial distrust of those who profited from gaming and the slow realization that people continued to gamble despite prohibition and that individual citizens viewed gaming legalization to be in their personal interest because of the prospect it offered of lower taxes. In the early twenty-first century the original arguments against legalizing gaming have been pushed out of the mainstream, as a $72 billion gaming industry has made itself a part of the United States. Or rather, the people of the United States have embraced it. By 2002 gaming advocates could argue that theirs was the true national pastime—that year, more Americans visited a casino than visited major and minor league baseball parks.[1] But if America is truly a nation of gamblers, one must understand the reasons that Americans once demurred on legalizing gaming. To do so will make the seemingly sudden embrace of gaming less perplexing.

When stripped of purely local or personal considerations, arguments against legal gaming in the United States tended to follow three prima-ry arcs. The first held that gaming, which permitted bettors to win something for nothing, defied the religious and moral principles of the nation and undercut the value of honest work and even social justice. A nation of gam-blers would assign no value to legitimate remuneration. The second argu-ment, advanced most strenuously after the Kefauver Committee's inves-tigations, centered on the supposed inexorable domination of gaming by organized crime; any gaming activity, legal or not, would inevitably lead to an increase in political corruption. This sentiment, of course, led to the passage of the Wire Act in 1961. The final argument against gaming posited that a small percentage of the population would become addicted to compulsive gambling and that the social costs incurred by these gaming addicts and others who could not control their gaming behavior were reason enough to deny gaming a place in a rational, caring society.[2]

To counter these arguments, gaming advocates formulated several ideas in favor of easing restrictions on a ubiquitous behavior and deriving some social benefit from it. In 1973, when the New Jersey Gambling Study Commission issued its final report, it cited three chief arguments favoring gaming legalization that directly rebutted the anti-gaming positions. To counter the religious/moral argument, the commission stated that most citizens no longer held compelling moral objections to gaming and that state-sanctioned, legal gaming "would remove restrictions on personal action which many people resent as puritanical, hypocritical, repressive and archaic." Adherents to the Kefauver thesis that gaming inevitably led to corruption were confronted with the proposition, unthinkable twenty years earlier, that state-sanctioned gaming would actually reduce the influence of organized crime by depriving it of its revenue from illegal gambling. Legal gaming would also eliminate "opportunities and temptations for the corruption of various public officials whose protection or connivance is necessary to the survival of most illegal gambling operations." Finally, legalizing gaming would free the police from investigating gaming crimes and allow them to concentrate on "both the 'organized crime' and the violent 'street crime' which alarm the citizenry and undermine social order," no small concern in years when crime rates rapidly rose.[3]

As if to rebut charges that the social costs of gaming were too high, the commission simply stated a stark truth: Gaming held the promise of "providing substantial revenues through as nearly a 'painless' method as can be conceived."[4] However severe the individual costs of problem gaming, the social costs—lost opportunities, misdirected spending, wasted time—were much harder to tabulate than the immediate social benefits—higher state revenue and more jobs.

By the twenty-first century, gaming had become both an interest group (in the form of an extremely well-organized and politically astute commercial casino industry) and a weapon in the arsenal of public officials seeking economic growth and revenue enhancement without the costly infrastructure improvements or higher taxes that a more traditional approach might entail. In many states, gaming expansion became a political football as public officials, trying to please constituents, sallied forth with proposals for slots at racetracks, video poker, Indian compacts, riverboat casinos, and full-blown gaming resorts.

Turning to gaming for salvation has become so deeply ingrained in the American political consciousness that one of California governor-elect Arnold Schwarzenegger's first gambits to bridge a possibly insurmountable budget deficit was to ask tribal governments to ante up their "fair share." When the tribes did not immediately pledge $1 billion in additional revenues, owners of racetracks and card rooms began assembling an amendment to legalize slot machines throughout the state, putting pressure on tribal governments to negotiate a new compact that would preserve their monopoly.[5] Through all this debate, no one questioned that gaming taxes were the solution to endemic budget shortfalls. The keepers of the world's fifth-largest economy, attempting to pull it out of an unparalleled economic crisis, almost instinctively turned to gaming as a solution.[6] Fifty years earlier, it would have been considered a big part of the problem.

Those who gambled might once have been considered deviant. But in today's America, a penchant for casinos and gambling is, if anything, a sign of normality. Harrah's Entertainment has conducted market research surveys of gambling behavior and annually compiled them into *Profile of the American Gambler*. When such surveys and anti-gaming writings of the Gilded Age, which depicted a simple dice game as the first step to perdition, are juxtaposed, the results are startling. In 2002 casino gamblers were more likely to have savings accounts, plan for their retirement, and invest in mutual funds than non-gamblers were—hardly the behavior of the fiscally dissolute.[7] Casino gamblers were more active socially than non-gamblers, visiting friends and seeing movies slightly more frequently, and they showed a consistently higher interest in spectator sports. Casino-goers were twice as likely to follow the relatively elite sport of golf than non-gamblers were, while non-gamblers evinced a slightly greater fondness for professional wrestling.[8] Casino patrons were more likely to own a personal computer, surf the Internet, exercise, play sports, contribute to charity, and entertain guests at home. Visiting a casino apparently even improved one's chances at romance: Gamblers reported having dated more in the past month than non-gamblers did. Gamblers, according to this survey, made ideal neighbors and friends, with one telling caveat. The only activities that non-gamblers engaged in more frequently than gamblers were praying and attending services at their place of worship.[9]

So is America's turn to gaming merely a symptom of a growing secularization of society? Most likely, it is much deeper than that. In *Something for Nothing: Luck in America*, historian Jackson Lears dissects the American devotion to chance, which he sees as a sort of anti-virtue, a shortcut to grace for those who are not willing to put in long hours at the hard work of self-betterment.[10] Lears sees an Apollonian/Hermetic dialectic throughout much of Western culture, with the trickster Hermes, patron of the lucky rounder, pitted against the rationalist Apollo. The rampant gambling found in most periods of American history is symptomatic of a deeper struggle within the American psyche between chance and control. This interpretation elides the fact that gaming casinos are among the most heavily regulated, surveilled, and controlled places in America, but it has powerful rhetorical resonance.

By the end of the twentieth century, collapsing expectations for achieving financial security meant that many Americans had more faith in chance than grace. Jack Engelhard's novel *Indecent Proposal*, from which Paramount Pictures produced the 1992 movie of the same name, takes as a central theme the ultimate consequences of a man seeking a shortcut to grace.[11] Engelhard's protagonist, Joshua Kane, is a classic American type. Brought to America as a child when his family fled Nazi-occupied France over the Pyrenees, Kane is a middle-aged former newspaperman who has surrendered all pretensions of artistic or ethical aspiration to work as a corporate speechwriter. Even so, his modest dreams far exceed his $31,000-a-year salary. Though his words spill from the mouths of CEOs, he does not share in their wealth or privilege.

Still imbued with the American immigrant work ethic of continuous self-betterment born equally of Benjamin Franklin's Philadelphia and the shtetls of Eastern Europe, Kane believes his chance will come, more likely at the casino than anywhere else. Nor is he alone; at the casino he is simply one of the crowd, one of the "financially lame," engaged in a last-ditch attempt to get rich. "We hadn't received it at birth, we had failed to earn it by the work of our hands, so we were here to wrest it from Lady Chance," Engelhard writes. "Heaven had forgotten to bless us. Maybe a slot machine or a blackjack table would hear our prayer."[12]

Though Kane is not poor, he is not rich either, which means, in his mind, that he is a failure. Watching high roller Ibrahim Hassan lose millions at blackjack, Kane concludes that this wealthy man was to money "what Beethoven was to music," which means something: "As literature, art, and music spoke for the past, money spoke for the present. We wagered billions on the stock market, lotteries, and casino, and in doing so we defined our culture. Our culture was money. Millionaires and billionaires, these were our heroes."[13] For Kane, simple proximity to the Arab high roller removes the "curse of tedium" from his life, a life in which nothing happened, and "every day was just another day." Even before they meet, Hassan represents to Kane possibility, or "the chance for something big," something that is lacking in Kane's life.

Like many in his generation, raised in relative comfort with the benefit of a college education and steady and remunerative, if not creatively challenging work, Kane feels that something is lacking. For most of human history and in many parts of today's world, even in the United States, Kane's life would be one to be envied. Yet for him it is marked by a lack of fulfillment and relative deprivation, something that can be cured only by visiting the casino. Kane resolves to take the chance to receive some of Hassan's "possibility." Though the results may be tragic, he has nothing to lose: "But in the vicinity of this Arab, something was bound to happen. What exactly, I did not know, except that greatness produced sparks, and these could light up another man. Burn him, too, of course."[14]

Eventually Kane completely loses interest in his own unsuccessful gambling, surrenders to temptation, and approaches Hassan's table to get a better look, setting into motion the events that lead to the eponymous proposal. But for all the drama of the novel, the characters never question the truth that compels them to act: Kane has no chance of "greatness" except through chance.

The apparent triumph of the culture of chance is not without its darkness. In his short story "Something for Nothing," Tim Gautreaux, with a somewhat overvivid pen, sketches the tale of Wayne, a former lifeguard who, after losing his job, car, and girlfriend to the vicissitudes of the postindustrial economy, finds a job manning the "suicide skiff" at a riverboat casino. His job is to deter and rescue despondent plungers who seek a more immediate self-destruction. For Wayne, the riverboat (improbably named the Something for Nothing) looks like "a wedding cake decorated by a lunatic" and represents a triumph of chance and disorder over his previous life at the truck factory, where he made $37.81 an hour "in a vast, clean plant in which everything made sense." And yet the ordered America has failed him and others; when he suggests that he will quit the casino and look for work at another truck plant, the casino manager frankly tells him he has few options, as the only plant nearby is closing down: "You've got to stay with us . . . check the want ads. We're the only game in town, anymore, unless you want to get scalded down at Exxon or elected to the legislature."[15] Some choose chance because it is the only option.

That option is now a nearly ubiquitous one. As late as the 1970s, public officials could argue with reasonable confidence that opposition to gambling was, in general, the policy of state and federal governments. With lotteries run by a small (though growing) number of states, pari-mutuel betting relatively static or even declining, and casino gaming restricted to one state, gambling was rightfully considered to be out of the mainstream. Though illegal gaming flourished, it was viewed as criminal at worst and a vice at best.

Yet a variety of circumstances combined to foster a complete realignment of American attitudes toward gaming. Chief among them was the restructuring of larger economic and political structures that saw states assume an increased burden of social services in years when their tax bases shrank. In a postindustrial America where the New Federalism reigned, it seemed, there simply wasn't enough money to go around.

Public officials quickly learned that this fiscal vacuum could be fed, if not always satisfied, with portions of gaming revenue. In many cases, gaming legalization seemed to be a proposition without discernible losers. States would get revenues they needed, taxpayers would face lesser burdens, gaming consumers would have the security of indulging their desire in a legal, regulated fashion, and operators would garner their share of the profits. Some even forecast that legal gaming could be a positive social good that would deprive organized crime of a chief cash cow. In a series of small decisions, public officials and American citizens moved from an atmosphere of gaming restriction to one of permission.

No single instance of gaming expansion stands out as particularly remarkable, but in sum the incremental creep forward of legal gaming from its 1920 nadir is one of the exceptional stories of legal and cultural transformation in American life. At no point did either side of the debate claim a decisive battleground where the struggle for the soul of the nation was won or lost. But at the end of the twentieth century, it was abundantly clear that the United States had become a nation of gamblers. State legislators tracked gross slot machine revenues as eagerly as racketeers once counted the take from their illegal operations. Though Americans continued to work and save and go to church, many indulged in their hopes for a better life by buying lottery tickets—usually at the urging of their own state governments. It is not surprising that, with the rise of a new medium of communications and commerce, Americans would eagerly embrace another permutation of gaming, though in doing so they would provoke a clash between their desires to wager and the ambivalent anti-gaming mechanisms remaining from the Kennedy years.

Commentator George F. Will discussed the unfortunate rise of gaming as an "electronic morphine" whose lure its victims cannot resist. But who is more dependent on a drug—the addict or the dealer? Will argued that the most aggressive promoter of American gambling was the government.[16] If gambling has become our national morphine, is the Internet simply another way for Americans to mainline hope? The military-sponsored researchers who created the telecommunications and computer infrastructure for the Internet certainly did not intend it to serve that purpose, but they didn't create the system in order to enable Americans to swap e-mail or buy books, either. The history of gaming should teach us that the use of new technologies to gamble is nothing new. Every advance in communications, probably as far back as the dawn of speech, has created new forms of gambling. So, in the grand pageant of American history, the fact that in the 1990s some Americans started gambling over the Internet is really not that spectacular.

But there are deeper issues than the Internet as a delivery system. The *Cohen* case touched on one of the most revolutionary aspects of the Internet—it dissolves national borders. While it is wonderful that gamers on different continents can share in the same virtual quests in fantasy games, troubling concerns arise as well, at least for those with more than a sentimental attachment to the nation-state. Technology has inverted the geopolitical reality—the mighty United States is apparently powerless to stop operators based in Antigua from directing gaming operations at its citizens.

Internet technology has increased the pace of globalization. Again, much of this is for the better—soldiers stationed abroad can post weblogs and instantly share their experiences with the world, a form of communication that was unthinkable in earlier times. But it also means that jobs in technology, once considered a mainstay of the postindustrial economy, can more easily be outsourced around the world. The idea of an Internet casino is only an extreme form of virtual outsourcing. If a casino company does not want to incur the expense of dealers, why not simply invest in a software package and place the casino online? For those with a stake in today's most intense form of public-interest gaming, commercial and tribal government casinos, gaming on the Internet is a potentially explosive phenomenon.

The failure of the American political system to articulate a true public policy on Internet gaming is dismaying, and it may be a consequence of the influence of the Internet on political life. In the early 1990s, citizens in various states realized that they wanted to gamble in casinos and that it might be a fair way for states to keep taxes low and, as an added benefit, to create jobs. So they voted to permit riverboat or land-based gaming, creating regulatory regimes that sought to balance the need for revenue with consumer protection. Personal choice had a necessary dimension of public responsibility. With the proliferation of the Internet, though, Americans no longer necessarily have to trade off personal desires with public obligations. If I want to bet on sports legally but do not live in Nevada, I no longer have to petition my representatives to change the law. I can now simply open a Web browser, click the mouse a few times, and get action down with a licensed sportsbook in Antigua or Australia.

The Internet frees Americans from the bounds of locality. For some, this means liberation from an otherwise parochial life, sometimes a difficult prospect. One online gambler profiled in a 2001 *New York Times* article complained about the number of deceitful online casinos but refused to stop gambling because in her Mississippi hometown there was nothing to do "except go to work and church."[17] For some, a life spent in honest work and spiritual growth would be ideal, but apparently for many it is no longer enough. The popularity of the Internet forces the question of whether, when Americans can shop, chat, flirt, and play online, the traditional idea of the community is extinct. And if it is, does that mean that our democracy, based on our community, is as outmoded as an LP record in an age of mp3 players?

Americans, needless to say, still spend most of their time interacting in significant ways offline, working and living in the terrestrial world. The problem is not that people will retreat to their computer screens and utterly abandon their communities—this is physically impossible outside the fantasy of *The Matrix* or a Phillip K. Dick novel. But there is the very real possibility that the proliferation of consumer and lifestyle choices available on the Internet will obscure the local consequences of those choices, be they social, cultural, legal, or economic. We may drive the same streets to work each day, but will we really be bothered to vote on a municipal bond issue to improve those streets when we are rushing home to get action on that night's game?

Americans have never fully confronted their paradoxical desires to gamble and to control gambling. Often, they just ignored the problem, and when they did pass laws against gambling, they often flouted those laws. The rise of public-interest gaming brought the body politic into the question of gaming as a partner, further complicating the issue in the twentieth century.

Yet Americans could still not say with one voice that gambling was good or bad—a welcome consequence, perhaps, of democracy. The use of the Wire Act, in the absence of any real legislative direction, to strike at online betting is only the latest manifestation of a habitual American inclination. It is probably unlikely that Americans, confronted by a world in which the prerogatives of nations to regulate their own citizens' conduct are eroded, will suddenly decide to gather a consensus and rationally administer the world of gaming offered by the Internet. But Americans have shown, time and again, that they cannot resist a long shot.

APPENDIX 1

THE WIRE ACT: FROM TITLE 18 OF THE UNITED STATES CODE

§ 1084. Transmission of wagering information; penalties

(a) Whoever being engaged in the business of betting or wagering knowingly uses a wire communication facility for the transmission in interstate or foreign commerce of bets or wagers or information assisting in the placing of bets or wagers on any sporting event or contest, or for the transmission of a wire communication which entitles the recipient to receive money or credit as a result of bets or wagers, shall be fined not more than $10,000 or imprisoned not more than two years, or both.

(b) Nothing in this section shall be construed to prevent the transmission in interstate or foreign commerce of information for use in news reporting of sporting events or contests, or for the transmission of information assisting in the placing or bets or wagers on a sporting event or contest from a State where betting on that sporting event or contest is legal into a State in which such betting is legal.

(c) Nothing contained in this section shall create immunity from criminal prosecution under any laws of any State, Commonwealth of Puerto Rico, territory, possession, or District of Columbia.

(d) When any common carrier, subject to the jurisdiction of the Federal Communications Commission, is notified in writing by a Federal, State, or local law enforcement agency, acting within its jurisdiction, that any facility furnished by it is being used or will be used for the purpose of transmitting or receiving gambling information in interstate or foreign commerce in violation of Federal, State, or local law, it shall discontinue or refuse, the leasing, furnishing, or maintaining of such facility, after reasonable notice to the subscriber, but no damages, penalty or forfeiture, civil or criminal, shall be found against any common carrier for any act done in compliance with any notice received from a law enforcement agency. Nothing in this section shall be deemed to prejudice the right of any person affected thereby to secure an appropriate determination, as otherwise provided by law, in a Federal court or in a State or local tribunal or agency, that such facility should not be discontinued or removed, or should be restored.

APPENDIX 2
TIMELINE OF FEDERAL GAMING LEGISLATION

1890 Act of September 19, 1890, prohibits postal authorities from delivering lottery material.

1895 Congress prohibits importation of lottery materials.

1909 Anti-lottery statutes are codified as 18 U.S.C. §§ 1301–07.

1934 Prohibition of radio broadcasting of lottery results is added as 18 U.S.C. § 1304.

1948 Prohibition of gambling ships, 18 U.S.C. §§ 1081–83, is passed.

1950 Johnson Act prohibits interstate transportation of gambling devices, 15 U.S.C. §§ 1171–77. Federal tax on slot machines is raised to $150.

1952 Wagering Tax Act places $50 occupational tax and 10 percent excise tax on bookmaking.

1961 18 U.S.C. § 1084 prohibits interstate transmission of gaming information via wire communications facility; 18 U.S.C. § 1953 limits interstate transportation of betting slips and paraphernalia; 18 U.S.C. § 1952 prohibits interstate travel or transportation in furtherance of racketeering; Johnson Act is strengthened.

1970 Organized Crime Control Act enacts or modifies 18 U.S.C. §§ 1511, 1955, 1961, 2516; these prohibit an illegal gambling business, make obstruction of state law enforcement unlawful, include syndicated gambling as a racketeering activity, and permit wiretapping for suspected syndicated gambling.

1978 Interstate Horseracing Act sets parameters for simulcast betting.

1992 Professional and Amateur Sports Protection Act prohibits betting on sports, except where already permitted, 18 U.S.C. § 3702.

1994 Loophole regarding lottery ticket messenger services is closed, 18 U.S.C. § 1301.

2000 Amendment to Interstate Horseracing Act of 1978 expands "interstate off-track wager" to include pari-mutuel wagers transmitted between states using electronic media.

NOTES

Introduction. Kennedy's War Continues

1. "Congress Enacts Five Anti-Crime Bills," *Congressional Quarterly Almanac*, 87th Cong., 1st sess., 1961, vol. 17 (Washington, D.C.: Congressional Quarterly, 1961), 381.

2. Ibid., 383.

3. *John F. Kennedy: Containing the Public Messages, Speeches, and Statements of the President, January 20 to December 31, 1961*, in *Public Papers of the Presidents of the United States* (Washington, D.C.: U.S. Government Printing Office, 1962), 600.

4. 18 U.S.C.A. § 1081.

5. 18 U.S.C.A. § 1084.

6. Ibid.

7. Testimony before Kefauver Committee, quoted in *Time*, May 8, 1950, 16.

8. Jeff Pelline and Courtney Macavinta, "Virtual Casinos Bet Big," CNET News.com, July 11, 1997.

9. Rebecca Quick, "Entrepreneurs Roll the Dice on a New Site," *Wall Street Journal*, April 10, 1997.

10. Ibid.

11. Steve Kanigher, "Caught in a Web: Future of Online Casinos Debated," *Las Vegas Sun*, March 7, 2003.

12. http://www.freejaycohen.com.

13. "Jay Cohen Convicted of Operating an Off-Shore Sports Betting Business," press release, U.S. Justice Department, February 28, 2000.

14. Kanigher, "Caught in a Web."

15. Brian Krebs, "U.S. Internet Gambling Crackdown Sparks WTO Complaint," *Washington Post*, July 21, 2003.

16. Howard McGrath, address at the Attorney General's Conference on Organized Crime, February 15, 1950, in *The Attorney General's Conference on Organized Crime, February 15, 1950* (Washington, D.C.: U.S. Department of Justice, 1950), 7.

1. Legal Vices and Illicit Diversions

1. Morris Ploscowe, "The Law of Gambling," *Annals of the American Academy of Political and Social Science* 269 (May 1950): 1–8; reprinted in Herbert L. Marx, ed., *Gambling in America* (New York: H. W. Wilson, 1952), 142–43.

2. Richard McGowan modified the three-wave theory by limiting the third wave to pari-mutuel and casino betting and adding a fourth wave, which began in 1964 with the New Hampshire lottery and continues today. See Richard McGowan, *State Lotteries and Legalized Gambling: Painless Revenue or Painful Mirage?* (Westport, Conn.: Quorum, 1994). This approach does not allow for a trough of prohibition between the third and fourth waves, so it can't be said to be any more accurate than the original three-wave model.

3. I. Nelson Rose, *Gambling and the Law* (Hollywood: Gambling Times, 1986), 1–2.

4. Jackson Lears, *Something for Nothing: Luck in America* (New York: Viking, 2003), 17.

5. John Findlay, *People of Chance: Gambling in American Society from Jamestown to Las Vegas* (New York: Oxford University Press, 1986), 13–15.

6. Gerda Reith, *The Age of Chance: Gambling and Western Culture* (London: Routledge, 1999), 58–60.

7. Henry Chafetz, *Play the Devil: A History of Gambling in the United States from 1492 to 1950* (New York: Bonanza Books, 1960), 15.

8. Quoted in *Development of the Law of Gambling* (Washington, D.C.: U.S. Government Printing Office, 1977), 42.

9. Ibid., 67–69.

10. Ibid., 239–40

11. Ibid., 25–28.

12. Chafetz, *Play the Devil*, 30–31.

13. Herbert Asbury, *Sucker's Progress: An Informal History of Gambling in America* (New York: Dodd, Mead, 1938), 72–76.

14. For a definitive historical study of the growth of the commercial economy in the Jacksonian period, see Charles Sellers, *The Market Revolution: Jacksonian America, 1815–1846* (New York: Oxford University Press 1991). For an overall history of the economy and industry of the United States (a backdrop for the expansion of gaming), see Stuart Bruchey, *Enterprise: The Dynamic Economy of a Free People* (Cambridge, Mass.: Harvard University Press, 1990).

15. *Development of the Law of Gambling*, 77–81.

16. Ibid., 87.

17. These years also saw a shift from special charters for corporations, granted on an ad hoc basis by legislatures and usually granting the holders a monopoly, to general incorporation laws that lessened the role of state legislatures in granting charters. See Kermit L. Hall, *The Magic Mirror: Law in American History* (New York: Oxford University Press, 1989), 98.

18. For a complete history of lotteries in America, see John Samuel Ezell, *Fortune's Merry Wheel: The Lottery in America* (Cambridge, Mass.: Harvard University Press, 1960).

19. Chafetz, *Play the Devil*, 48.

20. Ibid., 47.

21. For an account of the Murrell conspiracy and the Vicksburg lynching, see ibid., 55–63.

22. Asbury, *Sucker's Progress*, 185–86.

23. Ibid., 158–63.

24. Ibid., 109.

25. Portions of this chapter were originally published as "John Davis: Father of American Gaming?" *Global Gaming Business*, December 15, 2002.

26. *Development of the Law of Gambling*, 269.

27. Asbury, *Sucker's Progress*, 167–68.

28. Ibid., 456–57.

29. *Development of the Law of Gambling*, 250–56.

30. Asbury, *Sucker's Progress*, 161.

31. Cornell Law School, *Development of the Law of Gambling: Federal* (prepared for the Commission to Review the National Policy on Gambling, 1974), 12–13; hereafter cited as *Cornell Study*.

32. *Development of the Law of Gambling*, 276.

33. For a brief account of "the Serpent," see Chafetz, *Play the Devil*, 297–308. For an academic assessment of the lottery, see John J. White, "The History of the Louisiana Lottery" (master's thesis, Tulane University, 1939).

34. *Cornell Study*, 20–24.

35. Mark H. Haller, "Bootleggers and American Gambling, 1920–1950," in *Gambling in America*, Appendix 1 (Washington, D.C.: U.S. Government Printing Office, 1976), 104–6.

36. *Development of the Law of Gambling*, 10.

37. Roger Longrigg, *The History of Horse Racing* (New York: Stein and Day, 1972), 282.

38. *Development of the Law of Gambling*, 106.

39. Longrigg, *History of Horse Racing*, 282.

40. *Development of the Law of Gambling*, 291–92.

41. Thomas Dewey, reply to "Legal Betting on Public Sports Events," reprinted in Marx, *Gambling in America*, 178–79.

42. *Development of the Law of Gambling*, 297–99.

43. John Phillip Quinn, *The Highway to Hell* (Chicago: International Anti-Gambling Association, 1895).

44. Josiah W. Leeds, *Horse Racing. The Beginnings of Gambling. The Lottery* (Philadelphia: Josiah Leeds, 1895), 4–5.

45. Ibid., 4.

46. Quinn, *Highway to Hell*.

47. Ibid. This situation curiously parallels today's, where print and television media enthusiastically discuss the football spread, despite the fact that sports betting is ostensibly illegal in almost the entire nation and the major sports leagues officially oppose gaming on sports activities.

48. *Second Interim Report of the Special Committee to Investigate Organized Crime in Interstate Commerce* (Washington, D.C.: U.S. Government Printing Office, 1951); reprinted in *Mass Violence in America: Reports on Crime Investigations* (New York: Arno Press and the New York Times, 1969), 14.

49. Ibid.

50. Ibid., 14–15.

51. Leeds, *Horse Racing*, 26.

52. Ibid., 28.

53. Arthur Daley, "Sports Are Honest: A Defense," *New York Times Magazine*, March 4, 1951, 20; reprinted in Marx, *Gambling in America*, 88.

54. Richard O. Davies and Richard G. Abram, *Betting the Line: Sports Wagering in American Life* (Columbus: Ohio State University Press, 2001), 18–22.

55. Ibid., 47–48.

56. Ibid., 51–55.

57. Stanley S. Smith, "Lotteries," *Journal of Criminal Law and Criminology* 38:456–57; reprinted in Marx, *Gambling in America*, 61–66.

58. Deets Pickett, *Fools' Gold: The Truth About Gambling* (New York: Abingdon, 1936), 8–9.

59. "How Much Do Gamblers Take From Your Plant?" *Business Week*, August 21, 1948, 92; reprinted in Marx, *Gambling in America*, 33–34.

60. Albert Maisel, "Return of the Numbers Racket," *Collier's*, 123:21–23; reprinted in Marx, *Gambling in America*, 67.

61. See Johann Huizinga, *Homo Ludens: A Study of the Play-Element in Culture* (Boston: Beacon, 1955).

62. Hall, *The Magic Mirror*, 93.

63. Enoch Johnson Report, quoted in Jonathan Van Meter, *The Last Good Time: Skinny D'Amato, the Notorious 500 Club, and the Rise and Fall of Atlantic City* (New York: Crown, 2003), 63.

64. Enoch Johnson Report, 62.

65. *Development of the Law of Gambling*, 89.

66. Paul Gardner, "The Incredible Totalisator," *Nation's Business* 38 (May 1950):56–58; reprinted in Marx, *Gambling in America*, 97–99. For a more detailed biography of Straus and an in-depth description of the development of the totalisator, see John C. Schmidt, *Win, Place, Show: A Biography of Harry Straus, the Man Who Gave America the Tote* (Baltimore: Johns Hopkins University Press, 1989).

67. Leeds, *Horse Racing*, 15.

68. For a contemporary description of the multitude of slot machines available to

the public in 1895, see John Phillip Quinn, *Gambling and Gambling Devices: An Educational Exposition Designed to Instruct the Youth to Avoid All Forms of Gambling* (1912; reprint, Las Vegas: Gambler's Book Club, 1979), 188–226.

69. Leeds, *Horse Racing*, 25.

70. Quinn, *Gambling and Gambling Devices*, 188–89.

71. Shannon J. Bybee Jr., "Gaming Industry Trends 2001: New Directions, Faster Pace," in Dina Zemke, ed., *Evidence of a Serendipitous Career in Gaming* (Boston: Pearson Custom Publishing, 2003), 112–13.

72. Leeds, *Horse Racing*, 16.

73. There were, of course, myriad ways to cheat, defraud, and manipulate the results, all of which were aggressively explored by legions of con artists and cross roaders.

74. Haller, "Bootleggers and American Gambling," 107.

75. Davies and Abram, *Betting the Line*, 32.

76. Haller, "Bootleggers and American Gambling," 107.

77. John Landesco, *Organized Crime in Chicago. Part III of the Illinois Crime Survey, 1929* (Chicago: University of Chicago Press, 1968), 45.

78. Ibid., 46–51.

79. Ibid., 53.

80. Ibid., 58–70.

81. Ibid., 80–81.

82. Davies and Abram, *Betting the Line*, 32–35. For a full biography of Annenberg, see John Cooney, *The Annenbergs* (New York: Simon and Schuster, 1982).

83. Davies and Abram, *Betting the Line*, 36–37.

84. Ibid., 37–38.

85. According to Virgil Peterson, Ragen was the general manager for the Chicago distributor of the wire service. See Virgil Peterson, *Barbarians in Our Midst: A History of Chicago Crime and Politics* (Boston: Little, Brown, 1952), 278.

86. *Third Interim Report of the Special Committee to Investigate Organized Crime in Interstate Commerce* (Washington, D.C.: U.S. Government Printing Office, 1951).

87. Peterson, *Barbarians in Our Midst*, 280–81.

88. *Third Interim Report*, 155.

89. Paul Gardner and Allan Gould, "Brain of the Bookies," *Collier's*, October 25, 1947.

90. *Third Interim Report*, 155; Peterson, *Barbarians in Our Midst*, 281.

91. *Third Interim Report*, 156; Peterson, *Barbarians in Our Midst*, 284.

924. *Third Interim Report*, 156.

93. Ibid., 33.

94. Ibid., 33–34.

95. William H. Moore, *The Kefauver Committee and the Politics of Crime, 1950–1952* (Columbia: University of Missouri Press, 1974), 59.

96. *Third Interim Report*, 39–40.

97. *Second Interim Report*, 16.

98. Ibid., 15.

99. *Third Interim Report*, 160.

2. The Anxious Decade

1. Harry S. Truman, opening address at the Attorney General's Conference on Organized Crime, February 15, 1950, in *The Attorney General's Conference on Organized Crime, February 15, 1950* (Washington, D.C.: Department of Justice, 1950), 2.

2. Eric Monkkonen, *Murder in New York City* (Berkeley: University of California Press, 2000), 18.

3. John Bartlow Martin, "Al Capone's Successors," *American Mercury*, April 1949, 730.

4. "1950—Biggest Gambling Year Ever," *Scientific Digest*, January 1951, 33.

5. George Gallup, "Gambling, Betting Popular Pastime with 57%," *U.S. Public Opinion News Service*, June 11, 1950; reprinted in Herbert L. Marx, ed., *Gambling in America* (New York: H. W. Wilson, 1952), 25–26.

6. deLesseps Morrison, address at the Attorney General's Conference on Crime, February 15, 1950, in *The Attorney General's Conference on Crime, February 15, 1950* (Washington, D.C.: Department of Justice, 1950), 28.

7. Howard McGrath, address at the Attorney General's Conference on Crime, February 15, 1950, in *The Attorney General's Conference on Organized Crime, February 15, 1950* (Washington, D.C.: Department of Justice, 1950), 6.

8. The "allied rackets" of the slot owners were typically illegal gambling casinos, already declining in popularity. Morrison address, 28.

9. William H. Moore, *The Kefauver Committee and the Politics of Crime, 1950–1952* (Columbia: University of Missouri Press, 1974), 12–13.

10. Virgil Peterson, *Barbarians in Our Midst: A History of Chicago Crime and Politics* (Boston: Little, Brown, 1952), vii–viii.

11. "War on Syndicated Crime Urged of AMA," *American City*, January 1950, 86.

12. Peterson, *Barbarians in Our Midst*, 330–31.

13. In 1950 and 1951 the Kefauver Committee would identify this organization as part of a national mafia, and in the 1960s federal authorities, working from the testimony of Joseph Valachi, called the group La Cosa Nostra, but in its earliest incarnation it was simply called "the Syndicate."

14. Martin, "Al Capone's Successors," 728.

15. Mark H. Haller, "Illegal Enterprise: A Theoretical and Historical Interpretation," *Criminology* 28, no. 2 (1990): 221.

16. "West Fears Gang Invasion," *New York Times*, September 7, 1947.

17. "Bergen County—A Case Study," *New York Times*, December 4, 1951.

18. "War on Syndicated Crime Urged of AMA," 86.

19. Ibid.

20. Ibid.

21. Morrison address, 27.

22. Ibid.

23. Ibid.

24. See FBI file of Benjamin Siegel.

25. Ronald Kessler, *The Bureau: The Secret History of the FBI* (New York: St. Martin's, 2002), 102, 106.

26. "M'Grath to Bar Voter Fraud," *New York Times*, February 14, 1950.

27. Truman opening address, 4.

28. McGrath address, 5.

29. Ibid., 5–6.

30. Ibid., 9.

31. Executive session, the Attorney General's Conference on Organized Crime, February 15, 1950, in *The Attorney General's Conference on Organized Crime, February 15, 1950* (Washington, D.C.: Department of Justice, 1950), 12.

32. Ibid., 27–33.

33. Ibid., 41–42.

34. Ibid., 65.

35. Lewis Wood, "Truman Pledges to Campaign Against Forces of 'Vice and Greed,'" *New York Times*, February 16, 1950.

36. "Anti-gambling Bills Offered by M'Grath," *New York Times*, April 2, 1950.

37. U.S. Congressional Code Service, *Laws*. 81st Cong., 2d sess., 1950 (Washington, D.C.: U.S. Government Printing Office, 1950), 4242.

38. "Slot Machine Bill Voted," *New York Times*, April 20, 1950.

39. *Congressional Quarterly Almanac*, 81st Cong., 2d sess., 1950, vol. 6 (Washington, D.C.: Congressional Quarterly News Features, 1951), 434.

40. U.S. Congressional Code Service, *Laws*, 4245.

41. *Congressional Quarterly Almanac*, 434.

42. U.S. Congressional Code Service, *Laws*, 4246.

43. Ibid., 435.

44. Ibid.

45. Ibid.; "Slot Machine Bill Passed," *New York Times*, December 21, 1950.

46. U.S. Congressional Code Service, *Laws*, 548.

47. Senate Committee on Interstate and Foreign Commerce, Subcommittee, *Transmission of Gambling Information: Hearings on S 3358*, 81st Cong., 2d sess. (Washington, D.C.: U.S. Government Printing Office, 1950), 1–2; hereafter cited as McFarland Hearings.

48. Ibid., 2.

49. Ibid.

50. Ibid., 46.

51. *Congressional Quarterly Almanac*, 414.

52. McFarland Hearings, 47–49.

53. Ibid., 49.

54. Ibid., 50.

55. Ibid., 56.

56. *Congressional Quarterly Almanac*, 414.

57. Ibid., 324–31.

58. Ibid., 332–33.

59. Ibid., 345.

60. Ibid., 378.

61. "New York Aides Give Senate 'Bookie' Blueprint," *New York Times*, April 21, 1950.

62. McFarland Hearings, 469.

63. "Mayors, Police Tie 'Bookies' to Crime," *New York Times*, April 22, 1950.

64. McFarland Hearings, 377.

65. *Congressional Quarterly Almanac*, 416.

66. Ibid., 415.

67. For a more complete analysis of Kefauver's political career, see Joseph Bruce Gorman, *Kefauver: A Political Biography* (New York: Oxford University Press, 1971).

68. Estes Kefauver, *Crime in America* (Garden City, N.Y.: Doubleday, 1951), 1.

69. William Howard Moore. *The Kefauver Committee and the Politics of Crime*, 48.

70. *Congressional Quarterly Almanac*, 437.

71. "Senate Approves Inquiry Into Crime," *New York Times*, May 4, 1950.

72. *Congressional Quarterly Almanac*, 48.

73. *Third Interim Report of the Special Committee to Investigate Organized Crime in Interstate Commerce* (New York: Arco Publishing, 1951), 21.

74. McFarland Hearings, 65, 143.

75. Moore, *The Kefauver Committee and the Politics of Crime*, 183–84.

76. For a thorough rebuttal of the committee's characterization of the Mafia, see Joseph L. Albini, *The American Mafia: Genesis of a Legend* (New York: Irvington, 1979), which absolutely demolishes the committee's claims of a national mafia conspiracy.

77. *Third Interim Report*, 1–2.

78. Ibid., 2.

79. Ibid., 3–4.

80. Ibid., 8–11.

81. Ibid., 12–14.

82. Rufus King, *Gambling and Organized Crime* (Washington, D.C.: Public Affairs, 1969), 92–93.

83. "Gambling in Galveston," *Newsweek*, December 10, 1951.

84. "Bergen County—A Case Study."

85. Moore, *The Kefauver Committee and the Politics of Crime*, 231–32.

86. Evan Thomas, *Robert Kennedy: His Life* (New York: Simon and Schuster, 2000), 70–80.

87. George Stamos Jr., "Tropicana," *Las Vegas Sun Magazine*, August 26, 1979.

88. George Wolf with Joseph DiMona, *Frank Costello: Prime Minister of the Underworld* (New York: William Morrow, 1974), 253–54.

89. Ralph Salerno and John S. Tompkins, *The Crime Confederation: Cosa Nostra and Allied Operations in Organized Crime* (Garden City, N.Y.: Doubleday, 1969) 296–97.

90. John Drzazga, *Wheels of Fortune* (Springfield, Ill.: Charles C. Thomas, 1963), 27, 41.

91. Salerno and Tompkins, *The Crime Confederation*, 298.

92. Ibid., 300.

93. Thomas, *Robert Kennedy*, 82.

3. Camelot Strikes Back

1. "Robert Kennedy Urges New Laws to Fight Rackets," *New York Times*, April 7, 1961, 1.

2. "Anti-Crime Fight Is Pushed by U.S.," *New York Times*, February 2, 1961, 1.

3. Evan Thomas, *Robert Kennedy: His Life* (New York: Simon and Schuster, 2000), 59.

4. Ibid., 65–66.

5. Ibid., 66.

6. Ibid., 70–71.

7. Wallace Carroll, "Appointing a Relative," *New York Times*, December 17, 1960, 14.

8. Robert Manning, "Someone the President Can Talk To," *New York Times Magazine*, May 28, 1961, 22.

9. Jeff Sheshol, *Mutual Contempt: Lyndon Johnson, Robert Kennedy, and the Feud That Defined a Decade* (New York: Norton, 1997).

10. Thomas, *Robert Kennedy*, 79.

11. Robert Kennedy, *The Enemy Within* (New York: Harper and Brothers, 1960), 43.

12. Thomas, *Robert Kennedy*, 88.

13. Manning, "Someone the President Can Talk To."

14. Thaddeus Russell, *Out of the Jungle: Jimmy Hoffa and the Remaking of the American Middle Class* (New York: Knopf, 2001), 216.

15. Ibid., 213–14.

16. Thomas, *Robert Kennedy*, 116–17.

17. Senate Committee on the Judiciary, *Hearings on S. 1653, S. 1654, S. 1655, S. 1656, S. 1657, S. 1658, S. 1665*, 87th Cong., 1st sess. (Washington, D.C.: U.S. Government Printing Office, 1961), 2.

18. Ronald Goldfarb, *Perfect Villains, Imperfect Heroes: Robert F. Kennedy's War on Organized Crime* (New York: Random House, 1995), 42–43.

19. "Anti-Crime Fight Is Pushed by U.S.," 1.

20. Goldfarb, *Perfect Villains, Imperfect Heroes*, 18; "Anti-Crime Fight Is Pushed by U.S.," 1.

21. "Anti-Crime Fight Is Pushed by U.S.," 13.

22. Senate Committee on Interstate and Foreign Commerce, Subcommittee, *Transmission of Gambling Information: Hearings on S 3358*, 81st Cong., 2d sess. (Washington, D.C.: U.S. Government Printing Office, 1950), 56.

23. Bill Kaufman, "They Voted Against Mother's Day," *American Enterprise*, April–May 2002.

24. Senate Committee on Interstate Commerce, *Hearing on S. 3253, a Bill to Prevent the Nullification of State Anti-gambling Laws by International or Interstate Transmission of Race-Gambling Bets or Racing Odds*, 64th Cong., 2d sess., (Washington, D.C.: U.S. Government Printing Office, 1917), 62; hereafter cited as *1917 Hearing*.

25. House Committee on Interstate and Foreign Commerce, *Hearings on H.R. 25825, a Bill to Prohibit Interstate Transportation of Pictures and Descriptions of Prize Fights and H.R. 2160, a Bill to Prevent the Nullification of State Anti-gambling Laws by International or Interstate Transmission of Race-Gambling Bets or Racing Odds*, 61st Cong., 2d sess. (Washington, D.C.: U.S. Government Printing Office, 1911), 12; hereafter cited as *1910 Hearings*.

26. Ibid., 12–13.

27. Ibid., 15–19.

28. Ibid., 19.

29. Ibid., 17–18.

30. Ibid., 18.

31. Ibid.

32. *1917 Hearing*, 62.

33. *Transmission of Gambling Information*. Report Number 500, 83d Cong., 1st sess. (Washington, D.C.: U.S. Government Printing Office, 1953), 3.

34. Ibid., 7.

35. Ibid., 4.

36. Ibid.

37. Ibid., 2.

38. Ibid., 6.

39. House Committee of the Judiciary, Subcommittee Number 2, *Hearings on H.R. 7975, a Bill to Prohibit Certain Acts and Transactions with Respect to Gambling Materials*, 83d Cong., 2d sess. (Washington, D.C.: U.S. Government Printing Office, 1954), 2; hereafter cited as *1954 Hearings*.

40. Ibid., 25–27.

41. Ibid., 26.

42. Dwight Eisenhower, "Faith in the Individual: Limit the Powers of Government," in *Selected Speeches of Dwight David Eisenhower* (Washington, D.C.: U.S. Government Printing Office, 1970), 151.

43. "Congress Enacts Five Anti-Crime Bills," *Congressional Quarterly Almanac*, 87th

Cong., 1st sess., 1961, vol. 17 (Washington, D.C.: Congressional Quarterly, 1961), 381.

44. Ibid.

45. Russell Porter, "R. F. Kennedy Hits Greed of Public," *New York Times*, June 15, 1961, 1.

46. Ibid., 24.

47. "Robert Kennedy Urges New Laws to Fight Rackets."

48. *1961 Hearings*, 3.

49. *United States Code Congressional and Administrative News*, 87th Cong., 1st sess., 1961, vol. 2: *Legislative History* (St. Paul: West Publishing, 1961), 2666.

50. *1961 Hearings*, 38.

51. Ibid., 41.

52. Ibid., 8.

53. Ibid., 1.

54. Ibid., 3.

55. Ibid., 5.

56. Ibid., 6.

57. "Improve the Breed of Men," *New York Globe*, February 24, 1916.

58. *1961 Hearings*, 6.

59. Ibid., 11.

60. Ibid., 12.

61. Ibid.

62. Ibid.

63. Ibid., 12–13.

64. Ibid., 13.

65. Ibid.

66. Ibid.

67. Ibid., 47.

68. "U.S. Jury Indicts 13 in Betting Ring," *New York Times*, June 28, 1961, 20.

69. Cabell Phillips, "U.S. Crime Fight Nears a Climax," *New York Times*, July 23, 1961, 37.

70. *1961 Hearings*, 278.

71. Ibid., 45, 59.

72. C. P. Trussell, "House Votes Bill to Combat Crime," *New York Times*, August 24, 1961, 20.

73. C. P. Trussell, "Six Crime Bills Passed in Senate," *New York Times*, July 29, 1961, 17.

74. *John F. Kennedy: Containing the Public Messages, Speeches, and Statements of the President, January 20 to December 31, 1961. Public Papers of the Presidents of the United States* (Washington, D.C.: U.S. Government Printing Office, 1962), 600.

75. "U.S. Seizes 6 Here in Gambling Raid," *New York Times*, November 29, 1961, 35.

76. Anthony Lewis, "President Hails Anti-Crime Drive," *New York Times*, October 11, 1962, 22.

77. Joseph A. Loftus, "Racket Violence Is Found Waning," *New York Times*, February 27, 1962, 25.

78. The entire Ratterman affair is analyzed in Ronald Goldfarb's *Perfect Villains, Imperfect Heroes*, but even Goldfarb, the lead Justice Department attorney on the case, remains unsure of exactly what happened to Ratterman, and how a reform candidate for sheriff could have plausibly placed himself into such a situation.

79. Ibid., 100.

80. Loftus, "Racket Violence Is Found Waning," 25.

81. Robert F. Kennedy, "Robert Kennedy Defines the Menace," *New York Times*, October 13, 1963, 224.

82. Loftus, "Racket Violence Is Found Waning," 25.

83. *Gambling and Organized Crime*, Report of the Committee on Government Operations, U.S. Senate, made by its permanent subcommittee on investigations (Washington, D.C.: U.S. Government Printing Office, 1962), 46–48.

84. "Anti-Crime Bills," *Congressional Quarterly Almanac*, 87th Cong., 2d sess., 1962, vol. 18 (Washington, D.C.: Congressional Quarterly, 1962), 391.

85. Ibid., 390.

86. Ibid., 391.

87. "The Valachi Show," *New York Times*, October 6, 1963, 288. For the complete story of Valachi's career as an informant, see Peter Maas, *The Valachi Papers: The First Inside Account of Life in the Cosa Nostra* (New York: G. P. Putnam's Sons, 1966).

88. "Wiretapping," *Congressional Quarterly Almanac*, 87th Cong., 1st sess., 1961, vol. 17 (Washington, D.C.: Congressional Quarterly, 1961), 386.

89. Kennedy, "Robert Kennedy Defines the Menace," 108.

90. "Wiretapping," 385.

91. Emmanuel Perlmutter, "Robert Kennedy Cites Rise in Crime," *New York Times*, September 26, 1963, 27; Kennedy, "Robert Kennedy Defines the Menace," 108.

92. Goldfarb, *Perfect Villains, Imperfect Heroes*, 80, 130.

93. Edward A. Olsen, *My Careers as a Journalist in Oregon, Idaho, and Nevada; in Nevada Gaming Control; and at the University of Nevada* (Reno: University of Nevada Oral History Project, 1972), 338–39.

94. Jerome H. Skolnick, *House of Cards: The Legalization and Control of Casino Gambling* (Boston: Little, Brown, 1978), 124–26.

95. Victor Navasky, *Kennedy Justice* (New York: Atheneum, 1977), 80–81.

96. Olsen, *My Careers*, 346–48.

97. Skolnick, *House of Cards*, 129.

98. See David G. Schwartz, *Suburban Xanadu: The Casino Resort on the Las Vegas Strip and Beyond* (New York: Routledge, 2003), chapter 5, "Wiseguy Empire," for a more complete analysis.

99. "U.S. Fight on Organized Crime Brings Wide Rise in Convictions," *New York Times*, January 12, 1964, 47.

100. Goldfarb, *Perfect Villains, Imperfect Heroes*, 145–47.

101. "Philadelphia Parley Held," *New York Times*, November 17, 1961, 29.

102. Kennedy, "Robert Kennedy Defines the Menace," 224.

103. Ibid., 108.

104. Goldfarb, *Perfect Villains, Imperfect Heroes*, 302.

105. Ibid., 256.

106. Ibid., 302–3.

107. Kennedy, "Robert Kennedy Defines the Menace," 224.

108. Victor S. Navasky, "A Famous Prosecutor Talks About Crime," *New York Times*, February 15, 1970, 210.

4. Booking the Bookies

1. "Wire Bets Sifted by Western Union," *New York Times*, April 28, 1950, 32.

2. "Western Union Asks New Gambler Curbs," *New York Times*, June 4, 1952, 14.

3. Senate Committee of the Judiciary, *Hearings on S. 1653, S. 1654, S. 1655, S. 1656, S. 1657, S. 1658, S. 1665*, 87th Cong., 1st sess. (Washington, D.C.: U.S. Government Printing Office, 1961), 58–59.

4. Richard O. Davies and Richard G. Abram, *Betting the Line: Sports Wagering in American Life* (Columbus: Ohio State University Press, 2001), 46–47.

5. Paul Gardner, "The Incredible Totalisator," *Nation's Business* 38 (May 1950): 56–58; reprinted in Herbert L. Marx, ed., *Gambling in America* (New York: H. W. Wilson, 1952), 97–99.

6. Josiah Leeds reported that Pennsylvania backers triumphed over Yale bettors when the Quakers lost by less than the twenty points Yale men had offered them. See Josiah W. Leeds, *Horse Racing. The Beginnings of Gambling. The Lottery* (Philadelphia: Josiah Leeds, 1895), 28.

7. Davies and Abram, *Betting the Line*, 52–55.

8. William Barry Furlong, "Of Lines, Point Spreads, and Middles," *New York Times*, January 2, 1977, 142.

9. Paul Gardner and Allan Gould, "Brain of the Bookies," *Collier's*, October 25, 1947.

10. Furlong, "Of Lines, Point Spreads, and Middles," 143.

11. Gardner and Gould, "Brain of the Bookies."

12. Ibid.

13. Ibid.

14. Furlong, "Of Lines, Point Spreads, and Middles," 142.

15. Davies and Abram, *Betting the Line*, 135–37.

16. Ibid., 138–39.

17. "Sportsline.com, Inc. Announces Sale of Las Vegas Sports Consultants," CBS

Sportsline.com, Investors Relations, November 24, 2003, accessed online at: http://cbs.sportsline.com/info/ir/press/2003/lvscsale.

18. President's Commission on Organized Crime, *Organized Crime and Gambling: Record of Hearing VII, June 24–26, 1985* (Washington, D.C.: U.S. Government Printing Office, 1985), 188.

19. R. Phillip Harker, "Sports Bookmaking Operations," *FBI Law Enforcement Bulletin*, September 1978, 1.

20. Ibid., 2–3.

21. Lewis Wood, "Truman Pledges to Aid Campaign Against Forces of 'Vice and Greed,'" *New York Times*, February 16, 1950, 2.

22. For more on the Gross case, see Richard Sasuly, *Bookies and Bettors: Two Hundred Years of Gambling* (New York: Holt, Rinehart, and Winston, 1982), chapter 12, "Harry Gross Enterprises and the Law."

23. For more on the serious charges made against college basketball players, coaches, and tournament organizers, see Charles Rosen, *The Scandals of '51* (New York: Seven Stories Press, 1998).

24. "Previous Point-Shaving Scandals," CNN-SI.com, March 27, 1988, accessed online at: http://sportsillustrated.cnn.com/basketball/college/news/1998/03/27/gambling sidebar/.

25. For an in-depth analysis of the scandal, see David Porter, *Fixed: How Goodfellas Bought Boston College Basketball* (Dallas: Taylor Trade Publishing, 2000).

26. "Boston College Continues to Sort Out Mess From Gambling Scandal," *Las Vegas Review-Journal*, July 25, 1997.

27. "Previous Point-Shaving Scandals."

28. Raymond D. D'Angelo, "The Social Organization of Sports Gambling: A Study in Conventionality and Deviance" (Ph.D. diss., Bryn Mawr College, 1983), 94–102.

29. Steve Cady, "No Rest for the Weary Bettor as Sports Proliferate, Overlap," *New York Times*, July 23, 1974, 46.

30. Fund for the City of New York, *Legal Gambling in New York: A Discussion of Numbers and Sports Betting* (New York: Fund for the City of New York, 1972), 35–36.

31. Koleman Strumpf, "Illegal Sports Bookmakers" (paper presented at the Twelfth International Conference on Gambling and Risk Taking, Vancouver, B.C., Canada, May 2003), 2.

32. Ibid., 8–9.

33. Ibid., 49.

34. Fund for the City of New York, *Legal Gambling in New York*, 39.

35. Strumpf, "Illegal Sports Bookmakers," 25–31.

36. Fund for the City of New York, *Legal Gambling in New York*, 41.

37. President's Commission on Law Enforcement and Administration of Justice, *The Challenge of Crime in a Free Society* (Washington, D.C.: U.S. Government Printing Office, 1967), 188–89.

38. Ibid., 189.

39. Ibid., 197.

40. Ibid., 198–99.

41. Ibid., 200–203.

42. "Congress Clears 1970 Organized Crime Bill," *Congressional Quarterly Almanac*, 91st Cong., 2d sess., 1970, vol. 26 (Washington, D.C.: Congressional Quarterly, 1970), 545.

43. Organized Crime and Racketeering Section, *Racketeer Influenced and Corrupt Organizations (RICO): A Manual for Federal Prosecutors* (Washington, D.C.: U.S. Department of Justice, 1988), 1–3.

44. John Dombrink and James W. Meeker, "Racketeering Prosecution: The Use and Abuse of RICO," *Rutgers Law Journal* 16, nos. 3 and 4 (Spring and Summer 1985): 633.

45. Ibid.

46. Ibid., 652.

47. Ibid., 639.

48. G. Robert Blakey, "RICO: The Federal Experience (Criminal and Civil) and an Analysis of Attacks Against the Statute," in Robert J. Kelly, Ko-Lin Chin, and Rufus Schatzberg, eds., *Handbook of Organized Crime in the United States* (Westport, Conn.: Greenwood, 1994), 455, 481.

49. President's Commission on Organized Crime, *Organized Crime and Gambling*, 188.

50. Kevin B. Kinnee, *Practical Gambling Investigation Techniques* (New York: Elsevier, 1992).

51. "Gambling Investigations," *FBI Law Enforcement Bulletin*, July 1969; revised September 1979, 2.

52. President's Commission on Organized Crime, *Organized Crime and Gambling*, 189.

53. Robert F. Kennedy, "Robert Kennedy Defines the Menace," *New York Times*, October 13, 1963, 224.

54. *Illegal Gambling: Numbers, Dice, Bookmaking*, FBI Police Training Video, date unknown, likely early 1970s.

55. See "Gambling Investigations" and Captain George H. Bullen Jr., "Local Investigation of Illegal Gambling Operations," *FBI Law Enforcement Bulletin*, March 1971, for example.

56. Kinnee, *Practical Gambling Investigation Techniques*.

57. "Gambling Investigations," 2–3.

58. Ibid., 2.

59. Ibid., 3.

60. Floyd J. Fowler, Thomas W. Mangione, and Frederick E. Pratter, *Gambling Law*

Enforcement in Major American Cities (Washington, D.C.: U.S. Department of Justice, Law Enforcement Assistance Administration, 1978), 69, 77–78.

61. Kinnee, *Practical Gambling Investigation Techniques,* 33–34.

62. Fowler, Mangione, and Pratter, *Gambling Law Enforcement,* 144.

63. Kinnee, *Practical Gambling Investigation Techniques,* 124.

64. Department of the Treasury-Internal Revenue Service, Form 886A, 1.

65. *United States v. Miller,* 79-2 USTC Paragraph 16, 318, p. 7938 (N.D. Tex, 1979), cited in Form 886A, 2.

66. Form 886A, 3.

67. Bureau of Justice, *Sourcebook of Criminal Justice Statistics* (Albany, N.Y.: Hindelang Criminal Justice Research Center, 1974–2002), table 4.1.

68. Mary Breasted, "157 Indicted Here as Part of Gambling Network," *New York Times,* November 20, 1974, 94.

69. Selwyn Raab, "3 Accused of Running Mafia Betting Ring," *New York Times,* December 7, 1993, B3.

70. Ibid.

71. "U.S. Drive Opened on Bet Tipsters," *New York Times,* March 6, 1964, 64.

5. A Money Jungle From Sea to Sea

1. Howard McGrath, address at the Attorney General's Conference on Organized Crime, February 15, 1950, in *The Attorney General's Conference on Organized Crime, February 15, 1950* (Washington, D.C.: Department of Justice, 1950), 7.

2. I. Nelson Rose and David Staley, *Gambling and the Law: Indian Gaming in California* (Reno: Institute for the Study of Gambling and Commercial Gaming, 1994).

3. "Military Runs Slot Machines, Offers Little Help to Addicts," *Holland Sentinel,* January 14, 2001.

4. Senate Committee on Interstate and Foreign Commerce, Subcommittee, *Transmission of Gambling Information: Hearings on S 3358,* 81st Cong., 2d sess. (Washington, D.C.: U.S. Government Printing Office, 1950), 1–2, 715.

5. David Weinstein and Lillian Deitch, *The Impact of Legalized Gambling: The Socioeconomic Consequences of Lotteries and Off-Track Betting* (New York: Praeger, 1974), 17.

6. Ibid., 95–96.

7. Ibid., 98.

8. Michael Shagan, "The Relationship Between OTB and Racing," *OTB Journal* (Summer 1977): 6–7.

9. Jockey Club Fact Book at
http://home.jockeyclub.com/FACTBOOK/handle.html.

10. Maryland Department of Legislative Services, "Overview of Issues Related to Video Lottery Terminals" (Annapolis: Office of Policy Analysis, 1993), 9.

11. Patricia A. McQueen, "Match Made in Heaven," *International Gaming and Wagering Business* 24, no. 7 (July 2003): 1, 26.

12. Gerald Eskenazi, "Rise in Illegal Gambling Linked to OTB Climate," *New York Times*, January 10, 1974, 1.

13. Theresa La Fleur, *La Fleur's 2002 World Lottery Almanac* (Boyds, Md.: TLF Publications, 2002), 4.

14. Richard McGowan, *State Lotteries and Legalized Gambling: Painless Revenue or Painful Mirage?* (Westport, Conn.: Quorum, 1994), 14.

15. *Development of the Law of Gambling* (Washington, D.C.: U.S. Government Printing Office, 1977), 276; John J. White, "The History of the Louisiana Lottery" (master's thesis, Tulane University, 1939).

16. McGowan, *State Lotteries and Legalized Gambling*, 16–17.

17. Weinstein and Deitch, *The Impact of Legalized Gambling*, 15–16.

18. *Development of the Law of Gambling*, 118.

19. Ibid.

20. Weinstein and Deitch, *The Impact of Legalized Gambling*, 16.

21. *Development of the Law of Gambling*, 120.

22. Bryan Elwood and Hal Tennant, *The Whole World Lottery Guide*, 2d ed. (Toronto: Millions Magazine, 1981), 34–35.

23. Ibid., 75.

24. La Fleur, *La Fleur's 2002 World Lottery Almanac*, 6.

25. Elwood and Tennant, *The Whole World Lottery Guide*, 34.

26. La Fleur, *La Fleur's 2002 World Lottery Almanac*, 6–7.

27. Kim Masters Evans, *Gambling: What's at Stake?* (Farmington Hills, Mich.: Gale, 2003), 101.

28. La Fleur, *La Fleur's 2002 World Lottery Almanac*, 8–9, 23.

29. Evans, *Gambling*, 99.

30. "Happy Huskers," news release on Powerball Web site, accessed online at: http://www.powerball.com/powerball/winners/2003/102503mn.shtm. The story of the Minnesota sixteen illustrates a common pattern in lottery purchases: "Each group member contributes 25 cents every paycheck for Powerball tickets—enough to purchase one ticket for each of the four Powerball drawings held during the two-week pay period. The group has been pooling their money to purchase tickets since the Lottery began in 1990."

31. Evans, *Gembling*, 99.

32. Eric N. Moody, "Nevada's Legalization of Casino Gambling in 1931," *Nevada Historical Society Quarterly* 37, no. 2 (Summer 1994): 81–82.

33. For more on the creation and development of the casino resort, see David G. Schwartz, *Suburban Xanadu: The Casino Resort on the Las Vegas Strip and Beyond* (New York: Routledge, 2003).

34. Tom Alexander, "What Is Del Webb up to in Nevada?" *Fortune Magazine*, May 1965, 185.

35. Nevada Gaming Commission, *Gaming Nevada Style* (Carson City: Nevada Gaming Commission, 1981), 13–14.

36. Nevada State Gaming Control Board, Economic Research Section, *Nevada Gaming Abstract* (Carson City: Nevada State Gaming Control Board, 1972, 1981).

37. Frederick Hayes, *The Impact of the Resorts International Casino Hotel on the Atlantic City Economy* (prepared for Resorts International, February 1980), 3–4.

38. Ibid., 29, iii.

39. New Jersey Casino Control Commission, *2000 Annual Report* (Trenton: Casino Control Commission, 2000), 18.

40. New Jersey Department of Community Affairs, *Review of the Probable Impact of Atlantic City Casino Development* (Trenton: Bureau of Regional Planning, 1980), 3.

41. New Jersey Casino Control Commission. *2002 Annual Report* (Trenton: Casino Control Commission, 2002), 2.

42. Ibid., 24, 28.

43. Evans, *Gambling*, 63.

44. Janice Hernon and James R. Appel, "Riverboat Gaming Bonanza," *Real Estate Review* (Summer 1994): 41.

45. Kathryn A. Wendler, "Legalized Low-Stakes Gambling: The Colorado Experience" (master's thesis, University of Nevada Las Vegas, 1993), 5–8.

46. Ibid., 14–19.

47. Colorado State Gaming Statistics, 1991–1992, accessed online at: http://www.gaming.state.co.us/dogstats.htm.

48. Colorado State Gaming Statistics, 2001–2002, accessed online at: http://www.gaming.state.co.us/dogstats.htm.

49. "Higher Bets Help South Dakota Gambling Town Flourish," *Reno Gazette-Journal*, May 13, 2003, accessed online at: http://www.rgj.com/news/stories/html /2003/05/13/41913.php?sp1=rgj&sp2=News&sp3=Local+News.

50. For more about Colorado and South Dakota's gaming, see Katherine Jensen and Audie Blevins, *The Last Gamble: Betting on the Future in Four Rocky Mountain Mining Towns* (Tucson: University of Arizona Press, 1998).

51. Evans, *Gambling*, 64.

52. Ibid., 55.

53. Roger Gros, "Ten Years After," *Global Gaming Business* 1, no. 3 (August 1, 2002): 20–23.

54. George Loper, "Louisiana Politics: Is Edwin Edwards Running Out of Luck?" January 2000, accessed online at: http://www.loper.org/~george/archives/2000/ Jan/60.html

55. http://www.cnn.com/2000/ALLPOLITICS/stories/05/10/edwards5_10.a.tml/; for a book-length treatment of the Louisiana scandals, see Tyler Bridges, *Bad Bet on the Bayou: The Rise of Gaming in Louisiana and the Fall of Governor Edwin Edwards* (New York: Farrar, Straus, and Giroux, 2001).

56. "Illinois: When a New Casino Isn't Really a Gambling Expansion," accessed online at: http://www.polstate.com/archives/002865.html.

57. Alan Sayre, "Louisiana Casino Expectations Unfulfilled," *San Jose Mercury News*, November 7, 2003.

58. Evans, *Gambling*, 62.

59. "Casinos to Pay Tribe $79 Million," *Detroit News*, November 26, 2003.

60. Tom Walsh, "Words, Plans, Won't Build Classy Hotels," *Detroit Free Press*, November 6, 2003, accessed online at: http://www.freep.com/money/business/walsh6_20031106.htm.

61. Personal communication with Steve Wynn, September 2002.

62. Mirage Resorts, *Annual Report 1992*, 1; emphasis from the original.

63. Ibid., 1, 9.

64. Circus Circus, *Annual Report 1998*, 6.

65. American Gaming Association, *State of the States 2003*, accessed online at: http://www.americangaming.org/assets/files/AGA_survey_2003.pdf.

66. Alvin M. Josephy, *Red Power: The American Indians' Fight for Freedom* (New York: American Heritage Press, 1971), 15.

67. I. Nelson Rose suggested this to the author in a personal communication, September 2003.

68. s. Rep. No. 99–493, 3.

69. Ibid., 5.

70. Ibid.

71. William N. Thompson, "History, Development, and Legislation of Native American Casino Gaming," in Cathy H. C. Hsu, ed., *Legalized Casino Gaming in the United States: The Economic and Social Impact* (New York: Hapworth Hospitality Press, 1999), 46–47.

72. U.S. Supreme Court, *California v. Cabazon Band of Mission Indians*, 480 U.S. 202 (1987), accessed online at: http://caselaw.lp.findlaw.com.

73. Ibid.

74. Ibid.

75. Thompson, "History, Development, and Legislation," 49–50.

76. Senate Report 100–446, "Indian Gaming Regulatory Actc," cited in *The Indian Gaming Regulatory Act, Annotated* (Washington, D.C.: Hobbs Straus, Dean, and Wilder, 1989), A-3, Hereafter cited as *IGRA Annotated*.

77. Ibid., 3–5.

78. Evans, *Gambling*, 73.

79. "Foxwoods Reports a $66.6 Million Slot Win for Month of October," October 30, 2003, press release, accessed online at: http://www.foxwoods.com/Home/Press-Center/PressReleases.aspx#.

80. State of Connecticut Division of Special Revenue, *Annual Report 2001–2002*,

6, accessed online at: http://www.dosr.state.ct.us/PDFFolder/01-02%20Annual%20 Report.pdf.

81. *IGRA Annotated*, A-2.

82. Alan Meister, *The Economic Impact of Indian Gaming* (Los Angeles: Analysis Group, 2003), 1.

83. National Indian Gaming Commission, *Tribal Gaming Revenue*, 2002, accessed online at: http://www.nigc.gov/nigc/nigcControl?option=TRIBAL_REVENUE.

84. Meister, *The Economic Impact of Indian Gaming*, 13.

85. For an older analysis of Indian gaming, see Carl A. Boger Jr., Daniel Spears, Kara Wolfe, and Li-Chun Lin, "Economic Impacts of Native American Casino Gaming," in Cathy H. C. Hsu, ed., *Legalized Casino Gaming in the United States*.

86. Donald L. Barlett and James Steel, "Look Who's Cashing In at Indian Casinos," *Time*, December 8, 2002.

87. California Nations Indian Gaming Association, "Time Misses the Point of Tribal Government Gaming," December 12, 2002, accessed online at: http://www .cniga.com/media/pressrelease_detail.php?id=18.

88. "The Bookie Blues," *Newsweek*, November 12, 1951.

89. Richard O. Davies and Richard G. Abram, *Betting the Line: Sports Wagering in American Life* (Columbus: Ohio State University Press, 2001), 123.

90. Ibid.

91. Ibid., 129.

92. Emanuel Perlmutter, "City Studies Ways to Let Bet Parlors Cover All Sports," *New York Times*, August 24, 1970, 1.

93. Anthony Ripley, "Kuhn and Rozelle Caution Against Legal Sports Bets," *New York Times*, February 20, 1975, 1.

94. Donald R. Cressey, "Bet Taking, Cosa Nostra, and Negotiated Social Order," in Jackwell Susman, ed., *Crime and Justice, 1970–1971* (New York: AMS Press, 1972), 255.

95. William Barry Furlong, "Of Lines, Point Spreads, and Middles," *New York Times*, January 2, 1977, 142.

96. David Burnham, "Legal 'Numbers' Urged for State to Reduce Crime," *New York Times*, November 26, 1972, 80.

97. Furlong, "Of Lines, Point Spreads, and Middles," 142.

98. Interview with Jeff Bryson, Chief, Gambling Investigation, Department of Justice, Gambling Control Division, State of Montana, February 20, 2004.

99. Marvin R. Brams, *The Economics of the Unsuccessful Delaware Football Lottery* (Newark: University of Delaware, 1978), 1–4.

100. Ibid., 6–7.

101. "How to Play Sports Action," pamphlet from Oregon Lottery, 1989, in *Promotional and Publicity Materials: Oregon Lottery*, UNLV Special Collections.

102. *Congressional Quarterly Almanac*, 102d Cong., 1st sess., 1991, vol. 47 (Washington, D.C.: Congressional Quarterly, 1991), 178.

103. Ibid.

104. Benjamin Grove, "Panel Opens Debate on Betting Bill," *Las Vegas Sun*, March 29, 2000.

105. Ibid.

106. Laurence Arnold, "Senate Panel Passes Ban on College Betting," *Las Vegas Sun*, April 12, 2000.

107. "Ensign Says He Can Block Nevada College Sports Bet Ban," *Las Vegas Sun*, May 8, 2003.

108. Editorial on NCAA Gambling, *Reno Gazette-Journal*, March 14, 2002.

6. Point, Click, and Bet

1. Christos J. P. Moschovitis, Hilary Poole, Tami Schuyler, and Theresa M. Senft, *History of the Internet: A Chronology, 1843 to the Present* (Santa Barbara: ABC-CLIO, 1999), 52, 61.

2. Joseph L. McCarthy, ed., *Commerce in Cyberspace* (New York: Conference Board, 1996), 1.

3. Moschovitis et al., *History of the Internet*, 147.

4. Michael Krantz, "Click Till You Drop," *Time*, July 20, 1998, 37.

5. Joshua Quittner, "An Eye on the Future," *Time*, December 27, 1999.

6. Joshua Quittner, "Betting on Virtual Vegas," *Time*, June 12, 1995, 63–64.

7. Brett Pulley, "With Technology, Island Bookies Skirt U.S. Law," *New York Times*, January 31, 1998, A1.

8. http://www.antigua-barbuda.com/.

9. Pulley, "With Technology, Island Rookies Skirt U.S. Law."

10. Personal interview with Jay Cohen, December 15, 2003, Federal Prison Camp Nellis, Las Vegas, Nevada.

11. David Rohde, "Upstate OTB Wants to Put Horse Wagering on Internet," *New York Times*, December 26, 1996, B4.

12. David Kushner, "Racing's Brains: Handling the Bets at Tracks and Elsewhere," *New York Times*, January 28, 1999, G5.

13. "Tribe Starts New Business: Gambling Site on Internet," *New York Times*, July 5, 1997, 8.

14. Peter H. Lewis, "On the Net: Lawmakers Gear Up to Try to Control the Surging Online Gaming Industry," *New York Times*, September 2, 1997, D4.

15. Jack Boulware, "Online Pirates of the Caribbean," *SF Weekly*, December 15, 1999.

16. Trial Transcript, *United States v. Jay Cohen*, 814–18.

17. Cohen interview.

18. Rebecca Quick, "Entrepreneurs Roll the Dice on a New Site," *Wall Street Journal*, April 10, 1997.

19. Boulware, "Online Pirates of the Caribbean."

20. Pulley, "With Technology, Island Bookies Skirt U.S. Law," A1.

21. For more on competing jurisdictions in eighteenth- and nineteenth-century Europe, see Russell T. Barnhart, *Gamblers of Yesteryear* (Las Vegas: GBC Press, 1983).

22. Anthony Cabot, *The Internet Gambling Report* (Las Vegas: Trace Publications, 1997), 13.

23. Cohen interview.

24. National Gaming Impact Study Commission, "Final Report" (Washington, D.C.: U.S. Government Printing Office, 1999), 3–9, accessed online at: http://govinfo. library.unt.edu/ngisc/reports/pathch3.pdf.

25. Matt Richtel, "The Casino on the Desktop," *New York Times*, May 29, 2001, G1.

26. Dirk Johnson, "In a Legal Gray Area, Blackjack Is a Click Away," *New York Times*, September 22, 1999, G65.

27. James Sterngold, "Virtual Casino Is Coming, But Regulation Is Still a Big Question," *New York Times*, October 28, 1996, D1.

28. Richtel, "The Casino on the Desktop," G4.

29. Sterngold, "Virtual Casino Is Coming," D1.

30. Jon Kyl, *Backgrounder. Illegal Internet Gambling: Problems and Solutions* (Washington, D.C.: Republican Policy Committee, 2003), 1, accessed online at: http://kyl .senate.gov.

31. Elsa Brenner, "Internet Warning," *New York Times*, May 25, 1997, WC13.

32. Anthony Ramirez, "Judge Rules Internet Gambling Is Not Beyond Reach of State Authorities," *New York Times*, July 1, 1999, B3.

33. Matt Richtel, "For Internet Wagers, Shifting Legal and Financial Control," *New York Times*, March 29, 2001, G4.

34. Sterngold, "Virtual Casino Is Coming," D1.

35. Dave Foster, "Online Bettor Pleads Guilty," *Major Wager*, August 12, 2003.

36. Richtel, "The Casino on the Desktop," G1.

37. Sue Schneider, "The Market—An Introduction," in Mark Balestra, ed., *Internet Gambling Report*, 6th ed. (St. Charles, Mo.: River City Group, 2003), 56.

38. Sterngold, "Virtual Casino Is Coming," D6.

39. Jeff Pelline and Courtney Macavinta, "Virtual Casinos Bet Big," *CNET News. com*, July 11, 1997.

40. Schneider, "The Market," 56.

41. "Aspinalls Online to Outsource Casino Operations to Golden Palace," *Rolling Good Times Online*, April 3, 2002, accessed online at: http://www.rgtonline.com/ Article.cfm?ArticleId=34558&CategoryName=News&SubCategoryName=Featured.

42. Liz Bentsen, "Station Casinos Shelves Net Gambling Plans," *Las Vegas Sun*, August 26, 2002; Liz Bentsen, "Kerzner Drops Internet Gambling Operation," *Las Vegas Sun*, January 3, 2003.

43. Bentsen, "Kerzner Drops Internet Gambling Operation."

44. Roy Mark, "MGM's Online Casino Proves to Be a Mirage," *Internet News*, June 5, 2003, accessed online at: http://www.internetnews.com/bus-news/article.php/2217621.

45. Matt Richtel, "Place Your Bet: A Vegas Casino or a Virtual One?" *New York Times*, August 13, 2000, B11.

46. Home page of Senator Jon Kyl, "Crime and Justice Issues," accessed online at: http://kyl.senate.gov/legis_center/crime.cfm.

47. Kyl, *Backgrounder: Illegal Internet Gambling*.

48. Statistic cited online at: http://www.americangaming.org/Industry/factsheets/statistics_detail.cfv?id=7.

49. "Statement by Eliot Spitzer Regarding New York Racing Association," accessed online at: http://www.oag.state.ny.us/press/2003/jun/jun24b_03.html.

50. Michael Mell, "Officials Discuss Growing Dependence on Gambling," *Las Vegas Sun*, September 4, 2003.

51. Sterngold, "Virtual Casino Is Coming," D6.

52. Frank Fahrenkopf, "Testimony Before the House Financial Services Committee Re: Internet Gaming," July 12, 2001, accessed online at: http://www.american-gaming.org/Press/speeches/speeches_detail.cfv?ID=108.

53. Chad Hills, "An Introduction to the Consequences of Gambling," accessed online at: http://www.family.org/cforum/fosi/gambling/cog/a0029398.cf.

54. American Family Association, "Library Internet Filtering," accessed online at: http://www.afa.net/lif/.

55. Tony Batt, "Nader Says Gaming Targets Children," *Las Vegas Review-Journal*, June 13, 1998.

56. "Senate Approves Internet Gambling Ban," *Tech Law Journal*, July 23, 1998, accessed online at: http://www.techlawjournal.com/internet/80724.htm.

57. Anthony Ripley, "Kuhn and Rozelle Caution Against Legal Sports Betting," *New York Times*, February 20, 1975, 1.

58. Steven Crist, "All Bets Are Off," *Sports Illustrated*, January 26, 1998, 86.

59. Edward C. Baig, "Outlaw Online Betting? Don't Bet on It," *BusinessWeek*, December 15, 1997.

60. "National Indian Gaming Association Testifies on Future of Internet Gaming," press release, National Indian Gaming Association, accessed online at: http://www.indiangaming.org/info/pr/press-releases-2001/egaming.shtml.

61. Matt Richtel, "Las Vegas Casinos, in Shift of Position, Back Online Betting," *New York Times*, May 17, 2001, A1.

62. Moschovitis et al., *History of the Internet*, 206–7.

63. "The Legal Challenge to the Child Online Protection Act," Electronic Privacy Information Center, accessed online at: http://www.epic.org/free_speech/copa/.

64. Peter H. Lewis, "On the Net," *New York Times*, September 22, 1997, D4.

65. Ibid.

66. Sterngold, "Virtual Casino Is Coming," D1.

67. Johnson, "In a Legal Gray Area, Blackjack Is a Click Away," G65.

68. House Committee on Financial Services, Subcommittee on Financial Institutions and Consumer Credit, *Hearing*, 107th Cong., 1st sess., July 24, 2001, 5.

69. Tony Batt, "Congressional Legislation: Internet Gaming Bill Unlikely," *Las Vegas Review-Journal*, November 21, 2003.

70. Mark McClusky, "Longer Odds for Online Bookies," *Wired News*, September 8, 2003, accessed online at: http://www.wired.com/news/print/0,1294,60316,00.html.

71. Mark Balestra, "The Caribbean Basin," in Balestra, *Internet Gambling Report*, 511–12.

72. *United States v. Cohen*, 818–19.

73. Balestra, "The Caribbean Basin," in Balestra, *Internet Gambling Report*, 511–12.

74. Patrick O'Brien, "The Caribbean Basin," in Balestra, *Internet Gambling Report*, 135.

75. New Jersey Casino Control Commission, *2002 Annual Report*, 14.

76. E-mail communication, Daniel Heneghan, New Jersey Casino Control Commission, January 5, 2004.

77. See William N. Nester, *A Short History of American Industrial Policies* (New York: St. Martin's, 1998), and Thomas McCraw, *Prophets of Regulation: Charles Francis Adams, Louis D. Brandeis, James M. Landis, Alfred E. Kahn* (Cambridge, Mass.: Belknap Press of Harvard University Press, 1984).

78. Keith Furlong, "Self-Regulation," in Balestra, *Internet Gambling Report*, 503–8.

79. See http://www.igcouncil.org/.

80. See http://www.therx.com/index.html.

81. See. http://www.majorwager.com/home.cfm.

82. Isle of Man, Online Gambling Regulation Act 2001, accessed online at: http://www.gov.im/gambling/acts/gamblingregulation2001.pdf.

83. Jamie Nettleton, "Australia," in Balestra, *Internet Gambling Report*, 431–43, 449.

84. Erin Neff, "Lawmakers OK Internet Gaming Bill," *Las Vegas Sun*, April 27, 2001.

85. "New Jersey Settles Internet Sports Betting Suits," press release, Office of the Attorney General, June 11, 2002, accessed online at: http://www.state.nj.us/lps/ge/2002news/internet_settlement.htm.

86. Tony Batt, "Measure Back Proposing Study on Online Betting," *Las Vegas Review-Journal*, March 13, 2003.

7. March Madness

1. "Nixon Says No to Indian Internet Gaming," press release, Missouri Office of the Attorney General, December 29, 1997.

2. "Judge Issues TRO to Stop Internet Lottery in Missouri," press release, Missouri

Office of the Attorney General, January 29, 1998, accessed online at: http://www.ago.
state.mo.us/012998.htm.

3. Mark Balestra, *The Complete Idiot's Guide to Online Gambling* (Indianapolis: Que,
2000), 251.

4. Matt Richtel, "He Tries to Draw Legal Borders in Cyberspace," *Wired News*, August 11, 1997, accessed online at: http://www.wired.com/news/print/0,1294,5881,00.
html.

5. Sue Schneider, "State of the Industry: An Introduction," in Anthony N. Cabot,
ed., *The Internet Gambling Report III* (Las Vegas: Trace Publications, 1999), 111–12.

6. Anthony Ramirez, "Judge Rules Internet Gambling Is Not Beyond Reach of
State Authorities," *New York Times*, July 1, 1999, B3.

7. John McAlpin, "New Jersey Sues Internet Casinos, Claims Companies Operate
Illegally," *Las Vegas Sun*, June 19, 2001.

8. "New Jersey Settles Internet Sports Betting Suits," press release, Office of the
Attorney General, June 11, 2002, accessed online at: http://www.state.nj.us/lps/ge/
2002news/internet_settlement.htm.

9. Jay Cohen, "In His Own Words," accessed online at: http://www.freejaycohen.
com.

10. Anthony Ripley, "Kuhn and Rozelle Caution Against Legal Sports Betting,"
New York Times, February 20, 1975, 23.

11. Debevoise and Plimpton, "About Us," Web site accessed online at: http://www
.debevoise.com/about/about.asp.

12. Trial transcript, *United States v. Jay Cohen*, 528.

13. Ibid., 529.

14. Ibid., 534, 535.

15. Habeas Corpus, affidavit in support of 2255 petition (affidavit of Melinda Sarafa; 33 pp., MS Word), 2002, 23, accessed online at: http:/www.freejaycohen.com/
LegalCasePg.html.

16. Ibid., 23–24.

17. Ibid., 24–26.

18. *United States v. Jay Cohen*, 43–67.

19. "Online Sports Books Charged," *Las Vegas Review-Journal*, March 5, 1998.

20. *United States v. Jay Cohen*, 804.

21. http://web.archive.org/web/19970717153856/wsex.com/cgi/kyl_bill; July 1997.

22. *United States v. Jay Cohen*, 12–14.

23. Ibid., 16–19.

24. Ibid., 12–13.

25. Ibid., 14–15.

26. Ibid., 23–24.

27. Richard Sasuly, *Bookies and Bettors: Two Hundred Years of Gambling* (New York:
Holt, Rinehart, and Winston, 1982), 133–35.

28. *United States v. Jay Cohen*, 23–24.

29. Ibid., 26.

30. Ibid., 28–31.

31. Ibid., 31–32.

32. Ibid., 32–33.

33. Ibid., 36.

34. "United States of America v. Jay Cohen: Brief for the United States of America," Second Circuit Appeal, Docket No. 00-1574, 2002, 6–9.

35. *United States v. Jay Cohen*, 913.

36. Ibid., 910.

37. Ibid., 1130.

38. Ibid., 1202–14.

39. Ibid., 1316–18.

40. Sentencing transcript, *United States v. Jay Cohen*, 10.

41. Ibid., 61–62.

42. "Ruling on Appeal of *United States v. Cohen*," U.S. Court of Appeals, Second Circuit, 260 F.3d 68, July 31, 2001, 3–7.

43. *United States v. Cohen*, Appeal, 7–9.

44. Anne Lindner, "A Supreme Case for Cohen?" *Interactive Gaming News*, February 27, 2002, accessed online at: http://www.osga.com/artman/publish/article_44.shtml.

45. Ibid.

46. Penelope Patsuris, "Hard Time: Best Places to Go to Prison," ABCnews.com, September 24, 2003, accessed online at: http://abcnews.go.com/sections/business/DailyNews/forbes_prisons_020924.html.

47. Personal interview with Jay Cohen, December 15, 2003.

48. Ibid.

49. Ibid.

50. Matt Richtel, "Las Vegas Casinos, in Shift of Position, Back Online Betting," *New York Times*, May 17, 2001, A1; Cohen interview, December 15, 2003.

51. Cohen interview, December 15, 2003; Leon Mandel, *William Fisk Harrah: The Life and Times of a Gambling Magnate* (Garden City, N.Y.: Doubleday, 1982).

52. *United States v. Jay Cohen*, 12–13.

53. World Trade Organization, *United States—Measures Affecting the Cross-Border Supply of Gaming and Betting Services: Report of the Panel*, WT/DS285/R10, November 2004, accessed online at: http://www.wto.org/english/tratop_e/dispu_e/285r_e.pdf, p. 5; hereafter cited as WTO, p. 5.

54. "General Agreement on Trade in Services," *Wikipedia*, accessed online at: http://en.wikipedia.org/wiki/GATS.

55. WTO, *United States*, 1.

56. Ibid., 2–3, 10.

57. U.S. Trade Representative, *Before the World Trade Organization: Measures Affecting the Cross-Border Supply of Gambling and Betting Services*, January 9, 2004, accessed online at: http://www.ustr.gov/enforcement/2004-01-09-gambling-2ndwritten.pdf.

58. Liz Bentsen, "WTO 'Net Gambling Details Remain Secret," *Las Vegas Sun*, March 25, 2004.

59. WTO, *United States*, 272.

60. Ibid., 273.

Epilogue. Prohibition in a Borderless America

1. American Gaming Association, *State of the States 2003: The AGA Survey of Casino Entertainment*, 2.

2. William R. Eadington, "The Legalization of Casinos: Policy Objectives, Regulatory Alternatives, and Cost/Benefit Considerations," *Journal of Travel Research* (Winter 1996): 5.

3. State of New Jersey Gambling Study Commission, *Report to the Governor and Legislature*, February 5, 1973, 5–6.

4. Ibid., 5.

5. Dan Morain and Bill Dwyer, "Ballot Measure in Works to Spread Slots Beyond Casinos," *Los Angeles Times*, November 21, 2003.

6. See http://www.lao.ca.gov/2002/cal_facts/econ.html.

7. Harrah's Entertainment, *Harrah's Survey 2003: Profile of the American Gambler*, 4.

8. Ibid., 9.

9. Ibid., 10, 12.

10. Jackson Lears, *Something for Nothing: Luck in America* (New York: Viking Penguin, 2003).

11. Jack Engelhard, *Indecent Proposal* (New York, Pocket Books, 1988).

12. Ibid., 29.

13. Ibid., 4.

14. Ibid.

15. Tim Gautreaux, "Something for Nothing," *Harper's Magazine*, September 2002, 66–72.

16. George F. Will, "Electronic Morphine," *Newsweek*, November 25, 2002, 92.

17. Matt Richtel, "The Casino on the Desktop," *New York Times*, May 29, 2001, G4.

BIBLIOGRAPHY

Books

Albanese, Jay. *Organized Crime in America.* 3d ed. Cincinnati: Anderson Publishing, 1996.

Albini, Joseph L. *The American Mafia: Genesis of a Legend.* New York: Irvington, 1979.

American Gaming Association. *State of the States 2003.* Accessed online at: http://www.americangaming.org/assets/files/AGA_survey_2003.pdf.

Asbury, Herbert. *Sucker's Progress: An Informal History of Gambling in America.* New York: Dodd, Mead, 1938.

Balestra, Mark. *The Complete Idiot's Guide to Online Gambling.* Indianapolis: Que, 2000.

——, ed. *Internet Gambling Report.* 6th ed. St. Charles, Mo.: River City Group, 2002.

Barnhart, Russell T. *Gamblers of Yesteryear.* Las Vegas: GBC Press, 1983.

Block, Alan A. *The Business of Crime: A Documentary Study of Organized Crime in the American Economy.* Boulder, Col.: Westview, 1991.

Brams, Marvin R. *The Economics of the Unsuccessful Delaware Football Lottery.* Newark: University of Delaware, 1978.

Bridges, Tyler. *Bad Bet on the Bayou: The Rise of Gaming in Louisiana and the Fall of Governor Edwin Edwards.* New York: Farrar, Straus, and Giroux, 2001.

Bruchey, Stuart. *Enterprise: The Dynamic Economy of a Free People.* Cambridge, Mass.: Harvard University Press, 1990.

Bybee Jr., Shannon L. *Evidence of a Serendipitous Career in Gaming.* Edited by Dina Zemke. Boston: Pearson Custom Publishing, 2003.

Cabot, Anthony. *The Internet Gambling Report.* Las Vegas: Trace Publications, 1997.

——, ed. *The Internet Gambling Report III.* Las Vegas: Trace Publications, 1999.

Chafetz, Henry. *Play the Devil: A History of Gambling in the United States from 1492 to 1950.* New York: Bonanza Books, 1960.

Circus Circus. *Annual Report 1998.*

Cooney, John. *The Annenbergs.* New York: Simon and Schuster, 1982.

D'Angelo, Raymond D. "The Social Organization of Sports Gambling: A Study in Conventionality and Deviance." Ph.D. diss., Bryn Mawr College.

Davies, Richard O., and Richard G. Abram. *Betting the Line: Sports Wagering in American Life.* Columbus: Ohio State University Press, 2001.

Drzazga, John. *Wheels of Fortune.* Springfield, Ill.: Charles C. Thomas, 1963.

Eadington, William, and Judy Cornelius, eds. *Gambling and Public Policy: International Perspectives*. Reno: Institute for the Study of Gambling and Commercial Gaming, 1991.

Elwood, Bryan, and Hal Tennant. *The Whole World Lottery Guide*. 2d ed. Toronto: Millions Magazine, 1981.

Engelhard, Jack. *Indecent Proposal*. New York: Pocket Books, 1988.

Evans, Kim Masters. *Gambling: What's at Stake?* Farmington Hills, Mich.: Gale, 2003.

Ezell, John Samuel. *Fortune's Merry Wheel: The Lottery in America*. Cambridge, Mass.: Harvard University Press, 1960.

Findlay, John. *People of Chance: Gambling in American Society from Jamestown to Las Vegas*. New York: Oxford University Press, 1986.

Fowler, Floyd J., Thomas W. Mangione, and Frederick E. Pratter. *Gambling Law Enforcement in Major American Cities*. Washington, D.C.: U.S. Department of Justice, Law Enforcement Assistance Administration, 1978.

Goldfarb, Ronald. *Perfect Villains, Imperfect Heroes: Robert F. Kennedy's War on Organized Crime*. New York: Random House, 1995.

Gorman, Joseph Bruce. *Kefauver: A Political Biography*. New York: Oxford University Press, 1971.

Hall, Kermit L. *The Magic Mirror: Law in American History*. New York: Oxford University Press, 1989.

Hsu, Cathy H. C., ed. *Legalized Casino Gaming in the United States: The Economic and Social Impact*. New York: Hapworth Hospitality Press, 1999.

Huizinga, Johann. *Homo Ludens: A Study of the Play-Element in Culture*. Boston: Beacon, 1955.

The Indian Gaming Regulatory Act, Annotated. Washington, D.C.: Hobbs, Straus, Dean, and Wilder, 1989.

Jarvis, Robert M., Shannon L. Bybee, Jr., J. Wesley Cochran, I. Nelson Rose, and Ronald J. Rychlak. *Gaming Law: Cases and Materials*. Newark, N.J.: Lexis-Nexis, 2003.

Jensen, Katherine, and Audie Blevins. *The Last Gamble: Betting on the Future in Four Rocky Mountain Mining Towns*. Tucson: University of Arizona Press, 1998.

Josephy, Alvin M. *Red Power: The American Indians' Fight for Freedom*. New York: American Heritage Press, 1971.

Kaplan, Lawrence J., and Dennis Kessler. *An Economic Analysis of Crime*. Springfield, Ill.: Charles C. Thomas, 1976.

Kefauver, Estes. *Crime in America*. Garden City, N.Y.: Doubleday, 1951.

Kelly, Robert J., Ko-Lin Chin, and Rufus Schatzberg, eds. *Handbook of Organized Crime in the United States*. Westport, Conn.: Greenwood, 1994.

Kennedy, Robert. *The Enemy Within*. New York: Harper and Brothers, 1960.

Kessler, Ronald. *The Bureau: The Secret History of the FBI*. New York: St. Martin's, 2002.

King, Rufus. *Gambling and Organized Crime*. Washington: Public Affairs, 1969.

Kinnee, Kevin B. *Practical Gambling Investigation Techniques.* New York: Elsevier, 1992.

La Fleur, Theresa. *La Fleur's 2002 World Lottery Almanac.* Boyds, Md.: TLF Publications, 2002.

Landesco, John. *Organized Crime in Chicago. Part III of the Illinois Crime Survey, 1929.* Chicago: University of Chicago Press, 1968.

Lears, Jackson. *Something for Nothing: Luck in America.* New York: Viking, 2003.

Leeds, Josiah W. *Horse Racing: The Beginnings of Gambling. The Lottery.* Philadelphia: Josiah Leeds, 1895.

Longrigg, Roger. *The History of Horse Racing.* New York: Stein and Day, 1972.

Maas, Peter. *The Valachi Papers: The First Inside Account of Life in the Cosa Nostra.* New York: G. P. Putnam's Sons, 1966.

Mandel, Leon. *William Fisk Harrah: The Life and Times of a Gambling Magnate.* Garden City, N.Y.: Doubleday, 1982.

Marx, Herbert L., ed. *Gambling in America.* New York: H. W. Wilson, 1952.

Mass Violence in America: Reports on Crime Investigations. New York: Arno Press and the New York Times, 1969.

McCarthy, Joseph L., ed. *Commerce in Cyberspace.* New York: Conference Board, 1996

McCraw, Thomas. *Prophets of Regulation: Charles Francis Adams, Louis D. Brandeis, James M. Landis, Alfred E. Kahn.* Cambridge, Mass.: Belknap Press of Harvard University Press, 1984.

McGowan, Richard. *State Lotteries and Legalized Gambling: Painless Revenue or Painful Mirage?* Westport, Conn.: Quorum, 1994.

Meister, Alan. *The Economic Impact of Indian Gaming.* Los Angeles: Analysis Group, 2003.

Mirage Resorts. *Annual Report 1992.* N.p.

Monkkonen, Eric. *Murder in New York City.* Berkeley: University of California Press, 2000.

Moore, William Howard. *The Kefauver Committee and the Politics of Crime, 1950–1952.* Columbia: University of Missouri Press, 1974.

Moschovitis, Christos J. P., Hilary Poole, Tami Schuyler, and Theresa M. Senft. *History of the Internet: A Chronology, 1843 to the Present.* Santa Barbara, Calif.: ABC-CLIO, 1999.

Navasky, Victor. *Kennedy Justice.* New York: Atheneum, 1977.

Nester, William N. *A Short History of American Industrial Policies.* New York: St. Martin's, 1998.

Olsen, Edward A. *My Careers as a Journalist in Oregon, Idaho, and Nevada; in Nevada Gaming Control; and at the University of Nevada.* Reno: University of Nevada Oral History Project, 1972.

Peterson, Virgil. *Barbarians in Our Midst: A History of Chicago Crime and Politics.* Boston: Little, Brown, 1952.

Pickett, Deets. *Fools' Gold: The Truth About Gambling.* New York: Abingdon, 1936.

Porter, David. *Fixed: How Goodfellas Bought Boston College Basketball.* Dallas: Taylor Trade Publishing, 2000.

Quinn, John Phillip. *Gambling and Gambling Devices: An Educational Exposition Designed to Instruct the Youth to Avoid All Forms of Gambling.* 1912. Reprint, Las Vegas: Gambler's Book Club, 1979.

———. *The Highway to Hell.* Chicago: International Anti-Gambling Association, 1895.

Reith, Gerda. *The Age of Chance: Gambling and Western Culture.* London: Routledge, 1999.

Reuter, Peter. *Disorganized Crime: The Economics of the Visible Hand.* Cambridge, Mass.: MIT University Press, 1983.

Rose, I. Nelson. *Gambling and the Law.* Hollywood: Gambling Times, 1986.

Rose, I. Nelson, and David Staley. *Gambling and the Law: Indian Gaming in California.* Reno: Institute for the Study of Gambling and Commercial Gaming, 1994.

Rosen, Charles. *The Scandals of '51.* New York: Seven Stories Press, 1998.

Russell, Thaddeus. *Out of the Jungle: Jimmy Hoffa and the Remaking of the American Middle Class.* New York: Knopf, 2001.

Salerno, Ralph, and John S. Tompkins. *The Crime Confederation: Cosa Nostra and Allied Operations in Organized Crime.* Garden City, N.Y.: Doubleday, 1969.

Sasuly, Richard. *Bookies and Bettors: Two Hundred Years of Gambling.* New York: Holt, Rinehart, and Winston, 1982.

Schmidt, John C. *Win, Place, Show: A Biography of Harry Straus, the Man Who Gave America the Tote.* Baltimore: Johns Hopkins University Press, 1989.

Schwartz, David G. *Suburban Xanadu: The Casino Resort on the Las Vegas Strip and Beyond.* New York: Routledge, 2003.

Sellers, Charles. *The Market Revolution: Jacksonian America, 1815–1846.* New York: Oxford University Press, 1991.

Sheshol, Jeff. *Mutual Contempt: Lyndon Johnson, Robert Kennedy, and the Feud That Defined a Decade.* New York: Norton, 1997.

Skolnick, Jerome H. *House of Cards: The Legalization and Control of Casino Gambling.* Boston: Little, Brown, 1978.

Susman, Jackwell, ed. *Crime and Justice.* New York: AMS Press, 1972.

Thomas, Evan. *Robert Kennedy: His Life.* New York: Simon and Schuster, 2000.

Van Meter, Jonathan. *The Last Good Time: Skinny D'Amato, the Notorious 500 Club, and the Rise and Fall of Atlantic City.* New York: Crown, 2003.

Weinstein, David, and Lillian Deitch. *The Impact of Legalized Gambling: The Socioeconomic Consequences of Lotteries and Off-Track Betting.* New York: Praeger, 1974.

Wendler, Kathryn A. "Legalized Low-Stakes Gambling: The Colorado Experience." Master's thesis, University of Nevada, Las Vegas, 1993.

White, John J. "The History of the Louisiana Lottery." Master's thesis, Tulane University, 1939.

Wolf, George, with Joseph DiMona. *Frank Costello: Prime Minister of the Underworld.* New York: William Morrow, 1974.

Articles

"1950—Biggest Gambling Year Ever." *Scientific Digest,* January 1951.

Alexander, Tom. "What Is Del Webb up to in Nevada?" *Fortune,* May 1965.

Allensworth, Stephen. "You're in for Lotto Grief with Pirate Net Gambling." *New York Daily News,* December 1, 2004.

American Family Association. "Library Internet Filtering." Accessed online at: http://www.afa.net/lif/.

"Anti-Crime Fight Is Pushed by U.S." *New York Times,* February 2, 1961.

"Anti-Gambling Bills Offered by M'Grath." *New York Times,* April 2, 1950.

Arnold, Laurence. "Senate Panel Passes Ban on College Betting." *Las Vegas Sun,* April 12, 2000.

"Aspinalls Online to Outsource Casino Operations to Golden Palace." *Rolling Good Times Online,* April 3, 2002.

Baig, Edward C. . "Outlaw Online Betting? Don't Bet on It." *BusinessWeek,* December 15, 1997.

Barlett, Donald L., and James Steel. "Look Who's Cashing in at Indian Casinos." *Time,* December 8, 2002.

Batt, Tony. "Congressional Legislation: Internet Gaming Bill Unlikely." *Las Vegas Review-Journal,* November 21, 2003.

——. "Measure Back Proposing Study on Online Betting." *Las Vegas Review-Journal,* March 13, 2003.

——. "Nader Says Gaming Targets Children." *Las Vegas Review-Journal,* June 13, 1998.

Bentsen, Liz. "Kerzner Drops Internet Gambling Operation." *Las Vegas Sun,* January 3, 2003.

——. "Station Casinos Shelves Net Gambling Plans." *Las Vegas Sun,* August 26, 2002.

——. "WTO 'Net Gambling Details Remain Secret." *Las Vegas Sun,* March 25, 2004.

"Bergen County—A Case Study." *New York Times,* December 4, 1951.

"The Bookie Blues." *Newsweek,* November 12, 1951.

"Boston College Continues to Sort Out Mess from Gambling Scandal." *Las Vegas Review-Journal,* July 25, 1997.

Boulware, Jack. "Online Pirates of the Caribbean." *SF Weekly,* December 15, 1999.

Breasted, Mary. "157 Indicted Here as Part of Gambling Network." *New York Times,* November 20, 1974.

Brenner, Elsa. "Internet Warning." *New York Times,* May 25, 1997.

Bullen Jr., Captain George H. "Local Investigation of Illegal Gambling Operations." *FBI Law Enforcement Bulletin,* March 1971.

Burnham, David. "Legal 'Numbers' Urged for State to Reduce Crime." *New York Times,* November 26, 1972.

Cady, Steve. "No Rest for the Weary Bettor as Sports Proliferate, Overlap." *New York Times*, July 23, 1974.

California Nations Indian Gaming Association. "*Time* Misses the Point of Tribal Government Gaming." December 12, 2002. Accessed online at: http://www.cniga .com/media/pressrelease_detail.php?id=18.

Carroll, Wallace. "Appointing a Relative." *New York Times*, December 17, 1960.

"Casinos to Pay Tribe $79 Million." *Detroit News*, November 26, 2003.

Crist, Steven. "All Bets Are Off." *Sports Illustrated*, January 26, 1998.

Curry, Jack, with Adam Gershenson. "Even at Columbia, Gambling and College Athletics Collide." *New York Times*, February 16, 1998.

Dombrink, John, and James W. Meeker. "Racketeering Prosecution: The Use and Abuse of RICO." *Rutgers Law Journal* 16, nos. 3–4 (Spring/Summer 1985): 633–54.

Eadington, William R. "The Legalization of Casinos: Policy Objectives, Regulatory Alternatives, and Cost/Benefit Considerations." *Journal of Travel Research* (Winter 1996): 3–8.

Editorial on NCAA Gambling. *Reno Gazette-Journal*, March 14, 2002.

"Ensign Says He Can Block Nevada College Sports Bet Ban." *Las Vegas Sun*, May 8, 2003.

Eskenazi, Gerald. "Rise in Illegal Gambling Linked to OTB Climate." *New York Times*, January 10, 1974.

Foster, Dave. "Online Bettor Pleads Guilty." *Major Wager*, August 12, 2003.

"Foxwoods Reports a $66.6 Million Slot Win for Month of October." Press release, October 30, 2003. Accessed online at: http://www.foxwoods.com/Home/Press-Center/PressReleases.aspx#.

Furlong, William Barry. "Of Lines, Point Spreads, and Middles." *New York Times*, January 2, 1977.

"Gambling in Galveston." *Newsweek*, December 10, 1951.

"Gambling Investigations." *FBI Law Enforcement Bulletin*, July 1969 (revised September 1979).

Gardner, Paul, and Allan Gould. "Brain of the Bookies." *Collier's*, October 25, 1947.

Gautreaux, Tim. "Something for Nothing." *Harper's Magazine*, September 2002, 66–72.

Gros, Roger. "Ten Years After." *Global Gaming Business* 1, no. 3 (August 1, 2002): 20–23.

Grove, Benjamin. "Panel Opens Debate on Betting Bill." *Las Vegas Sun*, March 29, 2000.

Haller, Mark H. "Bootleggers and American Gambling, 1920–1950." In *Gambling in America*, appendix 1. Washington, D.C.: U.S. Government Printing Office, 1976.

———. "Illegal Enterprise: A Theoretical and Historical Interpretation." *Criminology* 28, no. 2 (1990): 207–35.

"Happy Huskers." News release on Powerball Web site. Accessed online at: http:// www.powerball.com/powerball/winners/2003/102503mn.shtm.

Harker, R. Phillip. "Sports Bookmaking Operations." FBI Law Enforcement Bulletin, September 1978.

Harrah's Entertainment. Harrah's Survey 2003: Profile of the American Gambler.

Hayes, Frederick. The Impact of the Resorts International Casino Hotel on the Atlantic City Economy. Prepared for Resorts International, February 1980.

Hernon, Janice, and James R. Appel. "Riverboat Gaming Bonanza." Real Estate Review, Summer 1994.

"Higher Bets Help South Dakota Gambling Town Flourish." Reno Gazette-Journal, May 13, 2003.

Hills, Chad. "An Introduction to the Consequences of Gambling." Accessed online at: http://www.family.org/cforum/fosi/gambling/cog/a0029398.cfm.

"Illinois: When a New Casino Isn't Really a Gambling Expansion." Accessed online at: http://www.polstate.com/archives/002865.html.

"Improve the Breed of Men." New York Globe, February 24, 1916.

Johnson, Dirk. "In a Legal Gray Area, Blackjack Is a Click Away." New York Times, September 22, 1999.

Kanigher, Steve. "Caught in a Web: Future of Online Casinos Debated." Las Vegas Sun, March 7, 2003.

Kaufman, Bill. "They Voted Against Mother's Day." American Enterprise (April–May 2002).

Kennedy, Robert F. "Robert Kennedy Defines the Menace." New York Times, October 13, 1963.

Krantz, Michael. "Click Till You Drop." Time, July 20, 1998.

Krebs, Brian. "U.S. Internet Gambling Crackdown Sparks WTO Complaint." Washington Post, July 21, 2003.

Kushner, David. "Racing's Brains: Handling the Bets at Tracks and Elsewhere." New York Times, January 28, 1999.

Kyl, Jon. Backgrounder. Illegal Internet Gambling: Problems and Solutions, 1. Washington, D.C.: Republican Policy Committee, 2003. Accessed online via http://kyl.senate .gov.

"The Legal Challenge to the Child Online Protection Act." Electronic Privacy Information Center. Accessed online at: http://www.e;kc.org/free_speech/copa/.

Lewis, Anthony. "President Hails Anti-Crime Drive." New York Times, October 11, 1962.

Lewis, Peter H. "On the Net." New York Times, September 22, 1997.

———. "On the Net: Lawmakers Gear Up to Try to Control the Surging Online Gaming Industry." New York Times, September 2, 1997.

Lindner, Anne. "A Supreme Case for Cohen?" Interactive Gaming News, February 27, 2002.

Loftus, Joseph A. "Racket Violence Is Found Waning." *New York Times*, February 27, 1962.

Loper, George. "Louisiana Politics: Is Edwin Edwards Running Out of Luck?" January 2000. Accessed online at: http://www.loper.org/~george/archives/2000/Jan/60.html.

Manning, Robert. "Someone the President Can Talk To." *New York Times*, May 28, 1961.

Mark, Roy. "MGM's Online Casino Proves to Be a Mirage." *Internet News*, June 5, 2003. Accessed online at: http://www.internetnews.com/bus-news/article.php/2217621.

Martin, John Bartlow. "Al Capone's Successors." *American Mercury*, April 1949.

"Mayors, Police Tie 'Bookies' to Crime." *New York Times*, April 22, 1950.

McAlpin, John. "New Jersey Sues Internet Casinos, Claims Companies Operate Illegally." *Las Vegas Sun*, June 19, 2001.

McClusky, Mark. "Longer Odds for Online Bookies." *Wired News*, September 8, 2003.

McQueen, Patricia A. "Match Made in Heaven." *International Gaming and Wagering Business* 24, no. 7 (July 2003).

Mell, Michael. "Officials Discuss Growing Dependence on Gambling." *Las Vegas Sun*, September 4, 2003.

"M'Grath to Bar Voter Fraud." *New York Times*, February 14, 1950.

"Military Runs Slot Machines, Offers Little Help to Addicts." *Holland Sentinel*, January 14, 2001.

Moody, Eric N. "Nevada's Legalization of Casino Gambling in 1931." *Nevada Historical Society Quarterly* 37, no. 2 (Summer 1994): 79–100.

Morain, Dan, and Bill Dwyer, "Ballot Measure in Works to Spread Slots Beyond Casinos." *Los Angeles Times*, November 21, 2003.

"National Indian Gaming Association Testifies on Future of Internet Gaming." Press release from the National Indian Gaming Association. Accessed online at: http://www.indiangaming.org/info/pr/press-releases-2001/egaming.shtml.

Navasky, Victor S. "A Famous Prosecutor Talks About Crime." *New York Times*, February 15, 1970.

Neff, Erin. "Lawmakers OK Internet Gaming Bill." *Las Vegas Sun*, April 27, 2001.

"New York Aides Give Senate 'Bookie' Blueprint." *New York Times*, April 21, 1950.

"Online Sports Books Charged." *Las Vegas Review-Journal*, March 5, 1998.

Patsuris, Penelope. "Hard Time: Best Places to Go to Prison." ABCnews.com, September 24, 2003.

Pelline, Jeff, and Courtney Macavinta. "Virtual Casinos Bet Big." CNET News.com, July 11, 1997.

Perlmutter, Emmanuel. "City Studies Ways to Let Bet Parlors Cover All Sports." *New York Times*, August 24, 1970.

——. "Robert Kennedy Cites Rise in Crime." *New York Times*, September 26, 1963.

Philadelphia Parley Held." *New York Times*, November 17, 1961.

Phillips, Cabell. "U.S. Crime Fight Nears a Climax." *New York Times*, July 23, 1961.

Ploscowe, Morris. "The Law of Gambling." *Annals of the American Academy of Political and Social Science* 269 (May 1950): 1–8.

Porter, Russell. "R. F. Kennedy Hits Greed of Public." *New York Times*, June 15, 1961.

"Previous Point-Shaving Scandals." CNN-SI.com, March 27, 1988. Accessed online at: http://sportsillustrated.cnn.com/basketball/college/news/1998/03/27/gambling sidebar/.

Pulley, Brett. "With Technology, Island Bookies Skirt U.S. Law." *New York Times*, January 31, 1998.

Quick, Rebecca. "Entrepreneurs Roll the Dice on a New Site." *Wall Street Journal*, April 10, 1997.

Quittner, Joshua. "Betting on Virtual Vegas." *Time*, June 12, 1995.

———. "An Eye on the Future." *Time*, December 27, 1999.

Raab, Selwyn. "3 Accused of Running Mafia Betting Ring." *New York Times*, December 7, 1993.

Ramirez, Anthony. "Judge Rules Internet Gambling Is Not Beyond Reach of State Authorities." *New York Times*, July 1, 1999.

Richtel, Matt. "The Casino on the Desktop." *New York Times*, May 29, 2001.

———. "For Internet Wagers, Shifting Legal and Financial Control." *New York Times*, March 29, 2001.

———. "He Tries to Draw Legal Borders in Cyberspace." *Wired News*, August 11, 1997.

———. "Las Vegas Casinos, in Shift of Position, Back Online Betting." *New York Times*, May 17, 2001.

———. "Place Your Bet: A Vegas Casino, or a Virtual One?" *New York Times*, August 13, 2000.

Ripley, Anthony. "Kuhn and Rozelle Caution Against Legal Sports Bets." *New York Times*, February 20, 1975.

"Robert Kennedy Urges New Laws to Fight Rackets." *New York Times*, April 7, 1961.

Rohde, David. "Upstate OTB Wants to Put Horse Wagering on Internet." *New York Times*, December 26, 1996.

Sayre, Alan. "Louisiana Casino Expectations Unfulfilled." *San Jose Mercury News*, November 7, 2003.

Schwartz, David G. "John Davis: Father of American Gaming?" *Global Gaming Business*, December 15, 2002.

"Senate Approves Inquiry Into Crime." *New York Times*, May 4, 1950.

"Senate Approves Internet Gambling Ban." *Tech Law Journal*, July 23, 1998.

Shagan, Michael. "The Relationship Between OTB and Racing." *OTB Journal* (Summer 1977).

"Slot Machine Bill Passed." *New York Times*, December 21, 1950.

"Slot Machine Bill Voted." *New York Times*, April 20, 1950.

"Sportsline.com, Inc. Announces Sale of Las Vegas Sports Consultants." CBS Sportsline.com, Investors Relations. November 24, 2003. Accessed online at: http://cbs.sportsline.com/info/ir/press/2003/lvscsale.

Stamos Jr., George. "Tropicana." *Las Vegas Sun Magazine*, August 26, 1979.

Sterngold, George. "Virtual Casino Is Coming, But Regulation Is Still a Big Question." *New York Times*, October 28, 1996.

Strumpf, Koleman. "Illegal Sports Bookmakers." Paper presented at the Twelfth International Conference on Gambling and Risk Taking, Vancouver, B.C., Canada, May 2003.

"Tribe Starts New Business: Gambling Site on Internet." *New York Times*, July 5, 1997.

Trussell, C. P. "House Votes Bill to Combat Crime." *New York Times*, August 24, 1961.

———. "Six Crime Bills Passed in Senate." *New York Times*, July 29, 1961.

"U.S. Drive Opened on Bet Tipsters." *New York Times*, March 6, 1964.

"U.S. Fight on Organized Crime Brings Wide Rise in Convictions." *New York Times*, January 12, 1964.

"U.S. Jury Indicts 13 in Betting Ring." *New York Times*, June 28, 1961.

"U.S. Seizes 6 Here in Gambling Raid." *New York Times*, November 29, 1961, 35.

"The Valachi Show." *New York Times*, October 6, 1963.

Walsh, Tom. "Words, Plans, Won't Build Classy Hotels." *Detroit Free Press*, November 6, 2003.

"War on Syndicated Crime Urged of AMA." *American City*, January 1950.

Will, George F. "Electronic Morphine." *Newsweek*, November 25, 2002.

"Western Union Asks New Gambler Curbs." *New York Times*, June 4, 1952.

"West Fears Gang Invasion." *New York Times*, September 7, 1947.

"Wire Bets Sifted by Western Union." *New York Times*, April 28, 1950.

Wood, Lewis. "Truman Pledges to Aid Campaign Against Forces of 'Vice and Greed.'" *New York Times*, February 16, 1950.

Government Documents
Federal

The Attorney General's Conference on Organized Crime, February 15, 1950. Washington, D.C.: Department of Justice, 1950.

Bureau of Justice. *Sourcebook of Criminal Justice Statistics*. Albany, N.Y.: Hindelang Criminal Justice Research Center, 1974–2002.

Congressional Quarterly Almanac. 81st Cong., 2d sess., 1950. Vol. 6. Washington, D.C.: Congressional Quarterly News Features, 1951.

Congressional Quarterly Almanac. 87th Cong., 1st sess., 1961. Vol. 17. Washington, D.C.: Congressional Quarterly, 1961.

Congressional Quarterly Almanac. 87th Cong., 2d sess., 1962. Vol. 18. Washington, D.C.: Congressional Quarterly, 1962.

Congressional Quarterly Almanac. 91st Cong., 2d sess., 1970. Vol. 26. Washington, D.C.: Congressional Quarterly, 1970.

Congressional Quarterly Almanac. 102d Cong., 1st sess., 1991. Vol. 47. Washington, D.C.: Congressional Quarterly, 1991.

Cornell Law School. *Development of the Law of Gambling: Federal*. Prepared for the Commission to Review the National Policy on Gambling, 1974.

Department of the Treasury-Internal Revenue Service. *Form 886A*.

Development of the Law of Gambling. Washington, D.C.: U.S. Government Printing Office, 1977.

Fahrenkopf, Frank. "Testimony Before the House Financial Services Committee Re: Internet Gaming." July 12, 2001. Accessed online at: http://www.american gaming.org/Press/speeches/speeches detail.cfv?ID=108.

Illegal Gambling: Numbers, Dice, Bookmaking. FBI Police Training Video. Date unknown, likely early 1970s.

"Jay Cohen Convicted of Operating an Off-Shore Sports Betting Business." U.S. Justice Department press release, February 28, 2000.

John F. Kennedy: Containing the Public Messages, Speeches, and Statements of the President. January 20 to December 31, 1961. *Public Papers of the Presidents of the United States*. Washington, D.C.: U.S. Government Printing Office, 1962.

Kyl, Jon. "Crime and Justice Issues." Accessed online at: http://kyl.senate.gov/legis_center/crime.cfm.

National Gaming Impact Study Commission. "Final Report," 3–9. Washington, D.C.: U.S. Government Printing Office, 1999. Accessed online at: http://govinfo.library.unt.edu/ngisc/reports/pathch3.pdf.

National Indian Gaming Commission. *Tribal Gaming Revenue, 2002*. Accessed online at: http://www.nigc.gov/nigc/nigcControl?option=TRIBAL_REVENUE.

Organized Crime and Racketeering Section. *Racketeer Influenced and Corrupt Organizations (RICO): A Manual for Federal Prosecutors*. Washington, D.C.: U.S. Department of Justice, 1988.

President's Commission on Law Enforcement and Administration of Justice. *The Challenge of Crime in a Free Society*. Washington, D.C.: U.S. Government Printing Office, 1967.

President's Commission on Organized Crime. *Organized Crime and Gambling: Record of Hearing VII, June 24–26, 1985*. Washington, D.C.: U.S. Government Printing Office, 1985.

Second Interim Report of the Special Committee to Investigate Organized Crime in Interstate Commerce. Washington, D.C.: U.S. Government Printing Office, 1951.

Selected Speeches of Dwight David Eisenhower. Washington, D.C.: U.S. Government Printing Office, 1970.

Third Interim Report of the Special Committee to Investigate Organized Crime in Interstate Commerce. Washington, D.C.: U.S. Government Printing Office, 1951.

Transmission of Gambling Information. Report Number 500. 83d Cong., 1st sess. Washington, D.C.: U.S. Government Printing Office, 1953.

United States Code Congressional and Administrative News. 87th Cong., 1st sess., 1961. Vol. 2: *Legislative History.* St. Paul: West Publishing, 1961.

U.S. Congress. House. Committee on Interstate and Foreign Commerce. *Hearings Before the Committee on Interstate and Foreign Commerce of the House of Representatives on the Bills H.R. 25825, to Prohibit Interstate Transportation of Pictures and Descriptions of Prize Fights and H.R. 2160, to Prevent the Nullification of State Anti-Gambling Laws by International or Interstate Transmission of Race-Gambling Bets or Racing Odds.* Washington, D.C.: U.S. Government Printing Office, 1911.

U.S. Congress. House. Committee on the Judiciary. *Hearings Before Subcommittee Number 2 of the Committee of the Judiciary, House of Representatives, on H.R. 7975, a Bill to Prohibit Certain Acts and Transactions with Respect to Gambling Materials.* 83d Cong., 2d sess. Washington, D.C.: U.S. Government Printing Office, 1954.

U.S. Congress. Senate. Committee on Government Operations. *Gambling and Organized Crime.* Report of the U.S. Senate Permanent Subcommittee on Investigations. Washington, D.C.: U.S. Government Printing Office, 1962.

U.S. Congress. Senate. Committee on Interstate Commerce. *Hearing on S. 3253, a Bill to Prevent the Nullification of State Anti-Gambling Laws by International or Interstate Transmission of Race-Gambling Bets or Racing Odds.* 64th Cong., 2d sess. Washington, D.C.: U.S. Government Printing Office, 1917.

U.S. Congress. Senate. Committee on Interstate and Foreign Commerce. *Transmission of Gambling Information: Hearings Before a Subcommittee of the Committee on Interstate and Foreign Commerce Committee, United States Senate, Eighty-first Congress, Second Session, on S. 3358.* Washington, D.C.: U.S. Government Printing Office, 1950.

U.S. Congress. Senate. Committee on the Judiciary. *Hearings Before the Committee on the Judiciary of the United States Senate, 87th Congress, First Session, on S. 1653, S. 1654, S. 1655, S. 1656, S. 1657, S. 1658, S. 1665.* 87th Cong., 1st sess. Washington, D.C.: U.S. Government Printing Office, 1961.

U.S. Congressional Code Service. *Laws. 81st Congress—Second Session, 1950.* Washington, D.C.: U.S. Government Printing Office, 1950.

State and Municipal

Colorado State Gaming Statistics, 1991–2002. Accessed online at: http://www.gaming.state.co.us/dogstats.htm.

Connecticut Division of Special Revenue. *Annual Report 2001–2002.*

Fund for the City of New York. *Legal Gambling in New York: A Discussion of Numbers and Sports Betting.* New York: Fund for the City of New York, 1972.

"How to Play Sports Action." Pamphlet from Oregon Lottery, 1989. In *Promotional and Publicity Materials: Oregon Lottery.* UNLV Special Collections.

"Judge Issues TRO to Stop Internet Lottery in Missouri." Press release, Missouri Of-

fice of the Attorney General, January 29, 1998. Accessed online at: http://www
.ago.state.mo.us/012998.htm.

Maryland Department of Legislative Services. "Overview of Issues Related to Video
Lottery Terminals." Annapolis: Office of Policy Analysis, 1993.

Nevada Gaming Commission. *Gaming Nevada Style.* Carson City: Nevada Gaming
Commission, 1981.

Nevada State Gaming Control Board, Economic Research Section. *Nevada Gaming Abstract.* Carson City: Nevada State Gaming Control Board, 1972, 1981.

New Jersey Casino Control Commission. *2000 Annual Report.* Trenton: Casino Control
Commission, 2000.

———. *2002 Annual Report.* Trenton: Casino Control Commission, 2002.

New Jersey Department of Community Affairs. *Review of the Probable Impact of Atlantic
City Casino Development.* Trenton: Bureau of Regional Planning, 1980.

New Jersey Gambling Study Commission. *Report to the Governor and Legislature.* February 5, 1973.

"New Jersey Settles Internet Sports Betting Suits." Press release, Office of the Attorney General, June 11, 2002. Accessed online at: http://www.state.nj.us/lps/ge/
2002news/internet_settlement.htm.

"Nixon Says No to Indian Internet Gaming." Press release, Missouri Office of the Attorney General, December 29, 1997.

"Statement by Eliot Spitzer Regarding New York Racing Association." Accessed online at: http://www.oag.state.ny.us/press/2003/jun/jun24b_03.html.

International

Isle of Man. *Online Gambling Regulation Act 2001.* Accessed online at: http://www.gov
.im/gambling/acts/gamblingregulation2001.pdf.

Judicial

"Ruling on Appeal of *United States v. Cohen.*" U.S. Court of Appeals, Second Circuit.
260 F.3d 68. July 31, 2001.

Sarafa, Melinda. "Jay Cohen, Petitioner, Against United States of America, Respon-
dent: Memorandum of Law in Support of Motion Pursuant to 28 U.S.C. § 2255."
Brafman and Ross, 2002. Habeas Corpus, Affidavit in Support of 2255 Petition
(Affidavit of Melinda Sarafa; 33 pp., MS Word), 2002, 23. Accessed online at:
http:/www.freejaycohen.com/LegalCasePg.html.

Sentencing Transcript. *United States v. Jay Cohen.*

Trial Transcript. *United States v. Jay Cohen.*

"United States of America v. Jay Cohen: Brief for the United States of America." Second Circuit Appeal, Docket No. 00-1574. 2002.

U.S. Supreme Court. *California v. Cabazon Band of Mission Indians,* 480 U.S. 202 (1987).
Accessed online at: http://caselaw.lp.findlaw.com.

U.S. Trade Representative. *Before the World Trade Organization: Measures Affecting the Cross-Border Supply of Gambling and Betting Services.* January 9, 2004. Accessed online at: http://www.ustr.gov/enforcement/2004-01-09-gambling-2ndwritten.pdf.

World Trade Organization. *United States—Measures Affecting the Cross-Border Supply of Gaming and Betting Services: Report of the Panel.* WT/DS285/R10. November 2004. Accessed online at: http://www.wto.org/english/tratop_e/dispu_e/285r_e.pdf.

Internet

http://www.antigua-barbuda.com/.
http://www.debevoise.com/about/about.asp.
http://www.freejaycohen.com.
http://www.igcouncil.org/.
5http://home.jockeyclub.com/FACTBOOKS/handle.html.
http://www.majorwager.com/home.cfm.
http://www.therx.com/index.html.

Interviews

Telephone interview with Jeff Bryson, Chief, Gambling Investigation, Department of Justice, Gambling Control Division. State of Montana. February 20, 2004.

Personal interview with Jay Cohen. December 15, 2003. Federal Prison Camp Nellis, Las Vegas, Nevada.

Personal Communications

Heneghan, Daniel, Director of Communications, New Jersey Casino Control Commission. January 5, 2004.

Rose, I. Nelson. September 2003.

INDEX

Accardo, Tony, 50
Accardo-Guzik-Fischetti syndicate, 71–72, 236n13. *See also* Syndicate
agricultural futures, 24
Alabama handbook operators, 89
Amazon.com, 177, 195–96
American Bar Association, 131
American Civil Liberties Union (ACLU), 102, 110, 190
American Coin Machine Manufacturers Association, 62, 63
American Gaming Association, 187–88
American Indians. *See* Native Americans
American Municipal Association, 52–53, 54, 56
American Net, 9
American Revolution, 17
Anne Arundel County (Md.), 27
Annenberg, Moses L. (Moe), 40–41, 118
Annenberg, Walter, 40
anti-betting bills: 1910, 87, 88–90; 1953, 90–92; 1954, 92; 1957–61, 93
antigamblers, 5–6, 49–50
antigambling laws: colonial period, 16–17; England, 149–50; South, 17, 24
Antigua: free-trade zone, 178; gaming operator regulation, 181; Internet betting sites, 8–9; legality of online bets, 1, 2; licensed sportsbooks, 180; limits to shelter from prosecution, 183; online gaming regulation, 193–94; suit against United States, 10, 215–17; as World Sports Exchange location, 179, 201, 205, 206, 209
Apalachin (N.Y.) meeting of mob leaders, 76–77
Arizona: lottery, 148; wide-open gaming, 150
Arkansas, 23
armed forces slot machines, 142
arrests, gambling, 137–38, 139
Aspinalls, 184–85

Assembly Bill 578 (Nevada), 197–98
Associated Press, 121
Association for the Suppression of Gambling, 23
Athletic Publications, Inc., 121–22
Atlantic City (N.J.): casino regulation, 194–95; casinos, 153–54, 159; federal raid, 112; horse rooms, 34
AT&T, 91, 98, 102–3
Attorney General's Conference on Organized Crime, 56–60, 61, 141
attrition strategy, 132
Auerbach, Red, 173, 174
Australia, 197

Balinese Room (Galveston, Tex.), 73
Bank of the United States, 18
Ban on Gaming Data bill, 60–61, 64, 65–69, 90
Barbara, Joseph, 76
Barbuda, 193
Baring, Walter, 62–63
Bartlett, Charles, 89
baseball, 30, 170, 189, 201
baseball pool cards, 30
basketball: college, 30, 125–26; lottery, 173; professional, 173, 201, 203
Beck, Dave, 75, 83
Bergen County (N.J.), 51–52, 73
betting on horses: cheating, 235n73; history, 12, 27–29, 142; legality of, 12–13, 23; off-track betting (OTB), 143–44, 145–46; organized crime, 124; remote wagering, 143–44; technological advances, 33–35. *See also* horse races; pari-mutuel wagering; race wire service
Bible, Alan, 58
Big Game (lottery), 149
Biloxi (Miss.): casinos, 157, 158; layoff bets, 103
bingo, Native American, 164–65, 167

sports betting, 169–75; bookmakers, 119, 120–23, 169, 171, 172; Delaware, 172–74; England, 170; France, 170; history, 29–30; and media, 234n47; Montana, 172; Nevada, 169, 171, 173–74, 175; New York City, 127; odds and handicapping, 119, 120–23; Oregon, 173; and organized crime, 128–29; scandals, 125–26; and television, 125, 126–27, 174; women in, 127. *See also specific sports*
Sports International, 179, 200
sports leagues, 9, 170, 173, 174–75, 189, 201–2. *See also specific leagues*
Stardust, 151, 162, 169
state attorneys general, 200–201
state gaming, 6–7, 11, 134–35, 149–50, 220–21
state lotteries, 11, 146–49. *See also specific states*
State of California v. The Cabazon Band of Mission Indians, 165–66, 212
Station Casinos, 185, 192
steamboat races, 33
Straus, Harry, 35
Supreme Court (U.S.), 109, 165–66, 190, 211–12
Sutton, Pat, 62
Syndicate, 41, 42–43, 44, 50–51, 236n13. *See also* Capone, Al; organized crime
syndicates: crime, 51–53
syndicates, gaming: history, 23, 25, 48; and slot machines, 35, 48, 236n8. *See also specific syndicates by name*

tax: on bookmakers, 137, 169; on slot machines, 64
Teamsters Union, 75, 83, 84. *See also* Hoffa, James R. (Jimmy)
technical innovations, 32–37. *See also* Internet; race wire service
telegraph, 33–34, 88–89, 91, 101, 103–4. *See also* race wire service
telephone companies, 91, 98, 101, 103–4
television, and sports betting, 125, 126–27, 174
Tennes, Mont, 38–40, 41, 118
Tennessee, legality of casinos, 12
Texas: lottery, 148; race wagering, 26
three-waves model (gambling legalization), 13–14, 232n2
three waves of lottery, 146–47
Time magazine, 121
tipsters, prosecuted under Wire Act, 138
Title 18 United States Code Section 1084. *See* Wire Act (1961)
Tobey, Charles, 70, 91. *See also* Kefauver Committee

totalisator, 35, 119
Touchdown/Touchdown II, 172
Trans-American Publishing and News Service, 41–43, 44
Trauman, Jeffrey, 183
Treasury Department, 56–60, 73, 130
tribal governments. *See* Native Americans
Tropicana casino resort, 75–76
Truman, Harry S., 46, 56–57, 63
Tunica County (Miss.), 158
turf clubs, 169

Union Plaza, 169
United Press International, 121
United States, Antigua's suit against, 10, 215–17
United States Independent Telephone Association, 97–98
United States v. Cohen: appeal of conviction, 210–12; conviction of Cohen, 209–10; defendant's case, 205–8, 209; jury instructions, 1–2; legacy, 213–15; prosecution's case, 204–5, 208; sentencing, 210; and Wire Act, 1–2, 9–10, 205, 206, 209–10, 211, 214–15. *See also* Wire Act (1961)
University of Kentucky, 125
University of Pennsylvania, 29, 120, 243n6
Unlawful Internet Gambling Funding Prohibition Act, 192
U.S. Attorney General, 80
U.S. Court of Appeals, Second Circuit, 210–12
U.S. Trade Representative, 216

Vacco, Dennis, 182–83, 200
Valachi, Joseph, 109, 236n13
Valachi hearings, 106, 109
Vicksburg (Miss.), 20, 158
video lottery terminals, 144–45
vigorish, 124
Virginia colonial gambling, 15–16
Virginia Company, 15–16
Volstead Act, 67, 213–14

Wagering Tax Act (1952), 73
Ware, Haden, 204
Washington (D.C.) gambling houses, 21
Washington, George, 17
Washington (state): lottery, 148; race wagering, 26
wave theory, 13–14, 232n2
wealth, redistribution of, 149–50
Western Union Telegraph Company, 37–38, 72, 91, 104, 118, 203